P9-CDX-977

Annapurna

The First Conquest of an 8,000-meter Peak
[26,493 feet]

Maurice Herzog

Leader of the French Himalayan Expedition

Translated from the French by
Nea Morin *and* Janet Adam Smith

Cartographic and Photographic Documentation by
Marcel Ichac

With Forewords by
Conrad Anker *and* Eric Shipton

LYONS PRESS
Guilford, Connecticut

To
LUCIEN DEVIES
WHO WAS ONE OF US

Copyright © 1997, 2010 by Maurice Herzog

All rights reserved. No part of this book may be reproduced or transmitted in any form by any means, electronic or mechanical, including photocopying and recording, or by any information storage and retrieval system, except as may be expressly permitted in writing from the publisher.

Lyons Press is an imprint of Globe Pequot Press.

The Library of Congress has cataloged the earlier printing as follows:
Herzog, Maurice, 1919–
[Annapurna premier 8,000. English]
Annapurna, first conquest of an 8000-meter peak: (26,493 feet) / by Maurice Herzog; translated from the French by Nea Morin and Janet Adam Smith; cartographic and photographic documentation by Marcel Ichac; with an introduction by Eric Shipton.
p. cm.
Originally published: New York: Dutton, c1952.
ISBN 1-55821-549-2 (pbk.)
1. Mountaineering—Nepal—Annapurna. 2. Herzog, Maurice, 1919–. I. Title.
GV199.44.N462H47 1997
796.52'2'095496—dc21 97-3203
CIP

ISBN 978-1-59921-893-9

Distributed by NATIONAL BOOK NETWORK

CONTENTS

LIST OF MAPS

FOREWORD TO THE 2010 EDITION

Since the dawn of human awareness, people have been drawn to high places: passes, ridges, mountains, and summits. Mountains represent inhospitable barriers to human habitation, but in their grandness we find a source of cultural heritage and a wellspring for our wildest dreams. The impenetrable vastness of the world's great mountain ranges makes us want to know more. This quest for knowledge was exemplified by the French expedition to the Himalaya sixty years ago, when 8,000-meter peaks were at the forefront of human exploration and possibility.

The ascent of Annapurna in 1950 by the French expedition was the first real foray of humans into this realm. The story of the climb, as recounted by Maurice Herzog in *Annapurna,* brings this time frame alive in the minds of readers. The awe-inspiring terrain the team explored before even setting foot on the mountain was just a prelude to what would become one of the twentieth century's most incredible adventures.

The team had two mountains to choose from, a quandary that proved to be both an advantage and a challenge: An advantage because if one peak was unsuitable they could choose the other, but a challenge because the team's precious time and resources were split. Which peak should they attempt? The decision would make all the difference.

The choice finally made, it took the team only two weeks to reach the summit of Annapurna. By modern standards this is a fast ascent; in 1950 it broke barriers and set the stage for the alpine-style climbing of the future. In hindsight, it's clear much of the progress made in Himalayan mountaineering over the ensuing decades is due to the pioneering efforts of the French expedition.

Annapurna was and still is the first climbing book for legions of climbers and adventurers, myself included, and in later years I would recall the story during my own Himalayan expeditions. In 2007 I attempted the east face of Meru Peak in the Garwhal Himalaya, and while the big-wall climbing on Meru was quite different than what the 1950 French expedition experienced, our hardships were some of the same. As our team shivered away in our sleeping bags, existing on meager rations, I dreamed of Herzog's epic on Annapurna and thought about how they had it much worse. We were lightweights compared to them.

The French expedition set the bar high for Himalayan expeditions of the future. The quickness with which the team solved the riddle of the approach, unlocked a route through the treacherous glacier-clad north flank of Annapurna, and made it to the summit is a testament to their skill and determination. Their return journey to civilization, fraught with swollen rivers and field amputations of frostbit fingers and toes, further demonstrates the fortitude of the team and the suffering they endured.

The relevancy of *Annapurna* is as important today as it was in 1952. Written in the months immediately after the climb, Herzog's account has been viewed with a critical eye by some, but regardless of the controversy, the book's ability to draw people out of their warmth and into the grip of a timeless expedition remains as strong today as it was when I first eagerly turned the pages as a young climber. These men, in their leather boots and woolen knickers, were climbing at a standard that exceeded their abilities but not their drive. *Annapurna* is a call for us as individuals to try harder, make a commitment, and stand on our own summit.

—CONRAD ANKER
January 2010

FOREWORD TO THE 1952 EDITION

Ever since the first World War, French mountaineers have been in the forefront in the field of Alpine achievement. They have been very largely responsible for the astonishing advance in climbing technique during the last thirty years. The names de Lépiney, Lagarde, de Ségogne, Vernet, Armand Charlet, Pierre Allain will live among the greatest in the history of mountaineering. It is fitting therefore that, with the climbing of the first 8000-meter peak, French mountaineers should now take a leading place in the field of Himalayan enterprise.

The story of the climbing of Annapurna is a remarkable one; in some respects it is unique. Those with experience of the problems of high altitude climbing know well how small are the chances of reaching the top of a peak of more than 25,000 feet in any given season. That the number of these giants to have been climbed can still be counted on the fingers of one hand is proof of this. In each case these few had yielded only after detailed reconnaissance in preceding years and several abortive attempts. But the approaches to Annapurna were quite unknown. The expedition had not only to find a practicable route to the summit; they had first to find a way of reaching the mountain. It is this triple accomplishment of successful exploration, reconnaissance and assault, all within the brief season between the melting of the winter snows and the onset of the monsoon, that places the achievement of the French expedition in a class by itself, and has won our wholehearted admiration and applause.

Certainly the party was fortunate in having two alternative objectives so close together from which to choose. But this advantage was also a handicap, for it tended further to disperse their energy and to dissipate the precious time at their disposal. The brilliant manner in which they succeeded in rallying their forces from the confusion and perplexity of groping through unknown country to concentrate on the final gruelling effort, is a measure of their resolution, their superb skill and their driving force.

It is a privilege to be permitted here to acclaim the splendid success of our French colleagues in the boundless field of Himalayan adventure; a success which, we may be sure, is the forerunner of many to come.

—Eric Shipton
August 1952

PREFACE TO THE 1952 EDITION

The conquest of Annapurna has stirred up general interest which is still increasing. It was, beyond all question, one of the greatest adventures of our times, and most nobly carried out.

Maurice Herzog and his companions have crowned a long series of attempts and successes, by climbing not only the highest summit yet attained by man, but also the first summit of over 8,000 meters, the first to be climbed of the very highest mountains of the world.

With this victory, achieved at a first attempt and in an unknown region, they have succeeded in an enterprise which the most experienced Himalayan travelers had considered impossible. That outstanding English climber, the late Frank Smythe, who had been on five Himalayan expeditions, had conquered Mount Kamet and had attained the highest point reached on Everest (8,500 meters), had declared that "Mountaineering in the Himalaya presents such difficulties that, as far as one can see, no expedition will ever succeed in climbing one of the twelve highest peaks at a first attempt."

This, however, is exactly what the Annapurna Expedition of 1950 achieved.

Victory in the Himalaya is a collective victory, for the party as a whole. Every member of the Expedition, each in his place, whether more or less favored by circumstances, has been worthy of the trust placed in him; one and all carried out with unswerving devotion their duty of bringing the two injured climbers safely down. We give them in full measure the gratitude they have so richly earned; but at the same time we realize that the victory of the whole party was also, and above all, the victory of its leader.

The other members of the party have been the first to confirm the wisdom of our choice of a leader by the affection, and even reverence, in which they hold him. But it was not the Himalaya that revealed Maurice Herzog to us, for his past record had convinced us that we had entrusted the Expedition to the most valiant of them all. The Himalaya did, however, provide him with the opportunity—ultimately, alas, in the most appalling circumstances—to be the very soul of a great adventure, and this he accomplished in the most moving and magnificent way.

What a range of gifts he has shown! His intelligence and character opened many fields of activity to him. His grasp of the practical side of life debarred him neither from the poetry of Mallarmé nor from the

Pensées of Pascal. He was as much at home in a city office as on one of the great Italian ridges of Mont Blanc. His great goodness of heart, which won him so many friends, did not prevent him from taking firm decisions, when necessary, or forming a clear-sighted judgment of people. A level head controlled the natural exuberance of abounding vitality.

The facts speak for themselves. His remarkable physical fitness throughout the Expedition, which surpassed even that of Lionel Terray and Louis Lachenal, "the two steam-engines," considered by all to be in a class by themselves, was the reflection of his will and of the faith in victory which he inspired in everybody, even in all of us at home, so many thousands of miles away.

Spending himself to the limit, reserving for himself the hardest tasks, deriving his authority from the example he set, always in the vanguard, he made victory possible. That last long stage to the top bears the stamp of his judgment and determination. The natural thing would have been to establish a sixth camp, but Maurice had the vision to realize that one more day spent on the climb might cost them the summit, and so he decided to make an all-out dash.

All France knows the price that had to be paid. And Maurice faced his ordeal with a resolution and courage perhaps even more admirable than that he displayed on the climb. He showed an utter disregard of self. It was typical of him that, as they emerged from the crevasse where they had bivouacked, his first thought should be for the others, and his first words a request that they should leave him behind, and increase their own chances of safety.

The endless return march in the monsoon rains, the succession of amputations, the long months of immobility and their accompaniment of pain—from all these he has emerged at last, standing on his own feet again, with a heightened simplicity and moral sensibility, as though purified by fire. It is with a sense of wonder and fulfillment that we see him turning again towards life as towards renewal, seeing more good in it because he himself is a better man.

And this book which we now hold in our hands is a triumph without parallel, a triumph of the heart and of the creative understanding. It is not like any other book. It reads like a novel, but it is truth itself, truth almost too elusive to grasp or to express. Its easy familiar tone, its straightforward presentation of people and events give it a striking authenticity. For the first time, we are all members of a Himalayan expedition, we are all present beside the leader and the rest of the party. You are taking us with you too, my dear Maurice, to the very end—to the end of the ordeal, to the end of an almost unbelievable experience.

It is impossible to read these pages without being overwhelmed by the sensitive awareness, and the kindliness, that went with so much courage and such dogged determination.

Thank you for being so well aware that one can put aside modesty without becoming vain. If it were not so, then every advance of the spirit would go unrecorded. It takes courage to draw the veil from those moments when the individual approaches most nearly to the universal.

That wonderful world of high mountains, dazzling in their rock and ice, acts as a catalyst. It suggests the infinite, but it is not the infinite. The heights only give us what we ourselves bring to them. Climbing is a means of self-expression. Its justification lies in the men it develops, its heroes and its saints. This was the essential truth which a whole nation grasped when it offered its praise and admiration to the conquerors of Annapurna. Man overcomes himself, affirms himself, and realizes himself in the struggle towards the summit, toward the absolute. In the extreme tension of the struggle, on the frontier of death, the universe disappears and drops away beneath us. Space, time, fear, suffering, no longer exist. Everything then becomes quite simple. As on the crest of a wave, or in the heart of a cyclone, we are strangely calm—not the calm of emptiness, but the heart of action itself. Then we know with absolute certainty that there is something indestructible in us, against which nothing shall prevail.

A flame so kindled can never be extinguished. When we have lost everything it is then we find ourselves most rich. Was it this certainty that all was well that gave Maurice Herzog the steady courage to endure his ordeal?

The summit is at our feet. Above the sea of golden clouds other summits pierce the blue and the horizon extends to infinity.

The summit we have reached is no longer the Summit. The fulfillment of oneself—is that the true end, the final answer?

—LUCIEN DEVIES
*Président du Comité de l'Himalaya et de
la Fédération Française de la Montagne.*

INTRODUCTION TO THE 1952 EDITION

This is the first time I have written a book. I never realized before what a long business it was. Sometimes the job was almost too much for me, but I have undertaken it because I wanted to set down, on behalf of all those who went with me, the story of a terrible adventure which we survived only by what still seems to me an incredible series of miracles.

The following pages record the actions of men at grips with Nature at her most pitiless, and tell of their sufferings, their hopes and joys.

I conceived it to be my duty to give a plain truthful account of what happened, and have tried—so far as lay within my powers—to bring out its human aspect, and convey the extraordinary emotional atmosphere in which everything took place.

The whole of this book has been dictated at the American Hospital at Neuilly where I am still having rather a difficult time.

The basis of the narrative is, of course, my memory of all that happened. In so far as the record is comprehensive and exact, that is due to the Expedition's log which Marcel Ichac so faithfully kept—an essential document, sometimes written up at the very moment of action. Louis Lachenal's private journal, and the details supplied by all my friends, have been of the greatest possible use. So this book is the work of the whole party.

The text, often colloquial in style, has been revised and put into shape by my brother Gerard Herzog, the sharer of my earliest mountain pleasures, as indeed of my earliest experiences of life. If it had not been for the confidence I had in his editing, and for the encouragement he gave me day by day, I doubt if I should ever have been able to finish my task.

The name of Robert Boyer, who did so much for our Expedition, does not figure in this record and yet his understanding friendship was a tonic in my darkest hours.

All the nine members of the Expedition will have more than one reason for cherishing this record. Together we knew toil, joy and pain. My fervent wish is that the nine of us who were united in face of death should remain fraternally united through life.

In overstepping our limitations, in touching the extreme boundaries of man's world, we have come to know something of its true splendor. In my worst moments of anguish, I seemed to discover the deep significance of existence of which till then I had been unaware. I saw that it was better to be true than to be strong. The marks of the ordeal are apparent on my body. I was saved and I had won my freedom. This freedom, which I shall never lose, has given me the assurance and serenity of a man who has fulfilled himself. It has given me the rare joy of loving that which I used to despise. A new and splendid life has opened out before me.

In this narrative we do more than record our adventures, we bear witness; events that seem to make no sense may sometimes have a deep significance of their own. There is no other justification for an *acte gratuit.*

—MAURICE HERZOG
Hôpital Américain de Paris
June 1951

Chapter I

Preparations

THE DAY FIXED FOR OUR DEPARTURE WAS CLOSE AT HAND. WOULD WE EVER manage to get everything done? The entire personnel of the French Alpine Club was mobilized. The lights burned late into the night at No. 7 rue La Boétie; there was a tremendous sense of excitement, and the Himalayan Committee sat nearly every evening. At nine o'clock, punctual to the minute, the men on whom the fate of the Expedition depended would arrive and at this stage vital decisions were taken at these secret councils: it is the Committee which settles the budget, foresees contingencies, weighs the risks and, finally, chooses the members of the expedition.

The names of the members of the party had been known for a few days. I was to have a splendid team. The youngest member was the tall, and aristocratic Jean Couzy, aged 27; he had been a brilliant student at the Ecole Polytechnique and was now an aeronautical engineer. He had not long been married but he had not hesitated to leave his young wife, Lise, to take part in the adventure. A quiet man, with a faraway look in his eyes, he always seemed to be turning over in his mind the latest problems of electronics. Couzy's usual climbing partner Marcel Schatz was going with us too. He was two years older than his friend, of a heavier build, and always well turned out, for the very good reason that he was manager of one of his father's prosperous tailoring establishments. He liked efficient organization, order and method. Whenever a bivouac was needed on a climb he was always the one to pitch in and get it ready. As he was unmarried, and an ardent climber, there was nothing to prevent him from spending all his holidays in the mountains; and although he lived in Paris, and so at some distance from his mountain paradise, he was rarely to be found in town at week ends.

Louis Lachenal had been an amateur, climbing for his own pleasure until he became, a few years ago an instructor at the National School of Skiing and Mountaineering. To the inhabitants of Chamonix he ranked as a "foreigner," which means that he was not a native of the Valley—he came from Annecy. In spite of this dubious origin, as it seemed to the local inhabitants, who are jealous of their mountains, he had succeeded, along with Gaston Rébuffat and Lionel Terray, in being admitted to the

Company of Guides of Chamonix, a body unique both for the number and quality of its members. He was of medium height, with piercing eyes, and in conversation could deliver a very sharp repartee. He loved to exaggerate and his judgments could be devastating. Absolutely honest with himself, he was perfectly ready, if occasion arose to declare himself in the wrong. As often as they could manage, he and Lionel Terray would go off together, as amateurs, to enjoy themselves on the toughest climbs in the Alps.

Lionel Terray, although a native of Grenoble, was also a Chamonix guide and he and Louis Lachenal formed a crack partnership; they were a couple of steam-engines. Like his friend, Lionel Terray had a weakness for dogmatic and exaggerated statements, and there was continuous rivalry between them to see who could go one better than the other. Terray was unbeatable and would never give in. Although the son of a doctor, and a highly cultured man, he liked to pass as an amiable tough, all brawn and nothing more. It was pure love of the mountains that brought him to his profession of Chamonix guide and he was entirely happy. He went over to Canada last year to teach the new French method of skiing, and brought back some notable additions to his repertory of swear words. "Just now," he wrote to me, "I am skiing *en tabernacle*"—skiing like hell. He was in Canada at the moment and would get back only a week before we sailed.

Gaston Rébuffat had a scandalous origin for a mountaineer, and even worse for a guide. He was born at the seaside! It would take the Company of Guides many years to live this down. Nevertheless, it was on the cliffs of the Calanques, between Marseilles and Cassis, that he made his first climb. He was the tallest man of the party—towering over the rest of us by nearly a head. He had done all the finest expeditions in the Alps, and thought nothing of going straight on from one big climb to another without a break. He young wife, Françoise, and his daughter seldom saw him during the season's round of Chamonix, Cortina d'Ampezzo, Zermatt, and other climbs. He was away in Italy giving a series of lectures, but I had asked him to return as soon as possible.

These men formed the assault teams, and no better men could be found in France. No one disputed our choice—not even secretly. If a vote had been taken among all climbers, the same names would have been selected.

Nor was there any question about our cameraman Marcel Ichac; he was one of our trump cards. He had already been to the Himalaya, in 1936, and had taken part in a great many expeditions. As soon as he arrived I should have the benefit of his advice. Now he was in Greenland with Paul-Emile Victor, and immediately afterwards he would be off to America to film the world ski championships at Aspen, Colorado, arriving back only a few days before we left for India.

He would have several jobs to do. Not only would he film the Expedition, he would be responsible for everything connected with our photography. We would each have a camera, but the maintenance, supply, and care of all the films would be his business. Collecting and documenting scientific observations would be another responsibility of this intelligent, enterprising and lively-minded man. Ichac had managed to solve one of the climber's biggest problems—a wife is always a problem!—by marrying another climber.

We hoped Jacques Oudot would be our Expedition's doctor. He was a first-class surgeon, and we should all be able to treat ourselves to the luxury of a fracture. But he was up to his eyes in work. He had very prudently given orders that he must not be disturbed at the Salpêtrière hospital where he performed vascular surgical operations under the direction of his chief, Mondor. The things he dared to do appeared so incredible to me that I constantly asked him "And d'you mean to say he didn't die?" My ignorance about surgery always seemed to cause him great amusement. There are not many surgeons who climb, and I knew from personal experience how invaluable Oudot would be to us.

"Oudot, have you made up your mind?"

"Just now I am very busy." His shrewd little eyes blinked cagily. "I'll tell you tomorrow," he would promise.

This performance had been going on for a week. Devies and I were on tenterhooks. Two days before our departure we finally dragged from him the longed-for "yes." His job would be to keep us all in good health, to deal with emergency ailments and accidents, and also to keep me constantly informed about the physical condition of the party and their degree of acclimatization. In addition he would exercise his skill upon the local inhabitants.

There was one thorny question: the liaison officer. Our preference was for one of our own countrymen whom we should be likely to get along with. Robert Tézenas du Montcel had spoken to us, a few days previously, of a young diplomat at the Embassy in New Delhi. A lot would be required of him. As well as English he must know and speak Hindustani and the principal local languages—Gurkhali and Tibetan. He would have to arrange all the transport and he would also be responsible for good diplomatic relations with the Nepalese authorities in the capital of Katmandu as well as in the regions through which we should be traveling. Francis de Noyelle seemed the ideal person. Furthermore he was entirely at home in the mountains, being himself an ardent climber—an indispensable requirement in our party.

Noyelle was the only one I did not know personally. But his parents and his sister talked to me and gave me such a clear picture of him that I had the feeling I was dealing with a friend. He was a well-built, keen-eyed, self-reliant young man, accustomed to dealing with the local high-ups. Not long ago he had made a trip to Katmandu with Monsieur Daniel Lévi, our ambassador to India and Nepal, who enjoys considerable prestige in these countries. He took part in the negotiations which succeeded in obtaining the rarely-granted permission to penetrate far into Nepalese territory. In India, Professor Rahaul, who had himself already taken part in several Himalayan expeditions, would help Noyelle in Darjeeling to recruit the Sherpas[1] whom, for the most part he knew personally.

That was our party—all hardened mountaineers, all men of marked individuality and strong character. All of them devoutly longed to go to the Himalaya, which we had talked about for so many years. Lachenal put it in a nutshell: "We'd go if we had to crawl there."

Let me put it clearly on record that their zeal for the adventure was entirely unselfish. From the start every one of them knew that nothing belonged to him and that he must expect nothing on his return.[2] Their only motive was a great ideal; this was what linked together mountaineers so widely dissimilar in background and so diverse in character.

In the few days remaining before our departure Marcel Schatz and I went round to speed up all the firms supplying our equipment. Our arms were sore from all the injections we had to undergo: yellow fever, cholera, smallpox. But who cared?

On the evening of March 28 the Himalayan Committee met for the last time with all the members of the Expedition. Lucien Devies, the President and chief promoter of the Expedition, outlined a history of Himalayan achievement and specified just what he expected of us.

"The Himalaya, by their size,[3] fully merit the title of 'the third pole.' Twenty-two expeditions of different nationalities have tried to conquer an 'eight-thousander.' Not one has succeeded."

Then he defined our objectives:

"Dhaulagiri, 8,167 meters (26,795 feet), or Annapurna 8,075 meters (26,493 feet) in the very heart of Nepal. Should these prove impossible—

and that would be no disgrace—'consolation' summits ought to be attempted. With the six tons of equipment and provisions, the Expedition must cross the Indian frontier and penetrate into hitherto forbidden Nepalese territory. After a march of three weeks up into the high valleys, the party should arrive at Tukucha, which enjoys a remarkable geographical situation; it lies between the two mountains Dhaulagiri and Annapurna.

"Until now other Himalayan expeditions have picked mountains in regions already known and explored. But we have absolutely no information about our two 'eight-thousanders.' We know nothing about the approach routes. The maps at our disposal are sketchy, practically useless above a certain height. As soon as the party reaches Tukucha, your headquarters, you must begin by exploring the two massifs. Only after you have become familiar with the lay of the land, and have drawn up a plan of attack, will the Expedition be able to launch the attempt . . ."

Then Devies went on to say that investigations must be carried out— medical, geological, ethnographical, meteorological and geographical.[4]

Clearly it was a tremendous undertaking; but I had complete faith in my colleagues. Our party was the best that could be assembled, and we all appreciated one another's individual qualities. Our supplies and equipment increased our confidence. French industry had made an exceptional effort, and in very few months had produced equipment which combined the maximum of strength, lightness and convenience.

The dull and dreary office in which we were meeting took on that evening a solemn air. There was nothing more to say. Soon we should be launched upon extraordinary adventures which we could not as yet picture but of which, as mountaineers, we could form an idea. There were now no barriers between those grave, thoughtful persons on the one side, and, on the other, the bronzed and vigorous members of the Expedition.

Then suddenly Lucien Devies stood up. After a moment, he spoke deliberately, enunciating each syllable.

"This, gentlemen, is the oath which like your predecessors in 1936 you must take—'I swear upon my honor to obey the leader in everything regarding the Expedition in which he may command me'."

Mountaineers don't much care for ceremonies. My colleagues stood up, feeling both awkward and impressed. What were they supposed to do?

"Now, gentlemen . . . your turn, Matha, since you are the senior"— and he turned towards Marcel Ichac.

Then Henry de Ségogne who had led the 1936 expedition, and had spared no pains to help this one was equal to the occasion. "Come on,

Matha," said Ségogne. Ichac began and Terray's almost timid response could be heard in unison. Each in turn, my colleagues swore to obey the leader of the Expedition in all circumstances, especially at moments of crisis. They were pledging their lives, possibly, and they knew it. They all put themselves completely in my hands. I should have liked to say a few words, but I just couldn't. There is no feeling to equal this complete confidence of one man in another, because it encompasses so many other feelings. In that moment our team was born. It was for me to keep it alive.

The Committee had acted in princely fashion. If they had given me all the responsibility, they had also given me an entirely free hand. As this memorable session drew to a close I felt very sad about one matter: Pierre Allain, that great figure of French mountaineering, who had done so much for us, would not be coming with us. His health, undermined during the war, no longer allowed him to undertake long expeditions. I knew better than anyone, just how much the Himalaya meant to him, and tonight was for him a Paradise Lost. But his face showed no hint of it; he even smiled.

Far away in Asia we would often think of our friend who had to stay behind.

Chapter II

The Himalaya

THE MOMENT WE TOOK OFF, OUR DOCTOR, JACQUES OUDOT, WHO WAS DEAD tired, fell asleep. He hardly woke until we reached Delhi though from time to time he would open an eye to grumble: "Damn all these stops." Or sometimes to ask Marcel Ichac, "How's my little mouse? Watch out she doesn't escape." This particular little mouse was going to be a godsend to Indian doctors. It belonged to a pure strain no longer to be found in India, which are essential in the study of certain types of malaria.

At last India! There was a perfect moment when, looking through a window at the panorama, I could conjure up the ancient city of Mohenjo Daro, the invasion of the Aryans, and that earliest milestone of humanity, the Vedas.

Ambassador Daniel Lévi and all his staff of the Embassy at New Delhi were on the landing-ground at Palem to welcome us and help us with all the official complications. The Indian Customs had never before seen an expedition arrive lock, stock and barrel by plane.

"I wish to see a complete list, in English, of everything you are taking with you, with details of the weight, value, size . . ."

"But there are more than 50,000 items!"

Without listening the haughty official added: "You will be admitted to the country in transit. Upon your return you must bring everything through the Customs again."

But weren't we going to eat while in Nepal? And suppose we were to lose or give away a gun or a tent—

It was a difficult situation. With an air of arranging everything the Customs officer made a new suggestion:

"Your equipment can all be held in customs for the duration of your expedition. It will come to no harm!"

"And what about us?"

"You can proceed on to Nepal. Then you can pick up your stuff on the way back."

I was horrified by the turn of events. "The Himalaya?" our Customs man seemed to say to himself, as he rolled his eyes. "It's all very well for pilgrims—"

We certainly were pilgrims, I thought to myself, pilgrims to the mountains. But I dared not interrupt his reflections.

"Well . . ." (I felt sure everything was going to turn out all right) "now in this case I shall hold in customs the airplane as well."

I turned round to see whether our pilot had fainted.

But like everything else in India, the problem would be solved, provided there was no hurry. Marcel Ichac kept to himself in a corner, for he is very quick-tempered and didn't trust his control. He took his revenge by drawing a skull of the Customs officer.

"A perfect geometrical figure, but difficult to express as an equation," Couzy whispered.

After two days of negotiation we eventually cleared the Customs. We proceeded to load up our gear at Old Delhi station but it was no light job. The work was done at night. Street lamps threw a dim light upon the dismal rows of shops. Our acetylene lamps with their bright, blinding glare and the flickering, smoky oil lamps, lit up the passing crowds, and threw fantastic shadows everywhere. I was sickened by the foul smell. Everywhere there was an infernal din and I was constantly in danger of being knocked over by bicycle-drawn rickshaws.

Gaston Rébuffat and Lionel Terray were given the job of going with all the equipment that could not go by air, while the rest of us took the plane for Lucknow. We were hardly in our places when three magnificent Sikhs got in, colossal figures, with a noble bearing and flowing beards. They wore enormous turbans, and with their swarthy complexions and deep-set eyes they looked very fine indeed. Beside them we felt like little boys in shorts.

"Ye gods, they're the pilots," cried Oudot.

We were all amazed by their competence, and by their smooth piloting during our short journey from Delhi to Lucknow.

At Lucknow I met for the first time Angawa, the youngest of our future team of Sherpas, and his chief, Ang-Tharkey. The rest of the Sherpas I met at Nautanwa, which is the last straggling Indian village before Nepal, and the terminus of the narrow gauge railway. It thrilled me to see these little, yellow men, with their plump muscles, so different from the lankier Indians. These Sherpas whose loyalty and unselfishness is proverbial, would in fact be our climbing partners, and I determined to see that they were treated as such. Their equipment and their comfort would be absolutely the same as our own, and their safety, like that of my teammates, would always be foremost in my thoughts.

8

Ang-Tharkey, their sirdar or chief, was very energetic and assumed undisputed authority over his companions and the porters. He was an ardent Buddhist, and his moral influence over the men was considerable. The other Sherpas who were going to join us—Ang-Tsering, known as Pansy, Dawatondu, Sarki, Foutharkey, Aila, Angawa, Adjiba—had all had a certain amount of experience. The expedition was to give them plenty of opportunity to show what they were made of.

With our new Sherpa friends, we got out of the plane at Nautanwa beneath a torrid sun. The four and a half tons of our equipment were added to the one and a half tons of food which, thanks to our liaison officer Noyelle's foresight, was already waiting for us at the railway station. On April 5 we were at last admitted within the gates of Nepal.

Nepal lies higher than any other country in the world except Tibet and numbers within its forbidden frontiers eight of the fourteen highest peaks in the world. This country of seven million inhabitants straddles the great Himalayan rampart for nearly four hundred miles; and is one hundred and twenty miles wide. On its Indian border is the Terai—the zone lying below the foothills—which is overgrown with tropical vegetation. It is an astonishing region sometimes sweltering under a burning sun that scorches everything, sometimes flooded by torrential monsoon rains.

The Nepalese-Buddhist in the north, Hindu in the south, (but all suspicious of foreigners)—have prospered within the shelter of this formidable natural fortress. Respectful of tradition, they have preserved intact the spiritual inheritance of their forefathers. From these hill-people we have learned to expect upright character and the ability to rise to a great occasion.

Our jeep took us about six miles along a dusty stony road to Kapilavastu, (now called Ruminndei)—a not particularly impressive place, at the foot of Kipling's beloved Siwaliks. There, thousands of years ago a man was born whose youth was as full of poetry as his whole life was of wisdom. Gautama Buddha spent his early years in this country which now lay before my eyes. He who had founded one of the wisest and most beautiful of all religions had perhaps trodden the paths we were now following.

At Butwal, the first village in Nepal, which marks the end of the great plain of the Ganges and the beginning of the mountains, we had to get our money changed, for in these mountainous regions, particularly in the remoter districts, the natives have no faith in paper money and insist upon silver, the standard coinage in most Asiatic countries.

Lachenal and Terray, who formed the advance-party, inspected the wretched horses brought out for them while the main party dragged on its endless preparations beneath a burning sun. The loads were gradually made up to weigh one maund each, eighty pounds. These were then distributed to some two hundred coolies.

"Bara Sahib, umbrella, please?"

A fine-looking Nepalese obligingly offered me his umbrella—a protection in these countries against sun as well as rain, and thus I made the acquaintance of G. B. Rana who soon became a real friend. G.B., as we all called him, was deputed by the Maharajah of Nepal to accompany the Expedition wherever it went. For many years G.B. had served as an officer in Gurkha battalions, crack units of the British Army.

Suddenly we heard wild galloping hooves drumming on the cracked sun-baked ground. The two horses belonging to Lachenal and Terray, without their saddles and covered with lather, rushed towards us from the gorges of the Gandaki[5] and made for their stables, riderless.

With dignity, Lachenal explained later, "Real mountaineers, you see, find such artificial means of locomotion obnoxious."

On the evening of this first march G.B. conducted us to a rustic bungalow.

"It belongs to His Highness," he informed me deferentially.

"We are indeed honored."

At this point the Maharajah seemed rather like the Marquis of Carabas. Little by little we were to learn that in Nepal everything belongs to the Maharajah personally.

On the 10th the main body of the Expedition reached Tansing, the capital of the province, and stopped for three days. As soon as camp was pitched and roped off to keep away the crowd of sight-seers, we climbed the hill overlooking the village to strain our eyes toward the far distant mountains. What a wonderful moment at last to see suddenly the goal of our dreams!

We had all read a great many books on the Himalaya, and had talked endlessly with our friends who had been to the Karakoram in 1936; we had put the most ridiculous questions to our cameraman, Marcel Ichac, the only Himalayan veteran among us. Everyone had formed his own personal idea of these mountains. Were we going to be disappointed?

The sight which awaited us at the top of the hill far exceeded anything we had imagined. First we could see nothing but a filmy mist; then, far away in the distance we could make out a terrific wall of ice rising above the mist to an unbelievable height. The horizon to the north was blocked out for hundreds and hundreds of miles. This shining wall appeared absolutely colossal, without fault, or without the slightest crack. The seven-thousand-meter peaks led up to the eight-thousanders, and were entirely overcome by their magnificence and grandeur. This was the Himalaya, our promised land. From now on we would always carry with us this vision.

11

The problem now seemed quite simple; to reach the mountains as quickly as possible and to battle with them. That night as we lay in our tents we all did a lot of thinking.

We left Tansing in two detachments, the advance party, consisting of Lachenal and Terray, going on a day ahead of the main body. Soon after we had started, about noon, I suddenly saw a wild figure loping towards me with long strides. With a shock I recognized Lionel Terray, dressed *a la népalaise,* in a minimum of clothes, his head shaven, his face gleaming with sweat. He was very angry, and vigorously brandishing his ice-axe so that everyone stood respectfully aside to let him pass.

What on earth could be the matter? Had there been an accident? Suddenly I felt anxious about his partner, Louis Lachenal—Biscante, as we called him (the Savoy word for cider). I called to Lionel:

"Where's Biscante?"

"He's back up there. The coolies have gone on strike."

"What about the loads?"

"Biscante is up there keeping an eye on them. Anyway I don't think the coolies mean any harm, but they want more pay. They want . . . I don't know what they want, I don't understand a word of their gibberish. There they are near Waiga at the side of the track. They've put down their loads and they won't budge an inch. It's blackmail," he added.

"That's G.B.'s department," I replied.

"I don't see how he can get us out of this mess."

"Now we'll see whether he has any real authority over these jokers."

We started off at once. By the end of the afternoon we came in sight of the strikers. Lachenal, usually so cheerful, looked thoroughly disgusted. When G.B. arrived, the porters drew closer together. They addressed him noisily, shouting their grievances. As for us, calmly we settled down to eat and drink at our leisure. We knew that our serenity would add considerably to our prestige. With remarkable nonchalance we took off our shoes to rest our feet, performing every movement with studied slowness.

Now it was up to G.B. For half an hour he treated the coolies to a flow of eloquence which we shall always remember, though it was quite impossible for us to understand. The quiet, measured tone in which he began grew steadily louder; then suddenly it rose like a tornado echoing through the cathedral-like gorge. As if by magic the loud complaints of the coolies were transformed into timid pleadings. G.B. replied with vigor and assurance. Now there was no question about his authority. Suddenly a coolie said something, probably abusive. We were amazed to see G.B.

hurl himself upon the offender and beat him until he took flight. This rough stuff produced quick results; one by one, as we watched, the coolies took up their loads and continued on their way.

As we approached the Sedhi Khola (Khola means river or torrent) we met some pretty Nepalese women on the road, dressed in all their finery. The light graceful creatures passed us quickly, walking barefoot with little steps. The further we went the more of them we saw dressed in their brightly colored saris. They were all making for the same spot. Ang-Tharkey explained to me that a great religious feast, the Kumbh-Mela, which they celebrate every twelve years, was taking place that very day.

We arrived and with great difficulty succeeded in making our way through the lively, noisy, crowd. At the foot of a large rock, a *sadhou* or holy man was fervently invoking his gods. Priests, surrounded by rapt multitudes, were reading out Vedic texts. Numbers of the faithful were making their way to Kali Gandaki, the sacred river. There they all undressed, both men and women, and plunged one after the other into the flood; then they dipped lotus leaves into the water and proceeded to beat their foreheads with them repeatedly. Some would take a few thick leaves and make a sort of conch-like affair in the center of which they placed little lighted candles. Then they carefully set these roving lights upon the waters which would carry them far, far away towards the Ganges.

On Sunday, April 16, we arrived at Baglung, the last considerable village before you climb to the high valleys. There remained only another three or four marches before Tukucha but those would be the hardest, for we should have to rise from about 2,000 feet to 8,000 feet.

Next morning Noyelle woke us early: "Look—look—Dhaulagiri! Dhaulagiri!"

Dhaulagiri at last! Noyelle was outside yelling for joy. Could he really see it? Everyone was out in a flash, covering up his nakedness with the first thing that came to hand. Some jumped out in their sleeping bags, hopping as in a sack race, others utilized a handkerchief for shorts. Lachenal distinguished himself by using his knitted cap.

An immense ice pyramid, glittering in the sun like a crystal, rose up more than 23,000 feet above us. The south face, shining blue through the morning mists, was unbelievably lofty, out of this world. We were speechless in face of this tremendous mountain whose name was so familiar to us, but the reality so moved us that we couldn't utter a word. Then slowly the reasons for our being here conquered our awe and our aesthetic pleasure, and we began to examine the gigantic outline from a practical point of view.

"Just look at the east arête, on the right!"

"Yes, it's impossible."

This was cold water on our hopes.

The sight was utterly magnificent, but from a mountaineering point of view we hadn't a prayer on this south face.

"If you're good, I'll show you Annapurna in two days' time," said our cameraman Ichac who, with Couzy, had just been making careful adjustments of his sights.

Seated in the shade of a great banyan tree, I presided over the coolies' payday which lasted all day long. The fascinated coolies shoved their noses close to the beams of the scales. Each of them received six rupees and one packet of "Red Star" cigarettes, acknowledged it with hands clasped, Hindu fashion, and then signed his name on G. B. Rana's list. (In front of what he is told is his name, written by the *babu,* each porter presses his thumb previously dipped in ink.) As the list lengthened, additional pieces of parchment were stuck on. By the time the operation was finished, it was nearly four yards long!

Terray allotted the loads to the coolies before they passed the check point. He felt their calves and their biceps, and inspected their lung-expansion, just as he would do if he were on his farm at Les Houches. The "strong man," as the Sherpas called him, handled the heaviest of the loads with disconcerting ease; the porters treated him with great respect. They came forward one by one, gauged the loads at a glance, and tested their burden, with sidelong glances in the direction of the others. With considerable ingenuity they made frames for the loads, out of bamboos and lianas, and in time everything was picked up. The coolies carry and balance the loads by bands round their foreheads, and in this way our six tons of gear were carried over 120 miles of mountainous tracks to the scene of action.

Now, on to Tukucha!

The coolies filed ahead of us as far as the eye could see, along the banks of the Kali Gandaki. Towards midday we came to a large tributary: the Mayandi Khola. Marcel Ichac couldn't figure it out.

"Why, it's as big as the Gandaki. If it drained only the south face of Dhaulagiri as the map indicates, it would be just a little stream."[6]

And in fact, judging from the map, the route up Dhaulagiri from our headquarters at Tukucha would, without any difficulty, follow a valley running up into the north face. But if, instead of going towards Tukucha, this valley should descend in a westerly direction, as we were now beginning to suspect—judging from the extent of the waters draining it and pouring into the Mayandi Khola—then there must be a ridge, not shown on the map, cutting Tukucha off from the north face of Dhaulagiri. This would certainly be an obstacle to our proposed plan of ascent.

"Well, yes," I had to admit, "the Mayandi Khola ought to be far smaller than this before the monsoon."

"I think I have it," suggested Ichac with remarkable intuition, "it drains all the north side as well as the west."

"But what about the map?"

"It must be wrong."

This struck me as plausible. However, before abandoning the map I would wait for more positive proof. This proof was to be given to us; a month later the mystery was cleared up.

Next day, April 20, as we passed through Dana we tried to discover in the distance the lesser peaks and ridges of Annapurna.

"Well, weren't you going to show us this Annapurna?" I reminded Ichac.

We couldn't see Annapurna, but right opposite us there opened out the deep winding valley of the Miristi Khola. On the map there was a clearly marked path which followed these gorges to the Tilicho pass, from which a short arête seemed to lead to the summit of Annapurna.

"This Tilicho valley doesn't look very attractive," said Marcel Schatz.

"There's a path marked on the map."

Our liaison man Noyelle, came back looking gloomy after having interrogated some *shikaris* or hunters. "Nobody heard of the Tilicho pass."

"That map again!"

"It would be too much to expect," said Rébuffat, "to find a pass over 19,000 feet high, with a good path and a 26,000 foot peak just at hand!"

Later, when we came to explore the country, we found that the Miristi gorges were impassable; the famous Tilicho pass was not where it was marked on the map.

Meanwhile our path skirted the cliffs. Looking down through the conifers we could barely make out the wild, rumbling waters of the Krishna-Gandaki. Tremendous waterfalls gushed here and there from the limestone cliffs. Slowly we gained height and realized it by the party's heavier step and deliberate pace.

At Ghasa it began to get chilly, for we were now about 6,500 feet up, with another 1,600 feet to climb up to Tukucha. There were no longer any bananas or rice, only a few poor-looking crops, mostly barley. A little farther on we saw the upper slopes of Dhaulagiri, streaked with blue ice.

15

The south-east ridge running down towards us, of which we had had some hope, extended endlessly, as sharp as the blade of a knife and bristling with ice pinnacles and snow cornices—absolutely impregnable.

We all craned our necks to get a view of the gigantic walls which disappeared nearly four miles up into the clouds and the blue sky. The rock was dark brown, the snow dazzling, and the light so intense it made us squint. To try to pick out a route at this point seemed absurd. Nevertheless we couldn't hide our excitement. We were as happy to be in the mountains at last and to be able, from now on, to devote ourselves to the real object of the whole expedition. As for myself, I should at last be able to give up a role which was more that of a carrier or impresario than the leader of a mountaineering expedition.

At Lete we passed, with some surprise and emotion, through a pinewood which reminded us astonishingly of our mountains—the same trees, the same scattered blocks of granite and cool mosses. How was I to know that two months later this beautiful idyllic place would witness my own sufferings?

We came out on to a long stony plain formed during the centuries by the impetuous and irregular flow of the Gandaki river which had cut a colossal canyon right through the great Himalayan chain. Tremendous gales blew down this funnel and held up our advance. These hurricanes rage all the year round, and prevent any kind of growth. Columns of dust whirled up into the air, the wind howled round this gloomy, rocky inferno, and Ichac, who was protecting himself as best he could, yelled in my ear, "We might be in the Karakoram!"

The barefoot coolies kept together in tight little groups for mutual protection as we all hurried to reach Tukucha.

Ang-Tharkey, an ardent Buddhist, soon caught sight of Larjung with its sacred streamers flying from the housetops, their prayers agitated by the wind.

In the distance, at the far end of the stony desert, we could see a village gay with hundreds of prayer masts and encircled by what looked like fortifications.

"Tukucha, Sahib!"

We all hurried on, forded the swirling torrent—the Dambush Khola, of which we shall hear more later—and so made our entry into Tukucha.

There were, after all, far fewer people than we had expected. Numbers of dirty children surrounded us, observing our every move with curiosity. They played about in the water conduit in the middle of the village in which the women washed their pots and got the water for their tea. The old men remained on their doorsteps, suspicious and mistrustful of these white men who were here with such very obscure intentions. We were through the village in a few minutes, and before us lay an open stretch. On a Buddhist temple with rose-colored walls, flags flapped in the wind. Although it was not a very attractive spot, with its naked gray cliff rising gloomy above us, it was the only suitable place for our camp.

The long approaching march was now over. The date was April 21 and we had taken just over a fortnight to travel practically right across Nepal.

Chapter III

The Hidden Valley

THE PROGRAM NOW BEFORE US WAS CLEAR-CUT. FIRST WE SHOULD HAVE TO establish camp, unpack, check and sort out the equipment and food. For the next forty-eight hours everybody would have a definite job. They were soon at it, dirty and noisy, and cheerful. Ichac delved into his precious crates of films and equipment; Dr. Oudot sorted his dressings and medical supplies, and the Sherpas pitched the tents, fixed up their kitchen, and helped the Sahibs stow everything away.

The weather was superb, and this first day at headquarters the mountains were looking their very best. It was marvelous to get at last a clear view of the peaks all round us! The Gandaki valley is a long rift between two immense mountain groups: The Dhaulagiri massif on the west rising to 26,795 feet, and the Annapurna massif on the east rising to 26,493 feet. A veil of mist lies in the depths of this rift, giving even greater majesty to these literally inaccessible walls that tower over us. The shapely Nilgiris,[7] the "blue mountains," glitter nearly 15,000 feet above us. Towards the north the sky is much clearer. As far as we could judge, vegetation is sparse up there towards Tibet.

The village of Tukucha is a maze of alleys, and the houses, regular little fortresses, are mostly caravanserais where passing travelers can find lodging for the night. The majority of the five hundred inhabitants are Buddhists whose piety can be judged from the number of prayer-wheels on the fifty-yard-long wall. Our Sherpas never omitted, when passing, to give a joyful turn to the metallic cylinders upon which sacred texts are engraved—a far more practical idea than the idea of reciting of lengthy prayers.

In the dark and evil-smelling courtyards or in the low-ceilinged rooms of the tumble-down houses, we saw a number of very primitive looms on which yak hair or sheep's wool could be woven into remarkably strong material. Here, the men spin as our shepherds of France used to.

At dawn the only sound in deserted Tukucha was the gong of the nearby temple, whose low harmonious booming floated weirdly on the air. A kind of drawn-out litany rose from the tent in front of mine. Sudden cadences in the monotonous chant made it seem like a dirge; then other voices would answer in the same monotone. Ang-Tharkey and his companions were saying their prayers.

A caravan surrounded by a host of children had assembled not far from our camp and everyone was talking vehemently—undoubtedly they were Tibetans. The women wore very becoming colored aprons, and their typically Mongolian faces were adorned with pats of cow-dung applied to both cheeks. Confident of their power to charm, they laughed, exposing all their teeth.

A crowd gathered and suddenly a wild dance started. The dancers were silhouetted against a magnificent background of snowy mountains. The ballet, which appeared to express the eternal dualism of joy and sorrow, life and death, was perfectly controlled. Its beauty was rough and primitive, for a dance always reflects the spirit of a people.

Abruptly they stopped. A Tibetan woman placed a copper dish in the center of the circle; the dancers began to mime most expressively, and their gaze traveled from the dish to us and back again. With great dignity the Bara Sahib generously tossed in a few rupees. This was a great success. Immediately the dance began again, even wilder than before. Again they all stopped suddenly. The Bara Sahib was obliged once more to display his generosity.

Since our arrival at Tukucha we had all nursed a secret hope of discovering a safe and easy ridge that would lead us straight to the summit of Dhaulagiri or Annapurna. The south-east ridge of Dhaulagiri, which was clearly marked on the map, and which we had seen from Baglung, gave us some slight encouragement, but no one was very certain. Then there was the north ridge; it was undoubtedly ice, but, judging from the general structure of the mountain, its moderate angle and slight rise in height would make it very suitable for an attempt. Now, by pitching a few intermediate camps, we might. . . . As for Annapurna, its proximity to the Tilicho trail seemed to make it easily accessible, and for that very reason it lost a good deal of its interest from the climber's point of view.

Next day Jean Couzy left with Pansy (Ang-Tsering) on a reconnaissance to make observations from the 13,000-foot point that overlooks Tukucha and which should command a wonderful view.

At 11 A.M. I was in radio communication with them.

"Coucou speaking. Just reached the top. The view is marvelous; Dhaulagiri towers above everything. The south-east ridge looks absolutely frightful. Very long, with lots of ice towers. Camp sites doubtful."

"What about the north ridge?"

"Ice all the way. Looks very steep. Certainly great technical difficulties. The ticklish part is toward the middle, but there is another snag, how to get on to the ridge. From here the East glacier,[8] which you would expect to be the normal approach, looks extremely broken up."

"Can you see the north face?"

"Those great walls of seracs make it a very dangerous proposition. At its foot there is a relatively easy slope, which ought to open onto the north-west ridge, but from where I'm standing I can't see very well."

"What do you think of the Nilgiris?"

"Absolutely sheer. Not a hope from this side."

"Thanks, Couzy. See you later."

"O.K., Maurice. Off."

This first report didn't do much to encourage optimism. When he returned we could proceed to an examination of the problem with the help of his sketches.

That evening in the mess-tent Couzy, between cups of tea, confirmed what he had told us by radio.

"We must find a way to the foot of the final pyramid," said Rébuffat. On this point everyone was agreed. But on the means of getting there, opinions differed.

What ought we to do? Ought we to go up this East glacier of Dhaulagiri, which was in a chaotic condition and undoubtedly extremely dangerous? Or skirt round the Tukucha Peak, which marks the end of the north arête and follow the Elbow Valley shown on the map,[9] in order to reach the northern basin of Dhaulagiri?

"We must reconnoiter in all directions," I said. "And to accomplish this we shall obviously have to split up. During this period of exploration, when we shall be working our way round Dhaulagiri and Annapurna, we need parties of two only."

"There's certainly work to be done on Annapurna," declared Schatz. Then, dreamily, "A pass at 20,000 feet, a track . . ."

"Dhaulagiri has a nasty look. I'd prefer the other fellow," admitted Couzy.

"Very well. Tomorrow, we'll all get going. You, Lachenal, and you, Rébuffat, will go and reconnoiter the East glacier. Doctor Oudot and Schatz will take horses, and go up above Lete to get a view of the Tilicho pass and Annapurna. Ichac and I will take a little trip up to the top of the

Elbow Valley, marked as the Dambush Khola. Perhaps we shall be able to see the north side of Dhaulagiri."

"And what about me?" said young Jean Couzy, deeply disappointed.

"You'll rest in camp. Don't worry, there'll be something for everyone to do. It's now April 23rd, we've plenty of time before the monsoon breaks, early in June. You, too, Lionel, try to keep warm."

"And stick to light food for the present," advised Dr. Oudot.

Terray who had been suffering from a stomach upset was feeling a bit better already, but I still thought he looked very drawn from illness.

"And I suppose I'm to twiddle my thumbs?" asked our liaison, Noyelle.

"Your excellency will be good enough to contact with the local bigwigs. And you and Couzy can finish organizing the camp."

At 5 A.M. we were awake. Lachenal and Rébuffat went off with two Sherpas who carried skis, and one high-altitude unit. This unit consisted of a nylon tent for two persons, two special sleeping-bags, two half-length air mattresses, an alcohol stove, and cooking utensils; the whole weighing roughly 22 lbs. A *shikari* would guide them over the lower slopes of the mountain where otherwise they might well lose time wandering in the valleys and forests.

Dr. Oudot and Schatz were up and about, and their horses were ready at seven o'clock. I hoped that during the day they would be able to go high enough to see the famous Tilicho pass and clear up the mystery about it. Then Ichac and I left camp, delighted at the thought of being in the mountains once more. In a few minutes we came to the Dambush Khola, whose valley we were to follow as high up as possible.

Our route took us through a wonderful stretch of thick jungle. We were greeted by the first rays of the sun, and at this early hour a delicate scent rose from some pink flowers, and recently felled fir trees gave out the familiar smell of resin. It was already pleasantly warm. Jumping from boulder to boulder, climbing the rocks that barred our path, scrambling over precariously balanced obstacles at the risk of falling into the stream, we rapidly gained height.

"The first snow!" shouted Ichac happily.

"More at home on this sort of ground, eh Matha?"

"What contrasts there are here, and how different from the Alps! Here it's only a step from jungle to snow."

By keeping to the cliffs on the true left of the valley we hoped to get some glimpses of the north face, and even perhaps a clear view. We had great hopes of this side, since we were aware that in the Himalaya north faces, for many reasons of geology and weather, frequently offer the least steep and least difficult means of access.

For some time we had been keeping along by the cliffs.

The Tukucha Peak, a "seven-thousander," completely blocked the view with its grand and terrifying walls. All round us cascades spouted from the rocks, and banks of rotten snow clung desperately to the flanks of the mountain. It was the end of winter.

Who knows the secret of the renewal of life in such places? From beneath the snow as it melted and slid off the vegetation appeared, stunted, twisted and flattened. Birds and insects were migrating to the heights which once again could nourish them.

"Another few weeks and summer will be here."

"The Expedition's arrived at just the right moment, don't you think?"

Ichac took some bearings. The altimeter registered 11,000 feet. "North Nilgiris 111° east. Tukucha Peak 270° west . . . This map is wrong! It's quite obvious. The great Dambush Khola *cirque* is contained on the north by a ridge coming from the Tukucha Peak. At the foot of Dhaulagiri on

The Ridges of Dhaulagiri—These sketch maps show the fundamental differences between the map of the Indian Survey, above, and the true lay-out, on the right. Tukucha had been chosen as our base on account of its proximity both to the Elbow Valley, which appeared to give access to the north face of Dhaulagiri, and the north side there is another basin, that's all. But if we've got to cross the ridge to get to that basin before tackling the north face, then we'll still be here until next year!"

I was beginning to be worried. But we had to leave it at that if we were to reach camp this evening.

We made some long glissades down the snow, stopped to take a few pictures and pick up some stones for the geologists, and at four-thirty, sunburnt and happy, were sipping wonderful tea with milk back in camp at Tukucha.

"What about Annapurna? Have you seen it?" I asked Dr. Oudot and Schatz who had just come back.

"Only the very top part."

"Ah, at last!"

"The little we saw looked all right. Getting there, however, is quite another matter. But of course we only had a very distant view."

"We were just able to pick out, above the gorges of the Miristi, a sort of depression which on this side looked possible. The other side is an unknown factor. We'd have to get a much closer view to be able to say anything."

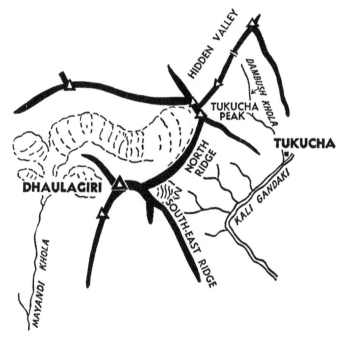

to the east face, where a small glacier lies wedged between the north-east and the south-east ridges. As Dhaulagiri has no true north ridge, we were accustomed to call the north-east ridge (which joins Dhaulagiri to the Tukucha Peak) by this name.

"As soon as you've rested," I said to Oudot, "you can go off again, this time for several days."

Noyelle came in with G. B. Rana and a native gentleman of forty or so, well-dressed, and wearing boots. He had fine drooping mustaches, and looked intelligent. It was the *Suba,* the head man of the district. There were Hindu greetings on both sides.

"*He* comes from Tinigaon," our friend G. B. Rana informed me with emphasis, pointing to a native who had held back until then. "He's a friend of the Great Man."

A searching interrogation began, for the man was a *shikari* who claimed to be perfectly well acquainted with the Tilicho pass. We had to take him to look at our map.

"Tilicho pass, at the foot of Annapurna? No?"

What *were* we to believe? There was only one thing to do—go and see the Tilicho. But this was all part of the exploration of Annapurna, and would be for later on. For the moment we were concerned with Dhaulagiri.

Next day Lachenal and Rébuffat returned, in high spirits. The guide had taken them well to the right of the East Dhaulagiri glacier, practically underneath the Tukucha Peak.

"The *shikari* is really tough," said Lachenal, himself a good judge of a guide.

"That's useful to know for the future. Well, what about this glacier?"

"We went up," Rébuffat explained, "to about the same height as Mont Blanc, after bivouacking at around 13,000 feet. The East glacier's just a great torrent of ice. It should be possible to get up it, but it would be tough."

"Even supposing we did succeed in getting up the glacier," continued Lachenal, "I don't quite see how we should get on the north ridge. My own view is that we shouldn't try. It's a regular Walker[10] with seracs stuck on!"

Clearly this demanded something beyond Alpine technique. A series of well-placed camps was called for, and individual initiative must give way to collective effort. Experienced as Lachenal and Rébuffat were they were beginning to realize just what Himalayan climbing is and what it requires—a team. While they hungrily devoured canned beef, we talked over the situation.

It wasn't at all encouraging. But these preliminary explorations had been the means of our making contact with the real Himalaya, and getting to the heart of our problems. There was no question of solving them in forty-eight hours. Now, however, we could begin to make a serious attack on our objectives. We decided that Couzy, Oudot and Schatz were to examine possible approaches to Annapurna by the Miristi Khola. Ichac, Terray and I were going to explore the north face of Dhaulagiri and the approach to it from the Dambush Khola.

At dawn on April 26 the two parties left for several days' reconnaissance. Each team was accompanied by Sherpas carrying high-altitude units and skis. Lachenal and Rébuffat's *shikari* guided us as far as the first *névés* which was as far as he had ever got. After a quick meal we sent the *shikari* down again. The heat was overpowering, the snow became like soup; we put on our skis so as not to sink. For the Sherpas, who went up to their waists, it was a horrible ascent.

At five o'clock the Sherpas, all except Ang-Tharkey, went down again and so it was time to pitch camp. We couldn't take off our special glasses— the glare was too powerful for our tired eyes. The light which poured down the immense north face of the Tukucha Peak overwhelmed us. This was our first night at high altitude. The tents, which we called "coffins," were so tiny that we had to wriggle in and out. They only weighed 2½ lbs., as they were made of nylon and duralumin, and they could be carried at the bottom of a rucksack. Lying on our stomachs on our air-mattresses, tucked in our sleeping-bags, Ichac, Terray and I did the so-called cooking. We had to be careful not to make any sudden movement, for every inch was taken. Under these conditions your morale needs to be good to cope with so oppressively restricted a world.

The next day Lionel Terray set a rapid pace from the start. During his illness he was so weak he had only been able to walk with considerable effort, but now it was as much as we could do to follow him. The slope was steep, at the maximum angle on which our sealskins would hold, and we were sometimes obliged to push with our sticks. The sun directly overhead made the ground more difficult. We stuck our skis upright in the snow, so as to be able to spot them on the way down. The height, which was about the same as that of Mont Blanc, was very tiring. In spite of a gnawing hunger we went on until we reached a little plateau. Terray was having heavy going. Had he over-estimated his returning strength? He had to summon up every ounce of energy to reach that plateau when he let himself fall heavily on the snow.

"I'm as weak as a kitten!" he said, "I feel like death."

After having drunk some good hot tea, to be on the safe side, we sent him back to the first camp. Ang-Tharkey after helping us to pitch our second camp would go down to join him. A little rocky island right in the middle of the slope offered a site for our tent. Ang-Tharkey went off quickly so as not to be overtaken by the dark.

We soon began to suffer from splitting headaches, which are frequent above 16,000 feet and were glad of the tablets of aspirin which Oudot had with foresight handed out. Although Ichac and I were both very tired, we could not sleep a wink. At sunrise we started in the direction of our wretched pass, leaving the tent up. We ascended much faster than the day before, and in barely an hour we reached the pass. The morning sun made the ridge ahead of us stand out in extraordinary relief and bathed it in lovely clear colors.

"Bad luck—this isn't the true pass yet," I said to Ichac, who was deeply disappointed.

Instead of looking out on to a valley, we had before us a basin of crusted snow.

"Maurice, look over there! The pass is the other side, at least two hours from here."

In spite of our preliminary marches, we were feeling our lack of training and acclimatization. It showed itself in our abnormal tiredness.

"Everyone, including the Sherpas, will have to go on reconnaissance and sleep out between 16,000 and 20,000 feet up," I said to Ichac. "Today has made me realize that without previous acclimatization, one can't go really high."

An icy wind greeted us as we approached the pass. We put on our nylon anoraks and trousers which were both snow- and wind-proof.

28 Avril 5

"Well I'm damned! A valley starting here—"

"It's not marked on the map," said Ichac. "It's an unknown valley."

"It runs down in a northerly direction, and divides into two great branches."

"No sign of Dhaulagiri! Surely it is not that pale impostor opposite us?" said Ichac pointing towards a 23,000 feet peak which had an odd likeness to Dhaulagiri.

Before us the "Hidden Valley," as Ichac called it—he loved giving things names—ran gently downwards. It was broad like a valley scooped out by a glacier, and the alternation of snow and yellow grass reminded one of a tiger's striped coat.

"To see the north face of Dhaulagiri, we'd have to go round to the left, right to the other end of the valley; it must be a terrific sight from there!"

"It's too late now," he replied, "and we haven't got the necessary camping gear."

"I suppose you're right."

On the other side of Tukucha, above the Nilgiris, there rose a mighty summit which Ichac identified as Annapurna. He made a rapid sketch of it while I was climbing up to him again. There was a keen wind from the north, and clouds were coming up, so after swallowing the contents of a tube of condensed milk, we started down.

Walking automatically, and looking straight ahead, we advanced in silence: we were both short of breath. Our minds wandered off into daydreams. I thought of the gentle valley of Chamonix with its trees, of so tender and restful a green, and its shady paths, so pleasant to stroll along. I felt my strength ebbing. The last rise before the pass was hard going, and Ichac made the trail. I tried to follow him; I just couldn't. Every ten steps I lay down in the snow. I couldn't go any further! Ichac cursed me roundly—the only thing that does any good at times like this. At last we got on to the ridge and what a relief! But we still had the whole descent before us.

To my great surprise, from the moment we started going down I felt as light as air. We went careening down to the camp, reaching it in a few minutes. This was a new experience for me: going up, one suffers from the height, the lack of oxygen and difficulty in breathing; coming down is quite a different story—everything seems easy.

While the water was heating for tea, Ichac told me a queer thing which had happened while we were on the plateau:

"As I was ploughing along heavily, I thought I heard someone else behind me . . . a third man. He was following us. I wanted to call out to

27

tell you. I couldn't. I glanced behind me rather furtively to set my mind at rest. But like an obsession, the feeling of someone else there kept on coming back to me. Then everything was all right again. It happened at the same moment that you felt so groggy."

"It just shows that when you're at a great height, your powers of clear thinking deteriorate very quickly."

We were all in, our legs like jelly and our heads like lead. Then the sun began to reach us, through the ceiling of evil-looking clouds.

"Ang-Tharkey is coming!" cried Ichac, who had just seen a little black speck on our tracks.

"Good! He'll help us carry all this stuff."

We were excited, and ready to put off for a while the joys of our super sleeping-bags. We got into our frozen boots as best we could, broke camp in record time and then burdened like donkeys we moved carefully down the slope of rotten snow.

I greeted him: "Salaam, Ang-Tharkey!"

"Tired, sir?"

He wanted to carry everything himself, and it was hard to resist the temptation. My shoulders were being sawn through by the straps, but on we went, striding down slopes which were just ready to avalanche and completely treacherous at this time of day. Here now was the ridge— Terray's nightmare—and our skis were still there. Ang-Tharkey strode on down to the lower camp on foot while we skied slowly down, describing elegant figures in the very uneven snow.

Next day we were given a triumphal reception at Tukucha. Terray, who had gone down the day before, was better, though still pretty exhausted. The others plied us with questions.

"Well, what do you make of Dhaulagiri?"

"Where do the waters from the north face drain?"

Solemnly we answered, "They drain into the moon!"

Chapter IV

The East Dhaulagiri Glacier

EVERYONE WAS BACK IN CAMP, EXCEPT COUZY AND SCHATZ, WHO WERE STILL off on the Annapurna reconnaissance, so it was a good opportunity to review the general situation. Oudot, who had only just left them, reported that on April 27 he had gone as far as the depression which we had first seen from Lete.

"It was hard work, but perfectly possible for porters. From there we saw Annapurna—but a long way off. From the higher ridges a spur runs down into the Miristi Khola valley."

"And the pass?"

"No sign of the Tilicho. I stopped there and let the other two go on."

"What it amounts to is this," I said after a moment, "there are three problems. For Dhaulagiri we must explore the north side, and the ways of getting there. The reconnaissance that Ichac and myself have just made gave us one glimpse into the unknown, but did not really clear up the problem."

"It's not a problem," said Ichac, "it's a mystery. I've my own ideas on the matter, but obviously we must go and see for ourselves."

"I'm ready to go," said Terray, "as soon as ever I can. I'm fed up with being sick. I want to get going again. In two days' time I'll be perfectly fit."

"I don't want to push myself forward," put in Oudot, "but I admit I'd like to go, too. I spend my time handing out Epsom salts to my native patients in Tukucha."

"All good for prestige. And anyway you've only just got back."

"Our prestige is so high it can stand my absence for a few days."

"Seriously," I added, "I don't care for the Expedition's medical officer to be too long away from Tukucha, but obviously it would be a good thing for you also to get acclimatized."

"Then we'll go together," decided Terray.

"Right you are."

"And what's the second problem?" asked Lachenal, who was obviously infected by Terray's fever to be up and doing.

"The second question is Annapurna. We'll have to go further into it, but before we can decide anything we must wait for Couzy and Schatz to come back. As for the third problem . . ."

"Ah, this is where we come in, Gaston," said Lachenal to Rébuffat.

"I don't think," Gaston said, to make us pretty dubious about it, "going straight up the glacier would be at all easy. Judging from what we saw, it's a huge slope of ice cluttered up with seracs and seamed with crevasses. Avalanches sweep it continuously. I don't much like the look of it."

"I shall go with you," I said to Lachenal and Rébuffat. "We'll ride up as far as possible on horseback, and pitch a small base camp at the foot of the glacier. I think we can clear up the problem."

The following day everyone rested. In the morning Ichac, Noyelle, Rébuffat and myself took the opportunity to climb up a hillock south of Tukucha from which we had a perfect view of Dhaulagiri. Through the glasses I picked out the frightful obstacles on the East glacier. By keeping to the left, that is to say on the true right bank of the glacier, we should be able to avoid most of the seracs, except in the upper section. The problem was to reach one of the two ridges.

Dhaulagiri, as seen from here, was magnificent. The morning mists were still lingering in the valleys, but high up the snow and ice glistened and made us blink. The sky was pastel blue. On another rocky point barely two hundred yards from us, a vulture was watching, motionless.

We had now been in Asia for a month.

Next morning we traversed the great rocky flats of the Gandaki on horseback. The Sherpas took us by way of Larjung, no doubt so that they could spin the prayer-wheels. This village, where the alleys are covered in by roofs—there must be a great deal of snow in winter—is extremely picturesque. Half a mile further on we left our mounts, and the party spread out over the grassy slopes. Numbers of yaks and cows were grazing hungrily on the lush grass. On the hillside our way was lined by trees covered with sweet-smelling blossoms that ranged from pink to red. It wasn't easy to keep to a schedule in a paradise like this. Today—and the Sherpas couldn't understand it—we let the porters have all the halts they asked for. It was fantastic that only a few hours after seeing these giant flowers and this inviting grass, we were to be walking upon glaciers of such a scale that our cheerful assurance would suddenly change to awestruck respect. All day we climbed upward.

We left the tree-line behind, and some patches of snubby grass were the only sign of vegetation at this height. The *névés* increased in number. The porters came up steadily with their loads, and when evening came we pitched our Base Camp on the last patch of earth. The radio was set up—it enabled us to receive and send messages at a distance of over six miles—and contact with Tukucha was established. I listened with almost childish delight to Marcel Ichac's voice as he gave me the latest news and the current village gossip.

"Hello, Matha," I said, using his nickname, "we've arrived safely. It's gloomy up here this evening in this weather. We're all spending the night here . . ."

He said, "Noyelle is leaving tomorrow to join you. Couzy and Schatz are back."

"Oh! What about Annapurna?"

"They went on for three days. They succeeded in reaching the bed of the Miristi Khola."

"Excellent!"

"They crossed it and then ran up against a subsidiary ridge coming down from Annapurna."

"The same one they saw with Oudot on April 27?"

"That's right. This ridge seems to be huge. After an easy beginning it probably links up with the main ridge, but this junction wasn't visible from below."

"Did they go any further?"

"No. They thought it would be quite impossible to skirt round the ridge to have a look at the north face."

"So they didn't see the Tilicho pass?"

"Not the ghost of a pass. If there really is a Tilicho pass leading to the foot of the north face of Annapurna, it's somewhere else."

"Then the man from Tinigaon was right! I hope they're not too tired."

"They're resting. What sort of weather have you got up there?"

"Very cold. We're in the clouds. Say hello to everybody."

"Good luck!"

Next morning at daybreak we proceeded rapidly in the direction of the great ice-fall. From close at hand, and in the half-light, it was extremely impressive. The party consisted of myself, Lachenal and Rébuffat, and the Sherpas—Ang-Tharkey, Foutharkey and Sarki. It would be the first time on this Expedition that they had come up against considerable technical difficulties.

The day was one long search for snow-bridges over the crevasses. We wound in and out between immense barriers of ice or alongside gaping crevasses. There was no alternative but to make our way beneath gigantic seracs that threatened to collapse at any moment. As we climbed, cutting steps, or walking up in our crampons, we often glanced up uneasily at these huge, precariously balanced blocks of ice.

The slope steepened considerably; we had to cut a great many more steps. The Sherpas labored beneath their forty-pound rucksacks. The weather had been threatening since eleven o'clock, and it now grew suddenly worse. We had to find a level spot, sheltered from falling seracs, on which to pitch camp. It was two o'clock, we were only halfway up the glacier, and it had started to snow. The night came on but most of us were restless and couldn't sleep a wink.

We were up very early in the morning, for every day the weather was liable to break any time after 2 P.M. Then the noise of the thunder would echo ceaselessly among the surrounding walls and rumble away relentlessly until the evening.

Day was breaking. Various bits of hardware—ice-pitons, hammers, and snap-links—clanked on our sacks; we were prepared for the worst. At this early hour the ice was very hard. As we had observed the day before from our lookout point, the best, if not the only, route ran along the true right bank of the glacier.

As we ascended to about 16,000 feet our breathing became labored. Now when the Sherpas halted they would double themselves up over their ice-axes and empty their lungs with a deep whistle to which we soon became accustomed. Even during the preliminary marches some of the porters had breathed like this.

Although I couldn't be too certain, it seemed to me that I suffered less from the lack of oxygen than Lachenal and Rébuffat: probably the result of those recent nights spent at 16,000 feet. This convinced me that everyone would have to go up to between 16,000 and 20,000 feet for conditioning before a major assault.

It was already midday, and we were still 300 yards from the plateau which marked the end of our difficulties. A glacier is like a river; the level places where it spreads out tranquilly are followed by turbulent falls. The possibility of crossing these 300 yards was doubtful.

"Looks bad," said Lachenal.

"Look at these blocks of ice that have come down already!" said Rébuffat.

"Bare ice everywhere," I said dejectedly. "And what a slope! We'll have to go right across the glacier and try the left bank."

"Before deciding on that side, we ought to have a look just above, and to the left near the rocks," advised Rébuffat.

"Go and see whether there's a way, both of you. I'll wait here with the Sherpas."

In a twinkling they were up the first slope which was green ice and extremely steep.

"Well done! Nice work!" I couldn't help calling out to them.

Their skill cheered me greatly, and the Sherpas were amazed. After a few minutes Lachenal shouted:

"Maurice! Don't go over to the left. You can come up, we're going to have a look over to the right."

"O.K. Be careful!"

The sky was livid—it was the daily storm coming up. Lachenal and Rébuffat were on extremely dangerous ground. At any moment they might be caught under a serac.

"Let's go on," I said to the Sherpas, who were not feeling too happy. I was obliged to cut plenty of big steps as well as holds for their hands, for the cumbersome sacks tended to tip them outwards. The angle was so steep that each man standing upright could lick the ice without the least difficulty.

"Nothing doing," a voice called to me from above.

"There's an enormous crevasse right across the glacier," yelled the other. I could hear them cursing.

"No luck?" I said, joining them behind a serac. "Well then, we'll have to cross over. Perhaps there's a way on the other side."

It was snowing a little, the cloud ceiling was low. Thunder growled ceaselessly, setting our nerves on edge. All six of us were in the middle of gigantic seracs; we were overwhelmed by the unexpected difficulties with which the mountain was confronting us. Sinister cracking noises shook the great blocks of ice on which we moved. The glacier was pallid; the light grew dim.

Although they were obviously uneasy, Lachenal and Rébuffat made a gallant attempt in the direction indicated, while the rest of us waited in complete silence, trying to keep cool and impassive when the glacier was shaken by ominous shocks and tremors. Lachenal and Rébuffat returned looking glum. "No way there."

"Maurice, we'd much better get down," insisted Rébuffat, "it's not healthy here."

Suddenly we heard a loud, prolonged cracking. We tucked our heads in: but it wasn't the end yet!

"Come on! We'll be caught," yelled Lachenal, "down we go."

"Let's get out of this," shouted Rébuffat.

The endless rumbling of the thunder added to the general alarm. It wasn't a retreat, it was a flight from the mountain which was preparing to strike.

Lachenal just had time to fling himself down the slope with a Sherpa on the end of his rope.

"Get a move on!"

I swore at my man, who was too slow for my liking. Down the ice wall we went, one after the other. Then a violent hailstorm broke. We had to check ourselves from going too fast for safety, in this slope where every move demanded care.

"Watch out for the Sherpas. Don't let them fall off," I called into the wind to Lachenal, who was setting rather too hot a pace for his man.

"We'd go a hell of a long way!" he flung back at me without slowing down.

Slowly the hail slackened: now, down the wall, we were safe, out of danger.

"Hell! We so nearly got there—!"

"You can't push on when it's like that."

I realized that even if we had reached the plateau, it would have been madness to try to bring the main body up this way. The risk was far too great; no victory would justify the loss of life resulting from taking such risks deliberately.

The hail turned to snow, and we were surrounded by mist, which reduced visibility to five yards. Gray shadows loomed up from time to time as ghostly figures went their headlong way down towards camp. Avalanches of fresh snow fell continually, with a frightful din. The inferno receded.

But for us this episode would always remain a nightmare.

About five o'clock, down at Base Camp, we were drinking tea which Noyelle had brewed as soon as he had spotted us.

"I found the way up quite easily," he said. "When I got here I sent young Angawa down to Tukucha, an unnecessary mouth to feed here, and Terray needed him."

"What day is it then? We've lost all notion of time."

"It's the third."

"What, May 3rd already! Just a month more before the monsoon."

"And nothing decisive has been discovered about Dhaulagiri. To settle the whole question once for all we'd have to explore those buttresses of the south-east ridge lying just in front of us."

"Perhaps we could go," exclaimed Lachenal.

"Right. As soon as your skis arrive, go and have a look at the big snowy point at the end of the ridge."

Noyelle suggested that we should get into radio communication with Tukucha.

"I spoke to Ichac a couple of hours back, but there was such a buzzing from the aerial that I thought it best to switch off."

A few minutes later communication with Tukucha was established.

"Herzog speaking. What's the news from Tukucha?"

"This is Ichac. All's well in camp. Nothing to report. Lionel Terray and Oudot went off this morning. Have you found a possible route?"

"Not on your life! These mountains are unclimbable! No expedition could ever get through this way."

"What are you going to do?"

"I'm going down tomorrow. Rébuffat and Lachenal will go on skis to a small point of about 18,000 feet on the south-east ridge of Dhaulagiri. From there they will be able to see the whole of the south face."

"Do they need anything?"

"Send up extra food supplies and three pairs of skis."

"O.K. If you come down tomorrow you'll have *thar* for lunch."

"*Thar?*"

"Himalayan chamois. G. B. Rana and the *Suba* have been hunting with our rifles and shot three. There's one for us."

"Well then I'll come down tomorrow for sure. And Lionel . . . did he go off without his share?"

"Don't worry—he took a good big hunk with him!"

"See you tomorrow."

"Say hello to everybody. *Off.*"

Early next morning I left the others upon the grass beside the camp, giving the Sherpas a lesson in ice-technique, and I made my solitary way back to Tukucha. The descent was pure delight. I tried not to lose too much time, but I couldn't resist stopping every hundred yards or so. My heart was full of joy as I passed beneath the trees with their wonderful red blossoms and then, humming to myself, went striding down grassy slopes covered with budding spring flowers.

Between two fir trees, and modestly concealed by wooded hillocks, lay a green lake in whose limpid waters was reflected the graceful picture of the Nilgiris. The larches round it looked more graceful than the firs, and its banks were covered with soft moss. Rough tracks led down to the stony plain of the Gandaki River. The waters had risen, and I knew I would have to get my feet wet. I didn't want to get blisters, and so I hesitated. By good luck a Tibetan came along just then, and took in the situation at a glance. In the admirable manner of the country, he lifted me gently on his back and then, despite his load and the current, he crossed the flooded streams of the Gandaki barefoot on the stones and deposited me on dry ground. How could I show my gratitude? I held out a rupee. Very respectfully he bowed to me several times in succession. One cannot often find opportunities to be generous in this wild part of the world. "Look, here's another." He couldn't believe his eyes. Bowing deeply, he came up and kissed my feet! I was rather embarrassed and didn't quite know what to do. I struck a dignified and lordly attitude, and then went off feeling a bit ashamed of myself. At one o'clock I reached Tukucha where Couzy and Ichac gave me a cheerful welcome.

"Fresh meat, for once," I said between mouthfuls. "Congratulations to G.B. for the *thar.*"

I was in splendid form, and my appetite rivaled Terray's.

"Was the East glacier all that bad?"

"Technically, it must be much about the same as the north face of the Plan, but incomparably more dangerous. That's what Lachenal thinks too. We had some really bad moments up there. We came whizzing down, the Sherpas all came off several times."

"Not very funny, that sort of thing," said Couzy.

"But at any rate no harm's been done."

"Yes it has! Time—the days are flying by. Dhaulagiri is putting up a very good defense."

"Perhaps we shall find a route tomorrow."

Ichac gave Couzy a long glance, then answered me:

"Tomorrow—that would surprise me. We've got to find a way, but what's worrying me is that none of us has yet seen even the glimmer of a hope. The reconnaissance stage is far from finished.

"There are still possibilities of access by the south-east ridge. On the other hand the East glacier, which stopped us yesterday, might be turned by the left-hand wall."

"Well," I said, "you shall kill two birds with one stone: get acclimatized to the altitude, like the rest of us, and make a final reconnaissance of the upper part of the East glacier."

"From one face to another, and one ridge to the next, we shall finish up by going all round Dhaulagiri," concluded Couzy. "So we'll be off tomorrow."

"Congratulations on the *thar*," I said to G.B. who had come into the tent. He was very proud of being a good shot.

I noticed he felt like talking that evening. He seemed to be at a loose end. With some difficulty we started a conversation about Nepal, the Ghurkas, and the Rana family who are all-powerful in this country. From his wallet he pulled out his instructions, which were now a month old: he might have shown them to me earlier! He held out some parchment (made of bamboo paper) covered with Sanskrit writing and adorned with several complicated seals: it looked like the ancient charters of our early kings.

The next day, May 5, at about eight o'clock Couzy and Schatz left camp. It was their turn to go and rub their noses on the East glacier! Suddenly everything became very quiet. Ichac and I alone remained at Tukucha.

"There's a soldier going down to Tansing! Any letters?"

Of course we had a whole pile. But where was our mail from France? For more than five weeks we had been without any news. With G.B.'s help we wrote a letter in Gurkhali for the postmaster to try and clear up the matter.

A telescope with a magnification of twenty-five diameters was mounted on the camera tripod, and we were not long in discovering our friends at about 16,000 feet, high up on the snowy peak we christened the White Peak. They were getting ready for the descent. Ichac and I wrangled for turns at the telescope. They were now giving a fine exhibition of the French style of skiing, in spite of the snow apparently being in poor condition. I recognized Lachenal by his style as he executed some dazzling turns before the startled eyes of the Sherpas who, themselves, preferred to descend on their backsides.

During the afternoon some fascinating processions went past. The village women, who had all put on their best dresses, carried vases or pitchers and sprinkled everyone with water. The purpose of the ceremony was, by invocations and prayers, to attract the all-too-infrequent rain. For though there was never a day without a storm in the mountains, down here in the valleys there was practically no rain at all, and the crops suffered badly.

In the main street Ichac mercilessly shot everyone point-blank with his movie camera. Our prestige did not protect us; amid general laughter we were thoroughly watered, and the camera was soon put out of action. Our dignity had suffered where it was least water-proof and we beat a prudent retreat towards camp.

On his return Rébuffat gave us an awestruck account of what he had seen from the White Peak.

"What's the south face like?" inquired Ichac, and without waiting for the answer I added:

"When we saw it from Baglung, it looked terrific."

"If you'd seen it from close up you'd have seen something! A monstrous slope, several miles high, and without a break, something like the north face of the Matterhorn, which as you know isn't exactly an attractive place, only this is three times as big."

We all looked at one another in consternation.

"The best thing is just to write off the south face."

"At least now we know where we are. What about the south-east ridge? The other day when we saw it from the East glacier, you were the most hopeful, you said . . ."

"I was absolutely wrong. To begin with, it's incredibly long, it's all very high up, and above all it's technically very difficult: great walls and towers of ice, some rock, broken ground, gendarmes—there's no end to it."

"Any possible camp sites?"

"None."

"Well," I said, "all that's not exactly encouraging."

"Oh," he replied, "there's absolutely no possibility of going *that* way."

"What's the verdict?"

"We must give up both these routes."

Dejectedly we went off to get ready for dinner in the mess tent.

The next day we received a visit from a Buddhist Lama whom we had already seen at Baglung. His claret-colored robe was of doubtful cleanliness, but his expression radiated jovial good nature. Ichac, who frankly enjoys the simplicity and naturalness of Buddhist Lamas, gave him a great deal to eat. Our Lama spoke enthusiastically of Muktinath. Our conversation with him was carried on with Ang-Tharkey as intermediary and was very quaint indeed. This is about how it went:

"Are you going there now?" we asked him.

"I'll be there tomorrow."

"But it's a long way from here." Even though he was a Lama, and a man of oracles and prodigies, I didn't think he would have seven-league boots!

"You must come there," he began again, "every day there are miracles: flames come out of the ground, the priests make prophecies."

"We'll certainly come. In a few days perhaps . . ."

Ichac suddenly had a wonderful idea: "Shall we climb Dhaulagiri?"

Here was a chance to show off his talents! The Lama reflected deeply. He began to tell the beads of an enormous rosary. He gazed up into the sky, then down at his hands. This went on for more than five minutes, while we remained silent and motionless. Were we about to witness some extraordinary feat of magic? Had we not been told that these Lamas were supernatural beings?

Very slowly, the Lama seemed to be coming back to earth: he brought himself to utter:

"Dhaulagiri is not propitious to you . . ." Then he added after a minute: "It would be best to give it up and turn your thoughts towards the other side."

"Which side?" asked Ichac.

For us the question was of some importance!

"Towards Muktinath," he said, as though it was obvious.

Did he mean Annapurna? The future would soon show us.

Lachenal, bronzed by the sun, returned to tell us that he had left Couzy and Schatz at the glacier camp and as the radio was out of order we should be without news of them for some days. About five-thirty Oudot and Terray "landed" (the word is no exaggeration) from the cliff overhanging the camp. Terray was wildly excited; he'd grown a beard which made him look frightful.

"As for Dhaulagiri, my lads! You can forget it!"

His lips were protruding more than usual in his efforts to find the right words. In a loud, exasperated voice he burst out:

"Look here, Maurice, it's absolutely unclimbable, that Dhaulagiri! It's fiendishly difficult!"

"Come and sit down and have a drink," I said this in hopes he would calm down a bit. "You're all dust and sweat!"

"I'll tell you what happened from the beginning," said Oudot quietly. "On the third we pitched our tents at about 14,700 feet, between your two camps. The next day we spent the night in the Hidden Valley. When we got to the pass the porters gave us a bit of trouble. They were frightened: they had never been beyond this point. Yesterday morning, very early, Lionel and I reached the pass which you had seen from a distance and which overlooks the northern basin of Dhaulagiri. And there . . ."

"Well?"

"It still gives me the creeps." Terray could not stop himself from shuddering. "And there below were the most terrifying gorges!"

"But where?"

"In front of us was Dhaulagiri," went on Oudot, "the real one—on the way up I had mistaken the false point for it—and straight down below us, was a huge glacier, very heavily crevassed . . ."

"The foulest-looking piece," put in Terray—

". . . flowing down a canyon with walls thousands of feet high!"

"You see, I was right," said Ichac, with modest triumph, "so it *does* all drain into the Mayandi Khola!"

"It's all on such a terrific scale, it's a world in itself," added Terray. "As for the north ridge, which separates this glacier from the East glacier up which you went, it's half rock and half ice, and very steep. The northwest ridge, which we had never seen before, runs down into the canyon."

This was most disappointing. "So you really think it's no go?" I asked.

"The Lama," said Ichac briskly, "has just informed us 'Dhaulagiri is not propitious for you. Go towards Muktinath.' Well?"

"We must go towards Muktinath," I said firmly, "and tomorrow morning at that!"

"Towards the Tilicho?" asked Gaston.

"We'll cross the Tilicho, the pass *north* of the Nilgiris, the one spoken of by the man from Tinigaon, and we'll take Annapurna in the rear."

"Why not make use of the Couzy-Oudot-Schatz reconnaissance of the Miristi Khola? They saw Annapurna."

"Yes, but only from a long way off. And they didn't see the north face. To reach it isn't going to be easy. And the ridge they saw there doesn't seem to me to be worth it. They don't think so either . . ."

"Look at the map," interrupted Ichac, "if we go by the Tilicho we shall save several days march."

"You'll see," said I, "we'll arrive plumb on the north face—and north faces in the Himalaya are often the easiest. We'll go just as far as is necessary to find Annapurna! As far as Manangbhot if need be."

"Well, so that's what we've come to!" concluded Ichac, quite disillusioned. "Just *looking* for Annapurna!"

Chapter V

Looking for Annapurna

"HURRY UP, OUDOT, I'M STARVING."

Lachenal and Terray were not enjoying themselves much that morning: Dr. Oudot was using them for various important tests—tests of metabolism, and Flack tests[11]—and the proceedings had gone on for an hour or more. The tests had to be done on empty stomachs, which was hard luck, for people have pretty good appetites after getting back from a reconnaissance. While Terray was being put through the tests, Lachenal, who had finished, cut himself enormous slices of *saucisson*. From time to time Terray cast a sidelong glance in his direction.

"Go away, Biscante, you hog, with your *saucisson*."

"Shut up, you'll spoil the results," said Oudot unsympathetically.

At first I'd been a bit apprehensive that Oudot might be keener on climbing than on doctoring, but I needn't have worried: he turned out to be a brilliant combination of both. He kept me regularly posted about the physical form of my party and about the progress of their acclimatization. May all future expeditions have an Oudot!

While Terray was feeling sorry for himself, Ichac, Rébuffat and I were getting ready to leave for Manangbhot. An attempt on Annapurna by the Miristi seemed very doubtful. From Manangbhot it should, on the contrary, be rather easier.

"You can give Tilman our love!" said Lachenal, who had finished his snack. Tilman is one of the great names in the Himalaya; it was he who had conquered the highest summit which had so far been climbed by man—Nanda Devi, 25,645 feet high, and we thought the world of him. On our departure we had been told that he was preparing to explore just this district round Manangbhot. I felt that, given the party he had with him, his objectives would be a reconnaissance of the approaches to Manaslu[12] and Annapurna. (Climbers always like to keep their plans dark beforehand, but it would be rather absurd if two expeditions were to attack the same summit.)

Foutharkey left in advance to get quarters ready at Tinigaon. We were taking supplies for eight days and before our return Oudot and Terray would have had time to go up to the Dhaulagiri glacier, if Couzy and Schatz should not meet with any success. These two rest days did me good; they gave me time to send news to France, to bring the expedition's accounts up to date, and to see that the organization of the camp was running smoothly. But the sedentary life really didn't suit me and I was very glad to be off again.

Along our route to Tibet there straggled a number of caravans carrying salt and rice. We made a triumphal march through the little village of Marpha, where the prayer flags were fluttering and the people crowded cheerfully round us. There were more Tibetans here than in Tukucha. All the Expedition's candies were distributed to the children who crowded about us. Later on we reaped the benefit of our open-handedness, for a great many coolies from the valley offered their services when we had need of them.

We came upon a number of prayer walls adorned with slabs of rock upon which we read the classic inscription: "*Om mane padme hum.*"[13] We were careful to respect the religious observances of these peoples, and to pass on the left of the walls. Little by little the look of the country changed; it became more desolate even than the regions we had just left. Northward the contours were softer; hills covered with reddish colored stones, a new luminosity in the atmosphere, and a growing feeling of desert country, showed beyond all doubt that we were approaching Tibet, though the frontier was a good day's march from this point.

At dusk we entered the wretched village of Tinigaon. The natives, extremely primitive and revoltingly dirty, stared suspiciously at us. A howling ragged mob, worthy of the *Cour des Miracles* of medieval Paris, escorted us to the only decent house in Tinigaon. A smiling Foutharkey was there to receive us; he had already made himself at home and was giving his orders, with his usual gentle kindliness, to numbers of women who crowded round him. We were in the house of the chief personage of the village whose home served as a halting-place for the caravans. He was an astute trader, adept at procuring at an advantageous rate all the supplies that the village needed.

The master of the house arrived and escorted us to the room which he had chosen for us. This was of very relative cleanliness, but a good scrubbing would soon make it habitable. A very pungent smell, at once sour and sickly, pervaded the room. Ichac rushed to open both windows which were shuttered fast. I proceeded to make a detailed inspection: skins tanned with urine were drying slowly, and in one corner there were barrels of butter which were allowed to become rancid.

It was time to eat. Ang-Tharkey served us with a ceremony which amazed and impressed all the villagers who gathered round to look on. Never before had any of them seen a sahib. Forks? What complex creatures these foreigners!

It was still dark when Ang-Tharkey brought us breakfast next morning and a few stars were shining in a very clear sky: a promising sign. There, in the distance, a beautiful and moving sight, was Dhaulagiri, rising solitary above the shadows and already lit up by the sun. Seen from this distance its massive grandeur stood out astonishingly.

The *shikari* who was to guide us professed to be quite familiar with the Tilicho pass, but he did not know how long it would take to reach it. We walked up in single file, bent under our loads. Ang-Tharkey, Foutharkey, Pansy and several Tibetan porters came with us. To enable them to go faster, we had lent them boots, but these, for economy's sake, they carried slung over their shoulders until we reached the snow.

After several hours' march the *shikari* no longer seemed very confident of his previous assertions. Though we plied him with questions he didn't appear to know where the Tilicho pass really was. In fact, this *shikari* was just an ordinary shepherd; and all he really knew was the way up to the grazing grounds. His role as guide and his self-importance tended to diminish with the altitude, and in the end he walked quite happily along behind us. In this manner we came to the much discussed Tilicho pass.

Here we had a surprise. According to the map we ought to have been at the opening of a deep valley coming up from Manangbhot. Where was the wonderful view of Annapurna we ought to have had on our right? In some bewilderment we gazed at a dazzling scene of snow and ice where a galaxy of summits scintillated against the clear sky. It was a winter landscape, with something fairy-like in its brilliance and clarity.

On our right, instead of Annapurna, rose a gigantic barrier of mountains with many summits of about 23,000 feet. Before us opened out no deep valley but a vast plateau, in the center of which was a great frozen lake covered with snow. On the left, cliffs fell sheer to the immense white expanse of the lake.

"But where the devil *is* Annapurna?" asked Ichac.

"It's almost certainly behind that handsome triangular peak, over there—look to the right, in the distance."

"I'm not so sure," said Ichac.

"Nor am I," said Rébuffat.

"And the Tilicho pass—where's that?" went on Ichac.

"At the far end of the plateau, on the other side of the lake. It must overlook the Manangbhot valley, which lies just beyond."

"Well, I shall have to verify that, but I'm not at all sure that you're right."

In any case we should have to go down towards the Great Ice Lake, as we already called it amongst ourselves. An hour later we were on its edge, and while Pansy cooked a meal, the discussion continued.

"No sign of a lake on the map! And it's at least four miles long."

"Oh, the map . . . Are all those summits marked on it?"

"Where do you think the waters flow down to?"

"I tell you the waters flow down towards Manangbhot!"

Everyone had his own idea, and he insisted on putting it forward.

The main thing was to get to the other end of the lake. We took up our sacks, and the party proceeded along the left-hand bank until the superb red cliffs forced us out on to the ice. The coolies weren't very keen on this detour. Ichac belayed me with a nylon rope and I ventured out some fifty yards from the bank. There I jumped up and down and danced, and banged with my ice-axe to break the ice and measure its thickness.

"It's like a billiard table," I shouted. "Come on, the lot of you!"

Just the same it was better to be safe than sorry; so we roped up into two long parties with the porters and Sherpas spaced out at intervals of at least twenty-five feet. They could not understand that we did this to secure the safety of one and all: being roped up like this prevented them from grouping together. The first rope started off after me. I began a wide circular sweep so as to come off the ice again safely on the other side of the cliffs. Behind me, one by one, the porters, bent under their loads, hesitantly approached the edge, then braced themselves to it as if they were plunging into water. Fervently gabbling prayers, they followed exactly in my tracks, the eyes of every one of them riveted to the ground. The operation went off all right, and henceforth the porters did not have the slightest wish to part company with us, for if they did they would be obliged to come back alone over the Great Ice Lake!

Safely across on the other side, we climbed up the slopes and reached a pass that corresponded to the one we had reached earlier that morning. We christened it the East Tilicho, its height was about 16,400 feet.

As I had suspected, there was no outlet here; this end of the lake was blocked. At our feet a deep valley opened out going down to Manangbhot. Here again I had made an error in estimating distances. I had imagined Manangbhot as lying at the bottom of a huge basin, but in fact the lay of the land was far more complicated: miles of moraines ran steeply down from where we stood. The valley was blocked by a high mound of rock debris. The only outlet here was a narrow defile which gave passage to the

Marsyandi Khola, a torrent which rises at the Tilicho pass and flows down beside the Great Barrier on which we hoped to find Annapurna. Beyond this obstacle, the ravine widened out gradually and here and there among the gray of the stones, shale and moraines were a few patches of green, islets of native cultivation.

To the right, along the continuation of the Great Barrier, were other peaks even more graceful and elegant than those we had seen above the Tilicho Lake. To the left, above the red cliffs, the Muktinath range rose to a number of 20,000-foot peaks. Behind us was the lake plateau over which we had just come, and at the far end the West Tilicho pass which we had crossed that morning.

We settled down to a council of war. Ichac was of the opinion that, contrary to the map, Annapurna was possibly not situated on the Great Barrier.

"These clouds have come just at the wrong moment. They're blocking out all the higher summits. We can't discuss anything we can't see."

"We had a glimpse just now," I said. "Of course I know the map's a bit erratic, but I doubt it could make quite such an error: one doesn't mistake the position of a peak over 26,000 feet high."

"So you think Annapurna's on the Great Barrier?"

"Yes, behind the big triangular peak in front of us."

"Well I'm prepared to bet the Great Barrier isn't marked on the map."

"Even though it's over twelve miles long and has about fifteen points of 23,000 feet or over?"

"Fifteen? Come, come," protested Ichac.

"Well, there are a lot."

"So you think the long ridge we see, and the ridge marked on the map, aren't the same. Then there'd be two long ridges, wouldn't there?" I asked.

"I suppose so."

Thereupon Ichac made some calculations about distances which, according to him, proved that it was quite impossible for Annapurna to be on this main ridge. I was shaken by his arguments, but not convinced.

Where *was* this Annapurna?

"Well," I said at last, "let's pitch camp here."

"And what are you and Gaston going to do?" asked Ichac.

"Go down to Manangbhot. No doubt Annapurna will turn up just there!"

"Right. We'll take advantage of our trip to buy *tsampa* for the porters. Foutharkey and Pansy will come with us."

"Perhaps we'll see Tilman, too!"

Next morning at dawn Rébuffat and I set off early with light supplies. We counted on finding provisions down at Manangbhot. Without bothering about the stonefalls that we started, we set off at a rush down the great ravine.

Jumping down from rock to rock, we soon lost height. We followed the turbulent waters of the Marsyandi Khola, which was fed by a big hanging glacier under the Triangular Peak. The lower down we went the more we realized the size of the cliffs barring the foot of the valley. Soon we were forced to admit that the bank we were following wasn't really a practical route, and that we should have to cross the river.

Rébuffat was over in a second. I hesitated. Let's see, if I stuck my ice-axe into the bed of the stream and used it as a pole . . . One foot on that rock . . . hum! that's not too safe . . . One . . . two! My muscles relaxed, the ice-axe twisted, the stone rolled over and into the frothing water I went.

After this experience the two Sherpas, Pansy and Foutharkey, had had a bright idea. They made for the top of the cliffs and we could see them going along a vaguely marked trail without any difficulty.

The great scree slopes which we had seen from the Tilicho pass now barred our way. From where we stood we could see no visible track or path. It was hard work climbing up as the slope seemed to be too steep for the stones to stay put, and the least movement was likely to start a regular avalanche. Far behind us we could see the Tilicho pass, where we had been a few hours earlier.

The stones were all the same size as though they had been put through a sort of sieve with an enormous mesh. When at last we reached the head of the gorge, we were suddenly brought up short by a steep ravine of hard earth.

"There's no doubt, we'll have to cut steps," I said to Rébuffat, somewhat puzzled.

"I'd rather it was ice!"

It was a chance to see how the Sherpas would manage. Foutharkey went ahead on the slope, ice-axe in hand. He stood in perfect balance and cut steps with quick blows. Pansy followed, quite at ease. We had only to follow in their tracks.

After this ravine we had thought to find grass slopes, but when we reached the crest, a second ravine confronted us, then a third, and a fourth. In the end we were obliged to cut steps for a good hour before we reached the easier slopes of green. We went down some immense screes, glissading in clouds of dust.

It was past midday, and we stopped by the edge of the clear waters at the lower end of the gorges, and made a quick lunch. It was rough going along the banks of the torrent. At times we had to climb up several hundred feet in order to find a way through the thick jungle growth.

This was a completely different world from the Tukucha valley: here it was much hotter, there was more vegetation and the contrasts were greater. From time to time flowering trees gave a softer and more friendly appearance to the scene.

Man had already penetrated here, and the various ill-defined tracks now converged to form a path. Manangbhot was still a good way off, and as we had no camping equipment and very little food we must reach it that evening. At a bend in the path we suddenly came upon some habitations, sheltered behind a dip in the ground. A Buddhist *chorten* adorned with prayer flags marked the entry to the village of Khangsar. Ragged children, black with filth, caught sight of us and rushed up. It was the first time they had seen white men and they stared curiously at these apparitions from the mountains. They could not conceive that we had come from the other side of the range. In fact they didn't know there was another side. The only path known to the natives here was the pilgrims' track to Muktinath which goes over the Thorungse.

Pansy asked for the *Suba*. A noisy procession preceded us along the foul-smelling lanes. The *Suba* came out to meet us. He showed no surprise whatever: for centuries Buddha has taught the art of remaining impassive in face of the most extraordinary happenings. I asked him to procure *tsampa* for our coolies who had remained up in the mountains. With loud lamentations he replied that Khangsar was very poor, not a pound of *tsampa* to spare, nor a handful of rice, much less a chicken. We must go on to Manangbhot: it was only an hour's march, he told us, and then the sahibs would find everything they needed. Manangbhot at once became our goal and a paradise. Without waiting any longer we continued on our way, in spite of the heat and our hunger and thirst.

As we left the village we came upon the completely bare skeleton of a yak, lying across the path. No one would dream of moving these sacred bones: there they had been for months and there they would stay until they turned to dust. Everyone reverently skirted round them.

A series of steps hewn out of the rock and a very steep slope, brought us down to the torrent again, and we made our way rapidly along its banks.

"Manangbhot!" said Pansy.

47

The town was perched on the cliffs after the manner of the ancient towns of Tibet. From the river we could see nothing but walls, and it looked as if we were going up towards a fortress. A plank across the stream showed that we were now in a civilized country.

We followed a series of alleys which brought us to the center of the town where we found an immense prayer wall about fifty yards long. The villagers came running up on all sides and surrounded us: the usual wretched-looking children, an old woman with a very curious portable prayer-wheel which she turned continuously, and young men—most of them very good-looking with a different type of face from those in the Tukucha district.

Here all were Buddhists. They were all crying out something, I couldn't make out what, but I didn't worry. I had learned that to say "good morning" in this country everyone finds it necessary to make a long speech at the top of his voice. After discussions lasting a quarter of an hour, a man went off in search of the *Suba*. Meanwhile Pansy had found us lodgings on the second floor of a barn. We climbed up to it by a ladder made of a thick plank in which notches had been cut. We all left our rucksacks there and Gaston and I returned to the square.

The villagers gathered round gesticulating:

"American?"

"No, French."

"Yes, French."

As if this were conclusive proof, they nodded approval:

"American!"

"No, there are Americans, and there are Englishmen, but we are French."

"Oh yes! But you're Americans all the same!"

I gave it up.

Most of them were Ghurkas who had served with the British army. We were the first white men to come here.

But as for Annapurna, not a thing was known about it.

A summit of 26,000 feet doesn't pass unnoticed. Even if it were further along the range the locals should at least have known of its existence. Perhaps its name here was different—perhaps it was called after some other god.

A group of men came towards me. They touched me and spoke to me, and yelled at me a few inches from my face. Were they cannibals? How did they want me dished up? All the same they were making meaningful gestures. Suddenly I made out what they were driving at in Gurkhali and bad English. The words "woman" and "rupees" were repeated. With the help of their gestures I reconstructed their offer, for it was indeed an

48

offer. They would be most honored if I would be so good as to become acquainted with the ladies of the district, in consideration for a sort of scheduled payment of five rupees.

I had great difficulty in preventing myself being borne off by them, for they were all tugging at me. The situation verged on the ridiculous.

The prudent Gaston Rébuffat chose this moment to go in search of something to photograph and basely abandoned his chief. I protested most vigorously. Moreover five rupees was a very high price. Ought a Bara Sahib really to pay anything at all? Now they were all pointing in my direction with their forefingers. What on earth was going on? Pansy winked an eye at me but didn't dare say a word.

"Pansy, what is it?"

Like the rest of them I put my two forefingers together. Tremendous applause from the crowd: I had made a hit! Pansy was doubled up and choking with laughter. At last he explained to me in his comic English that every member of the population was offering me one of his own household as a mark of respect. I could choose whichever one I liked best. It would cost the Expedition only the modest sum of ten rupees. If I so wished I could even take a superb Ghurka maiden back to India!

I pretended to be very choosy.

The men proceeded to discuss the matter, and the women went into a huddle together over it. The villagers closed round me once more, making guttural noises and wild gestures.

"Bibi . . . Bibi . . . Bibi!" This name was repeated again and again. The crowd fell back to let through a young man with an attractive, even charming, face. His appearance had its comic side. He had on a brown frock-coat with a long mauve silk shawl wound tightly around his waist, from which there hung a chased silver Tibetan sword. Long black boots came up to his calves. On his head was a khaki bowler hat with a high brim, and adorned with a band of the same material as the shawl. With frenzied enthusiasm everyone intoned, in the monotonous chant of Nepal,

"Bibi . . . Bibi! Fifteen rupees!"

I left Gaston, who had just arrived on the scene, to choose for himself. Anyway we hadn't enough rupees on us, so that settled the matter. We had firmly to say No.

The sun was sinking; it had already gone behind the splendid summit— our Triangular Peak—which towered above Manangbhot. Through Pansy, who questioned the inhabitants closely, we learned that the mountain in question was Ganga Purna. The two other summits on the left were

49

Tchongor and Sepchia. Coming back from a stroll through the narrow alley-ways of the village, which had at last quieted down, Rébuffat and I met our Sherpas who reported sadly that the country was very poor. It would be extremely difficult for us to find supplies.

At that moment along came the *Suba,* an old man with a long beard, dressed very simply, and looking intelligent. After being introduced we sat down. Immediately the conversation opened on very practical lines. He would provide ten kilos of *tsampa,* and that was all. He gave us so many reasons that he got quite muddled himself. No hens, only four ridiculously small eggs, no milk and no rice. It was a very small amount of the *tsampa* so essential for our porters at the Tilicho pass.

This serious news compelled me to send Foutharkey back to the pass first thing next morning. I scrawled a note to Ichac.

Dear Matha,

Foutharkey is just off on his way back to you. It's a very very long way down here. Results up to date:

Beyond the great Triangular Peak, which is called Ganga Purna, is another summit, Tchongor, a snow and ice peak of 23,000 feet. Then the range appears to drop down to the valley at a distance of about two miles from here, near a junction with another river, the Choundikiou, at the little village of Chindi. From where we are we can see another big summit on the right bank of the Choundikiou—this is Sepchia.

But where is Annapurna? It's still a mystery. Nobody here knows of it. Program! *Gaston, Pansy and I are going to Chindi in the hope of collecting information to place Annapurna. If we get it we shall examine the possible approaches and estimate the difficulties, then return immediately by way of Muktinath.[14] If what we discover makes it clear that we ought to proceed with our intended reconnaissance to the top of the Great Barrier, which should be easily accessible and which we should do together, then we will return to the camp on the 12th, that is to say, tomorrow.*

If we don't turn up, you break camp on the morning of the 13th and return to Tukucha.

Yours ever,

Maurice.

Meanwhile Ichac, after having seen us off to Manangbhot, set out with Ang-Tharkey at about nine o'clock the same day from the camp on the East Tilicho pass. His objective was a point to the north-east of the camp, on the Muktinath Himal, looking towards the Great Barrier. When he reached a suitable spot at about 18,000 feet he took a series of compass-bearings and photographs. While he was engrossed in this, Ang-Tharkey set to work to build a cairn, with such skill that he managed to construct an impressive monument over eight feet high. The clouds which had covered the sky at dawn now returned and the party had to make its way back to camp.

Lying flat on his stomach in his tent Ichac, with as much accuracy as the conditions and his equipment allowed, transferred the triangulations he had made on to the map.

"There we are—I've got it clear at last."

He had collected evidence that the chain stretching to the south of the camp, which we called the Great Barrier, was in fact the Annapurna Himal. Our famous Triangular Peak—the Black Rock whose topographical importance we had suspected—was the starting point of the further system of ridges from which rose Annapurna. So the only possible conclusions was that Annapurna must lie on the other side of the Great Barrier from the camp.

Rébuffat and I, therefore, had gone off after a ghost mountain. If only we had realized. But that is exploration: a great deal of hesitation, doubt, error, and then, quite suddenly, a discovery.

Up in the pass it was a very cold night. Dawn shone through the tent and heralded fine weather. Ichac took advantage of the clearness of the atmosphere to take bearings of the enormous peaks to be seen beyond Manangbhot, among them Manaslu, one of the eight-thousand-meter peaks of Nepal, a formidable pyramid that stands out strikingly from the other summits.

The clouds came down and the wind began to blow. The party either remained in the tents or kept a lookout through glasses for the return of the Manangbhot party. Towards three o'clock Foutharkey arrived and gave Ichac my message. Ichac read it quickly, he knew already that he would learn nothing from it. There would be no point, he reckoned, in going up the easily accessible summit of the Great Barrier. It was preferable to go in the other direction as high as possible up a glacier he had discovered the previous day, and try to see Annapurna over the top of the Great Barrier.

On the morning of the 12th the weather was magnificent. Ichac explained to Ang-Tharkey that they would go up together in the direction

51

The Annapurna range according to the map of the Indian Survey with the Tilicho pass incorrectly situated.

of the Muktinath Himal. At seven o'clock they reached the cairn built the day before; at eight-thirty, with clouds beginning to cover the sky, they set foot upon a gently sloping glacier and started to climb it. A layer of new snow covered the ice and made the going slow. The altimeter showed a steady rise gradually. Soon they came to a zone of crevasses.

It was not the moment to embark upon anything difficult but simply to get as high as possible in the shortest possible time. Here and there a few steps had to be cut in the ice, but the difficult bits were short and finally they emerged on to the upper slopes where the ridge was enveloped in thick mist.

Where was Annapurna? Visibility was zero. Ichac didn't even know exactly where he was himself. He waited in vain for an improvement in the weather. It was twelve-thirty and the altimeter registered 20,300 feet. He and Ang-Tharkey did not suffer much from breathlessness, which showed that they were beginning to get into training. This point reached by Ichac was the highest so far attained by the Expedition, and was our first summit of over 20,000 feet.

The weather didn't improve, and at three-fifteen they began the descent, following in the tracks made on the way up, which remained

The Annapurna range shown correctly.

visible in spite of the sleet. It was four-thirty when they reached the camp. Here they found the leader of the Expedition snoring heavily in his sleeping-bag! Now just what had happened?

At Manangbhot, at dawn on the 11th, the little party had wakened with difficulty. After a frugal breakfast Foutharkey went off with his sack and my note to Ichac. Rébuffat and myself, with Pansy, left shortly afterwards to go down the valley of Marsyandi Khola in search of our elusive Annapurna.

Ahead of us, and a good distance off, a peak stood out which we identified as Manaslu. Our intention was to skirt round the Great Barrier as far as possible. But we had to be back at Manangbhot that evening. At midday the little village of Chindi came into view and beyond it the valley narrowed and I could guess at the deep gorges that enclosed the river. To go further would have been useless. I was quite sure we were not on the right track—Annapurna was not down in these parts.

The inhabitants, and the *shikaris* from whom we asked for information, had never heard of it. They explained at some length that the word meant "Goddess of the Harvests." There was nothing to do but to return to

53

Manangbhot, which we had to do on empty stomachs as our provisions were all gone.

Clouds collected over Tchongor and Sepchia and prevented us from taking the photographs which we should have liked to bring back as evidence. A halt was suggested to give them a chance to clear; everybody found a comfortable nook, and Rébuffat was not long in falling asleep. Pansy smoked his last cigarettes. I kept watch like a sentry ready to give the alarm the moment the clouds should part and our summits appear.

Suddenly I heard strange sounds coming down the road. A group of women appeared along the path. They wore brightly colored petticoats and carried empty sacks and baskets. They chattered, and laughed, and settled themselves comfortably on the ground. They were all barefoot.

Pansy opened one eye, and then, with interest, both. He explained to me that they were porters who were going down the valley in search of work. The men cultivate the soil, the women carry. That is the rule but I hadn't long to wait for the exception which proves it—for the celebrated and charming "Bibi" came forward in all his splendor. The women seemed to treat him as one of themselves. As soon as he saw me he hurried up. His walk became even more graceful and a smile lit up his face. Without a word he sat down near me. After a brief halt the group of women went on down the valley. Silence descended once more. At last Bibi got up and regretfully departed. He turned round at every step and waved his hand sadly at me.

At last the mountains Tchongor and Sepchia came out of the mist. Rébuffat took photographs and then we went on our way back to Manangbhot.

It was hot and we found it pretty hard going. Every time we met anyone Pansy would ask about the possibility of getting some provisions, but it was hopeless. The afternoon was well advanced when we reached our barn.

"So we're going back empty-handed," said Rébuffat dejectedly.

"At least we know it's not over here."

"We'll have to get back at once."

"There's scarcely any food. Take what there is and push off with Pansy to Muktinath over the Thorungse. That will save you the ascent to the Tilicho pass and you'll be back a day earlier at Tukucha. You'll be tired after traveling on an empty stomach, so with the remaining rupees you can hire ponies . . ."

"What about you?"

"Don't worry, with a slab of chocolate I'll manage to get up to the Tilicho camp."

"It's the hell of a long way."

"I'll be there tomorrow morning. I'd like to go up with Ichac to his 'accessible' summit."

We had a little to eat, then we left on our separate ways.

I was alone. With a slab of chocolate as my only food I should have to step lively to get up from 9,000 feet to over 16,000. My plan was to go as fast as I possibly could, to run when possible, until I couldn't go a step further.

An hour later I was at Khangsar. Without losing a minute I followed the path which gradually faded out along the left bank of the torrent. I made my way between the cliffs, going up and down to avoid obstacles. The hours went quickly by.

I found the steps which Foutharkey had cut in the limestone. Then I started up the great scree-slope and at last came to the stream which had to be crossed. Jumping was out of the question so I took off my boots and hung them over my shoulder. It was getting dark and a slip into the icy water would be extremely disagreeable. I entered the water gingerly, testing every stone with my feet.

The current was very strong. Suddenly I slipped, tried to save myself only to fall in deeper, and ended by going right in altogether. This time I was soaked to the skin. With considerable difficulty I got up on the opposite bank and began wringing out my clothes and emptying my boots. Still shivering and with my teeth chattering I got dressed again. Now it would take me four hours to reach the camp and I had scarcely more than an hour of daylight left. Staggering on, I crossed a long steep slope of hard earth, where more than once I narrowly avoided slipping.

A piercing wind blew up from the valley and I shivered with cold. I could no longer see to go on. I looked for a grassy place where I could spend the night, and ended by sitting down on a tuft, spreading my cape so that it covered me completely. My legs were icy cold and shivered violently against each other.

With my hood over my head, I hesitated between eating my last bit of chocolate and keeping it for the morning. I chose the first course and then I indulged myself in my last cigarette.

I was lost in the heart of the mountains, over 14,000 feet up, soaked through, weary and very hungry. Should I have the strength to climb up the last fifteen hundred feet? A treacherous wind found its way through every gap in my clothing; snow began to fall. I closed my eyes, relaxed my muscles, and composed myself as I always try to do in mountain bivouacs.

Long and monotonous, the hours crawled by. Below me the angry rumble of the torrent shook the ground and the noise echoed back and forth incessantly in the valley. The damp rose up and went right through me—a horrible feeling when one is already chilled to the marrow, and I tried to fight against it. From time to time I had a look around. The weather was not improving. If the clouds came down, I shouldn't be able to find the way.

Though numb and half asleep, I welcomed the first streaks of dawn with hope. I should have to wait for it to get a bit lighter, and how hard those last minutes were. Folding my anorak, I started off again with a painfully empty stomach. It was very cold and I hoped to warm up as I walked. The weather had improved slightly; I frequently stopped on the pretext of picking out the way ahead. My legs were trembling and refused to make any effort, but all the same I managed to gain some ground. I could see patches of sunlight shining on Manangbhot, but down here I was still in shadow.

At every halt, before starting off again, I picked out above me a comfortable stone for the next stop. The stops became more frequent, and longer. I began to wonder if I should ever get up.

Whenever I came to a flat rock I sank down, and immediately felt a bit better. After a few seconds' rest I would see the absurdity of the situation: how could I possibly give up with only a few more yards to climb? I would pick out another rock, drag myself up and take a few steps. To myself it was as though I were racing along, but actually I was going extremely slowly, and I would throw myself down the moment I reached my objective. Yard by yard, I gained height, and presently there remained only two hundred yards to the camp, which was just not visible from this point.

I tried to call out, but no sound came from my throat. It was difficult to stand up without swaying; it was safer and easier, down on all fours. My head swam; I wanted to sleep. Then mustering my last ounce of strength, I threw myself heavily down on a rock on the ridge. Time slipped by. When finally I opened my eyes it seemed as though a lifetime had passed; I raised my head above the ridge. There was the camp, barely twenty yards away! In vain I tried to attract somebody's attention, but the coolies were chatting quietly around a good fire. If only they could see me! If only one of them would turn his head. I dropped some stones in the hope of making them look up, but they didn't hear, and I couldn't call them. My head was like lead and my ears were buzzing.

Now that I was certain of getting there, I gritted my teeth fiercely and managed to crawl along on all fours like an animal. Suddenly Foutharkey turned round.

"Bara Sahib!"

Quite thunderstruck, he watched me crawling along. Then everyone got up and came running towards me.

They laid me down, trembling all over, on an air mattress. I drank, and ate a little, and learned that Ichac had not yet returned, but that he wouldn't be long. I asked them to get a meal ready for me. With the assistance of the porters, Foutharkey opened an impressive number of cans. The fire burned merrily and the capacious cooking-pots began to simmer, giving off such an appetizing smell that to control myself I had to remain motionless and half drugged with sleep.

When the meal was ready I began to eat straight out of the pots which was not what Foutharkey had been expecting—he had been cooking for the whole camp!

For over an hour and a half, without stopping, and voraciously, I consumed the biggest meal of my life. I was like the snake who swallowed a fat sheep in the dream of the Little Prince, in St. Exupéry's story. I fell back in my sleeping-bag with relief.

The next words I heard were Ichac's:

"Hello, Maurice, good morning!"

I pulled myself together.

"Matha!"

"We've just come down from a peak of over 20,000 feet!"

We exchanged news. Everything fitted in with Ichac's deductions and confirmed them, and the whole northern side of the Annapurna massif had been explored.

"There's no question about it," I said. "The key to Annapurna lies in the south, along the route that Couzy, Oudot and Schatz took on April 27th, up the Miristi Khola."

"So there is nothing more for us to do here," concluded Ichac. "We must get back quickly to Tukucha."

Next day we packed up. The porters were delighted to be leaving this spot where they had spent three days completely cut off and with nothing to do. We didn't have to hurry them on or show them the route. In a few minutes the loads were made up and allotted, and while Ichac and I set out, still talking, the porters went off quickly under the supervision of Ang-Tharkey who led them straight towards the Great Ice Lake. This time, without any hesitation, they traversed its entire length.

In the past three days the snow which had formerly covered the ridge leading to the West Tilicho had melted. At the pass, we paused a little to look at the Great Ice Lake, the immense amphitheater surrounding it, and above all at the remarkable Great Barrier. Never would we see it all again. We ran down the hillside and came out on to the lower slopes in the middle of a magnificent forest of deodars. A strong wind arose, but it was blowing the right way, and soon afterwards we reached Tinigaon.

Next morning we passed through Marpha and after six exhausting days we were very glad indeed to get back to headquarters at Tukucha. As we neared the camp Oudot came toward us.

"Hello, Doctor! Any news?"

"Everybody's here and feeling fine. What about you?"

"Have you seen Rébuffat?"

"He got back yesterday."

"Good. It is May 14th, we'll have to make up our minds. We'll have a meeting this afternoon."

Meanwhile what had been happening on Dhaulagiri during our absence? On the evening of Monday, May 8, Noyelle had come racing down from the camp on the East glacier. Excitedly he explained that while going up the glacier with a Sherpa, he had seen the Couzy-Schatz rope in a very steep snow couloir. The point of this route was that it ought to enable us to bypass the enormous and dangerous seracs of the upper part of the East glacier. Actually it was just as difficult and as dangerous as the other route since the couloir was threatened by avalanches. One look upward revealed tremendous walls of blue ice, towering fifteen hundred feet above. At the very moment when Noyelle was watching the movements of the other two, an enormous unstable block of ice heeled over. Tons of ice shot down the slope with a fearful noise, just missing our liaison officer, and were pulverized on the plateau of the East glacier lower down.

"And to think my camera wasn't set," Noyelle said regretfully.

Couzy and Schatz had insisted upon going on. They were not going to give up for a little thing like an avalanche; however, their efforts to get out of the couloir and set foot on the rocks proved fruitless. They pressed on with their attempt but were unable to advance more than a dozen yards: the rocks were slippery and unsafe. Schatz had one small satisfaction: he was able to hammer in his first piton in the Himalaya at over 16,000 feet. After having exhausted all the possibilities, they gave it up, and on the 9th they came down.

The following day Oudot and Terray went up in their turn, and though they met the Sherpas coming back this did not deter them. They pitched a camp on the East glacier, at a height of 16,500 feet, up against a big rock wall on the right bank. During the night a stone tore right through their tent.

On the 11th Oudot and Terray broke camp early at 3 A.M. and so they had all day before them to devote to the problem. Putting on their crampons, they started up and with great difficulty succeeded in advancing a few yards. After considerable effort they reached the foot of the big ice wall which the first reconnaissance parties had climbed, and which Couzy and Schatz had passed on their right. Instead of going up the wall, up which steps had already been cut for a good part of the way, they went towards the left bank of the glacier. Cutting steps and climbing up with considerable difficulty, they reached the same height as the previous parties' furthest limit. Soon they saw a possible way that had been invisible from the point the previous parties had reached. As they went up they were able to skirt around a number of seracs and gain height, and, taking considerable risks they reached the place where the glacier leveled out.

In front of them stretched a tangled maze of crevasses and snowfields with no way through. Further away on the right the slope steepened again and ran up into the north ridge of Dhaulagiri, which rose before them, clear cut and inaccessible.

Oudot and Terray rightly judged the difficulties and dangers to be far too great. What was the use of going on, only to be forced to give up later? The way up Dhaulagiri did not lie over this glacier, and if there was no other way, then the mountain would never be conquered. Having thus reduced our visionary hopes to their proper proportions, and realizing very well the bitter disappointment it would be to us all, the two decided to give up the attempt. That evening they made their way wearily back to Base Camp at the foot of the East glacier, and the following day to Tukucha.

If we were to launch the full strength of the Expedition against Dhaulagiri, it would be a tremendous hazard, full of uncertainty and danger; and we could only decide on this course after very carefully weighing all the reasons for and against it. We should have to examine the whole question calmly and wisely.

On May 14 the entire Expedition assembled in the mess tent at Tukucha for a solemn council of war.

Chapter VI

Council of War

THE HEAT WAS OPPRESSIVE, AND THE GLARE OUTSIDE BLINDING; THE GREENISH light that filtered through the canvas of the mess-tent where we assembled offered a soothing change. Throughout our deliberation Ang-Tharkey kept us supplied with torrents of coffee.

Everyone was very serious. I realized that behind all Lachenal's light-hearted joking and nonsense there lay a very understandable impatience and uneasiness. Well, in an hour's time we should have come to some decision.

The Sherpas made themselves busy. They knew that something was up—all the sahibs were there.

"It is now May 14th," I began. "In spite of all our efforts since April 22nd, no real possibility has turned up: we have no route in prospect; we aren't even clear in what direction we ought to set out. We aren't sure of anything. Time's short. The moment has come to take major decisions."

Nobody said a word.

"These mountains are extremely tough propositions. The climbing possibilities are limited, in every direction. As for Dhaulagiri by the Dambush Khola and the Hidden Valley, it would be pretty risky to plan a route which would involve crossing two passes at 16,000 feet, and then traversing a huge and extremely difficult glacier—and all this just to get to the foot of the mountain. A route up the East glacier would be even more problematical. I don't wish to take the risk of sending the Expedition over such dangerous ground. There will be plenty of danger, wherever we go, without deliberately courting it at the start.

"There remains another possibility: the Tukucha Peak, which we haven't yet reconnoitered. But must we really first get up a seven-thousand-meter peak in order to climb an eight-thousander? It would be a desperate decision—and the longest route, if not the most dangerous."

"I'm never going on that mountain again," said Terray firmly—his recent experience among the rickety seracs and treacherous snow bridges of the East glacier fresh in his mind. "Dhaulagiri will never be climbed," he declared forcefully. "I wouldn't go up there at any price."

Schatz made a face. "The chances seem pretty slim. I, for one, don't really see any possibility: the south-east ridge is out of the question. What about the north ridge?"

"The north ridge!" exclaimed Terray. "No one will ever get up it—it's bare ice and the angle is so steep that handholds would have to be cut."

"When Couzy, Oudot and Schatz were up above the Miristi gorges on April 27th," I continued, "they brought back sketches showing the average angle of the north ridge of Dhaulagiri. It looked perfectly reasonable. Moreover the steep part didn't look to me to be more than twelve or fifteen hundred feet high. On the left flank, looking towards the mountain, there are crevasses which would give shelter for camps. And why not place some fixed ropes?" Although my argument was based on reasons of a technical nature, it didn't convince anyone.

After a long silence Rébuffat replied:

"In any case we'd have to reach this ridge. Somehow. So what?"

None of this was encouraging, but I wanted to appear to be defending possibilities which I really knew were hopeless, because I felt a tacit and unanimous opposition to these plans. Once we'd abandoned Dhaulagiri, I did not want the party to have any regrets on the score of not having fully explored the question. Before turning the page I wanted the problem of Dhaulagiri to be well and truly settled.

Another long silence; everyone was thinking but no one wanted to be the first to speak. Then Couzy leaned forward, and looked hard at me, searching for the right words:

"Maurice, on Annapurna there are at least *some* possibilities."

The tension relaxed, and tongues were loosened. Everyone thought it rather courageous of Couzy to have opened the question. There was now no question about it, we must now turn our attention to Annapurna.

"What we *do* know about Annapurna," I added, "is that the only possible line of attack is from the north. But we must first get there. The way to the upper basin of the Miristi Khola is a problem we have already solved. From the farthest point reached, three routes were seen: first, the north-west ridge, and it is on this ridge that, in theory, we ought to launch our first attack. Secondly there is the west glacier of Annapurna— it looks as if we ought to be able to follow a couloir from it up to the spur with the main ridge. And finally there is the glacier that no one has yet seen, but which, we can infer, flows down the whole of the north face of Annapurna."

"You see," said Oudot, "that spur is the shortest route. In two days we ought to be able to reach the summit ridge at a height of 20,000 feet to 21,000 feet. Of course between the top of this spur and Annapurna itself there is a bit that we haven't yet seen. If there should be a gap, it would always be possible to get around it by taking to the west glacier, that is to the right of the spur when you face the mountain."

"Yes," added Couzy, "I'm all in favor of this route, because we ought to be able to gain considerable height without any special difficulty."

"And, after all," continued Schatz, "it is only the middle part of the route which is still an unknown quantity. The upper slopes of Annapurna appear to be quite easy. There seem to be places level enough for tents, I'm sure. Let's have a try at it; in three days we'll have it in the bag!"

I was in complete agreement with Schatz; it struck me as an entirely reasonable plan.

"What's your view, Matha?" I queried Ichac.

"I'm not here as a climber, Maurice. I'm your cameraman."

"When you go out on reconnaissance you're a climber all right. What do you think, Oudot?"

"It strikes me that Dhaulagiri is altogether too dangerous. I'm for Annapurna."

Noyelle was of the same opinion.

I turned to Rébuffat.

"Do you think there'd be any chance of getting up the Tukucha Peak?"

"I've already told you, Maurice: I think we ought to have begun by going up it: the summit must be a perfect viewpoint. But now it's out of the question."

Once a decision had been taken, the Expedition would, single-heartedly, throw all its strength into the attack. Every voice had been heard; now it was for me, alone, to decide. It was a very heavy responsibility.

"Instead of immediately making an all-out attempt on Annapurna, we'll send out a large reconnaissance party to find the best route up. This party will carry ten days' food, and will be re-provisioned, on a limited scale, until further notice. As soon as the advance party see a possible route the whole reconnaissance will, upon definite orders from me, be transformed into an assault party. And right now we'll make arrangements to ensure that this transformation can be effected without wasting a single day."

"Well, now that it's all settled," exclaimed Schatz, "let's get going."

"Wait a minute!"

Everyone was quiet.

"It's a long way from being settled. You must all know exactly what you've got to do. Three of us know the route taken on April 27. Each of these three will accompany a party during the four days' preliminary march.

"Ichac, Rébuffat and myself are only just back from Manangbhot, and we are very tired. And I've got a lot to do here, with letters and accounts—I must bring them up to date so as to know whether we shall need more money for our return journey. Lachenal and Terray will leave today, with the Sherpas Adjiba, Angawa and Dawatondu, and Schatz to show them the way.

"A second group—Rébuffat and myself, guided by Couzy—will follow a day later. Noyelle will see to the regular provisioning of these groups. Ichac and Oudot will wait for instructions from me before coming on, and as this won't be before six days at least, they will have time to go over together to Muktinath."

"What about Ang-Tharkey?" asked Ichac.

"You can take him with you. And Noyelle and G. B. Rana will constitute the rearguard, and must not move up until I send word. Noyelle, you must prepare all the loads needed for the reconnaissance, for the assault and the return, and organize the recruiting of porters against the time they're needed."

"What about our equipment?" inquired Lachenal.

"Divide everything into four lots. The first, which you will take with you, must be very light—you must reserve your strength. The second lot—climbing gear, warm clothes, toilet things, etc.—will be carried by porters. The third lot will consist of everything necessary in the event of the reconnaissance being transformed into a full scale assault. This will consist of spare clothes, heavy equipment such as camp boots and sweaters. Finally the fourth lot, which will consist solely of what we need on our valley-marches, will be put into containers labeled with your names and will remain at Tukucha."

So everybody knew just what was in store for him, and what he must do. I called Ang-Tharkey over and explained the plan. The camp immediately became a hive of tremendous activity. The first party was due to leave as soon as it was ready. Though they weren't carrying much weight, the diversity of the objects they were taking gave rise to consultations, preparations and visits from tent to tent.

The doctor collected everything needed by the first group for a fairly long trip, through the jungle or high up on the mountains, in good or bad weather: the anti-toxic serum and the aspirin, sunburn cream and maxiton, vitamin B$_2$ and bicarbonate of soda. He passed everyone as fit; it had taken three weeks for us all to get acclimatized and back to our normal form.

Terray sorted out his belongings most conscientiously: he painted his name on the container which would remain at the camp, and then got busy with the provisions. Lachenal, the Expedition's equipment man, measured ropes and sorted out pitons.

Noyelle looked a bit worried: the negotiations with the *Suba* and G. B. Rana were difficult. He explained to them again and again that the horses asked for must really be produced at once. Eventually he got his way, but the wretched animals didn't inspire much confidence. One was bandy-legged, another too old and his head nodded dismally. They didn't look as if they could hold up even long enough to get out of the village!

Rucksacks were closed and the horses saddled—with what saddles! Our steeds were certainly not "pawing the ground impatiently"—still, they were horses. Everyone ran through his list of things in his head, praying that nothing had been forgotten. The Sherpas took up their loads, with a lot of kindly help from their friends, and shouts of "Good luck" from those who were staying. Then they were off.

While waiting for dinner in camp, I brought my accounts up to date and wrote a letter to Paris.

Tukucha, May 15th, 1950.

My dear Devies,

We are just back from a long and tiring reconnaissance to the north of Annapurna, and I am writing to you at once to give you our news.

To begin with, you can tell all our families that we are very well indeed. Everybody's in grand form, and Dr. Oudot's tests confirm it. We're all working splendidly together as a team. I can now report that the period of exploration is practically at an end.

Climbing: Upon my return we went thoroughly into the technical situation: the various routes on Dhaulagiri are not only extremely difficult but also, on certain sections, highly dangerous. On the other hand Annapurna offers several possibilities.

So yesterday I took the decision to direct the expedition's efforts towards this objective, and to send off a large-scale reconnaissance at once, which can be transformed without loss of time into a definite assault.

Actually, while Dhaulagiri rises alone like a monstrous pyramid, Annapurna dominates a mighty range comprising about fifty summits over 23,000 feet high, some very high ridges, and an almost inaccessible upper basin, with probably only one line of weakness—a depression by which we shall make our attack.

Yours ever,

Maurice Herzog.

Why did we all feel so melancholy? Was it because some of our friends were already off on the adventure? Or was it because there was still some element of indecision? Or was it simply that we were tired? I couldn't say. So while Gaston snored away conscientiously in his sleeping-bag, I worked late on figures, making estimates and drawing up my budget till my eyes closed.

The camp slowly came to life next morning; people got up and began to get busy.

The first job I'd set myself that morning was to shave off my eight days' growth of beard, which I found quite unbearable. Ichac and I proposed to go up to the village spring, a little trickle of water which spouted out barely a couple of hundred yards away, just beside the only tree in the neighborhood. Like a couple of Spartans, in shorts and thin shirts, with our washing kit in one hand and our cameras, which never left us, in the other, we made our way to the "waters" of Tukucha.

Two particularly pretty and graceful girls were doing their laundry in the spring; they were clean, their hair was carefully done, and they wore work-day saris of calico. Their movements as they beat their washing allowed us to admire their supple, well-made bodies.

"They're charming," I said to Ichac as I approached.

"Wait a minute," he whispered. "I'll try to take a picture of them."

We were greeted with loud squeals! But very soon, reassured at seeing us put away the ungodly "boxes," they set to work again on their laundry, beating it harder than ever on the stone. It is the classic method in all these parts and the linen doesn't stand up to it for long. Ironing is unknown.

Children were playing by the spring, throwing water and pushing each other about; most of them were little Buddhist girls. In spite of their tender age they already had jewels in their ears, nostrils, foreheads, and round their necks and wrists. I was very taken with one of them, a really lovely child who never stopped smiling. She burst out laughing to see me cleaning my teeth with a strange, colored paste, and then shave with a sharp instrument she didn't at all like the look of. But I knew something that would interest her: the eau de Cologne! I made her sniff it and then I put some on her hair. She was in transports of delight. In this part of the world scents appear to be much sought after. The little girl was certainly no longer shy. This little rogue of eight years old felt very sure of her charms. But what few moments of real happiness this child can ever have known, living in such a state of destitution, though luckily unconscious of it.

Suddenly her smile vanished. I turned round: click! Ichac had just taken a picture, and she had had a fright. Long might I have gone on combing her hair, and long would she have continued to laugh, but however sweet and touching this brief friendship, we had to be on our way. We packed up our things and left the spring, and my little friend departed. Poor little soul, she limped terribly, and walked in a horribly twisted way, through one leg being much shorter than the other. My heart ached as I watched her disappear.

Everything was bustle in the camp when we got back. The second party was due to leave early in the afternoon. The kitchen smoked and the Sherpas bustled around the tents, while the village children stared wide-eyed. One of the locals placidly twirled his distaff as he looked on; another had his eye on a can which spelled treasure to him, and a third blew into an old tube of condensed milk and burst it with a frightful pop.

The porters began to arrive one by one. They had been told to come in the afternoon so of course they turned up in the morning; they would just have to wait and watch us. Pansy, Sarki and Aila had their heads deep in their wide-open sacks. I kept an eye on them because, with an excess either of prudence or mistrust, they tended to take all their belongings along with them. I thought it quite unnecessary for them to be burdened with three pairs of trousers, but on the other hand I did not hesitate to load them up with extra ropes.

Sounds of Indian music reached me from the mess-tent where Noyelle was trying to get the news on the radio. This renewed contact with the world beyond turned our thoughts away for a moment from our tasks. What news had they of us in France? Here we had heard nothing from home—not a word; in spite of all our inquiries, complaints to the Nepalese, and special messengers, the mystery of our mail remained unsolved.

When our meal appeared we threw ourselves upon the food, making free, while we had the chance, of all condiments, vinegar and anything spicy.

Now it was time for the second party's departure; yesterday's scenes were repeated in an atmosphere of mounting excitement. Rébuffat supervised the provisions and Couzy the equipment. The horses arrived; by good luck the porters were there.

The afternoon was already well advanced, hot and thundery. Saying goodbye to Ichac, Noyelle, and Oudot, we dug our heels into our horses' flanks.

It was our turn to set out on the great adventure.

Chapter VII

The Miristi Khola

WE PASSED ALONG TUKUCHA'S MAIN STREET AT A GENTLE TROT, THROUGH A crowd of lousy children, women scouring their pans, and old men who observed us from their doorways; the sahibs were up to something new.

The crossing of the Dambush Khola was a tricky operation. Perched up on our mounts we tried to avoid getting our boots wet, and might have managed it if we had not been obliged to keep close up to our horses' heads so as to guide them firmly through the rushing river, and if the local saddles had not had the disagreeable habit of slipping round the animals' bellies, or the over-taut girths had not chosen the most inconvenient moments to give away. Rébuffat, who has long legs, crossed over boldly, with his feet hanging in the water.

"It's better to get your feet wet," he explained, "than to be soaked all over."

On the broad plain of Tukucha we urged our steeds to a decent pace. One of the straps of Rébuffat's saddle broke and he completely lost his balance; he didn't seem to be aware of the comic figure he cut as he clung to his horse. I offered to change mounts with him but eventually we got things straight and galloped on.

Passing through the familiar villages of Khanti and Larjung we came to the little village of Dhumpu—extremely primitive, but with most friendly inhabitants—and then started up the slope to Lete. The *garawalas* or grooms who were waiting for us there were getting anxious: it was late—how were they going to get the horses back to Tukucha? Since the path was good, why should we not proceed with the horses and so save time? The grooms could trot along behind us. The moment came when we really had to dismount. The *garawalas* came up dripping with sweat and did not conceal their satisfaction at seeing the end of the gallop—nor did we, for that matter.

We started off along a sparse track which struck off to the left and which, according to Couzy, should lead us to the hamlet of Choya. Soon we came in sight of the village; there was a great deal of coming and going at the first house, and coolies were climbing up and down a ladder. The sounds of laughter, singing and general hilarity led me to suspect that *chang*—rice

68

alcohol—was being generously distributed. Its sale is forbidden in Nepal; but that was no good reason for giving one's guests a poor welcome!

Not long after we had left the village we came upon the main body of porters—whom I had sent on ahead, in view of the long march—comfortably settled in the cool grass with their loads lying round them. We shouted at them, and in the twinkling of an eye the loads were picked up and the porters disappeared with a rapidity of which I should not have thought them capable. As darkness fell we skirted some large boulders and came out on to an alp perched on the edge of a precipice. Sarki and Aila quickly got the tents up, unpacked the evening's provisions and lit a great fire. It was late, and we ate our meal in silence and afterwards needed no urging to get into our sleeping-bags.

Next morning, we soon found ourselves all bunched together on a narrow track leading down to the river-bed. It was at this spot that, later on, Marcel Ichac and Jacques Oudot met a band of monkeys going up the valley. We now took to a path along the side of the cliff and after a steep descent found ourselves suddenly beside the Chadziou Khola, not, at this season, a very large stream. There was no difficulty about crossing it, but even for those who had been there before, it was quite impossible to make out the slightest vestige of a track on the other side, where a stretch of thick and apparently impenetrable jungle seemed to run far up the mountain side. Couzy informed us that this was the last water until the evening of the next day, so we filled up every available container. The Sherpas and the porters went on drinking indefinitely, like camels.

The ascent began with a climb up a vertical slab of rock. The track went up in steep zig-zags, obstructed by bamboos, dead tree-trunks and trees which straggled over the path in an attempt to reach the light; the air was damp and heavy. Couzy and I embarked on a long discussion: we had got as far as Bergson and Jünger when we came upon a delightful meadow bright with snowdrops and a variety of other flowers.

"It was here that Oudot, Schatz and I bivouacked on April 27," said Couzy. Mountaineers are great lovers of habit, so we had lunch there. Tubes of condensed milk were passed round. Those who weren't sick of this form of nourishment sucked concentrated fruit tablets, and while the last of the sweating porters were still arriving, the smoke curled up from our cigarettes. Couzy had grown meditative as a result of our discussion, and Rébuffat thought of his little Dominique, of whom he had received no news. Resuming our march, we suddenly found ourselves at a turning of the path, in a grove of trees resplendent with brilliant colored flowers whose names I did not know. No vaulted cathedral roof could have been more magnificent. The track went on across a beautiful clearing. Round us was a cemetery of charred deodars whose trunks rose well over a hundred feet high, and giant rhododendrons bordering our path, hung out great clusters of pink and red flowers. The Sherpas rushed up to some trees like red birches, made holes in the trunks with their ice-axes, fixed an empty tin underneath and so got a few mouthfuls of fresh water.

We now climbed painfully up a desperately long and steep couloir full of loose stones.

"There are lots of marmots here," said Rébuffat.

But though I kept my eyes peeled I didn't see a single one. At the top, which must have been about 13,000 feet high, we stopped again to smoke a cigarette while we waited for the porters. They had gone splendidly so far, but I could see they were tired. The ground was becoming more difficult and their loads, which were held by straps round their foreheads, tended to make them over-balance downhill. It was rough and painful for their bare feet and they didn't feel at all safe. Further on, we had to cross a large patch of snow where we enlarged the track and stamped it down, but our porters, doubled under the weight of the containers, looked most unhappy. I felt guilty as I walked along in my comfortable boots.

The weather turned really bad and it rained solidly. We kept together so as not to lose each other and advanced by guess-work over the gentle slopes of an alp, up the cairn, which marked the pass which was the goal of this day's journey. We pitched the tents in an indescribable muddle; our only thought was to get under cover the minute they were up. We climbed over 6,000 feet that day to reach the pass which we decided once for all to call "Pass of April 27." Couzy, Oudot and Schatz, who discovered it, deserved great credit for picking out the various vague tracks and following them up to the end.

The day's route was planned to cross the buttresses of the Nilgiris, always keeping well above the Miristi Khola. Where impassable ravines barred our way we went higher up and then descended again right to the river's edge where the gorges became practicable once more. Endlessly we carried out these flanking movements, going up and down the ravines, crossing streams, large and small. Here and there, by good luck, we found boulders which had been up-ended. These guiding marks were dotted along the route taken by the first party the day before, and on a patch of snow I read the time at which they had passed, written by Schatz. Roughly speaking, we were keeping to the same timetable.

We were covered in cloud and I could get no general view of the ground over which we were passing. Early in the afternoon we got to a point from which any further progress appeared very difficult. We hailed Couzy, our guide: he hesitated a bit, retraced his steps, then called to us triumphantly. On a small boulder, held in place by some stones, was a pennant of the Club Alpin Français, which marked the beginning of the descent to the Miristi Khola. We started down very steep grassy slopes where the porters, whose morale was not very good, kept on slipping. It rained and snowed and the way seemed interminable. Suddenly I heard a shout, and as I went forward I saw a wood fire, and round it, the porters of the first party who, having deposited their loads, were returning to the valley. Conversations began in Gurkhali. Once more I noticed how well this language of short words and guttural sounds can be understood at a great distance.

The slope continued over steep rock slabs, and then skirted along cliffs in which we could make out some enormous caves. Couzy assured me that the previous time he had been that way, a herd of *thar,* taking things easy by the entrance to these grottoes, did not even trouble to move as he went by. But today I had the rifle, and of course there was not an animal to be seen.

A few minutes later we were all assembled on the banks of the Miristi Khola, a turbulent river that drains all the waters from the upper basins of Annapurna, the Great Barrier and the Nilgiris. From now on the route lay along the opposite bank, so we had to cross over. I spotted some tree trunks which the others had placed the day before, but our coolies refused to venture on them with their loads. Rébuffat and I did not hesitate; we decided to take the stuff over ourselves.

Now Rébuffat was transformed into a porter; he had the straps supporting the containers placed round his forehead, and his head, his neck and his long body swayed dangerously. He approached the torrent, started across with Couzy's support, then balancing by himself took a few steps over the foaming water, and stretching out his arms reached me where I was standing on a boulder sticking out of the water: from that point I could take the loads on safely.

This maneuver was repeated a number of times, but one of the loads made me anxious; it was very heavy and very awkward, consisting of two base camp units and one high-altitude unit. Rébuffat advanced, hesitated, lost his balance, just managed to regain it, advanced again, slowly. Then the strap round his forehead slipped, the load was hurled into the water and in a flash I foresaw the irreparable loss of our tents.

71

Couzy and I reacted in the same way: from our opposite banks we each tried to grab the tents, and madly hopped about from boulder to boulder. I missed once, jumped along further, and then just before a big eddy which held up the load, managed to stick the point of my ice-axe into a bit of stuff, and pulled the load out. The rest of the operation went off perfectly.

Next day, in considerably better weather, we left early. I went on about an hour ahead of the rest of the party and towards midday, met Marcel Schatz who had come out to look for us. He gave me the latest news: Louis Lachenal and Lionel Terray had left that morning on a reconnaissance of the north-west spur of Annapurna. Near the Base Camp the moraines flattened out, the valley of the Miristi widened and there was a better view of our surroundings. The spur which ran down and petered out a few hundred yards from where we were did not look too bad, but without quite knowing why, I didn't feel keen on this route. Ever since our experiences on Dhaulagiri I was suspicious of ridges. I was afraid that even if it did not present any insurmountable difficulties, this ridge would be troublesome, and I could not bring myself to turn the reconnaissance into a full-scale assault until we had completed our exploration. This meant, practically speaking, not before we had set foot upon the upper plateau of Annapurna. Schatz and I arrived at Base Camp which was pitched among the moraines in the midst of a vast stony desert with little blue-green lakes dotted about in the hollows. From here it would be a day's march to the Great Barrier which blocked the horizon to the east, or to the Nilgiris on the north. Snow was falling and we sheltered in one of the tents, where hours passed in prolonged discussions.

There were sounds of stones displaced, ice-axes clanging against the rocks, bad language—evidently the Lachenal-Terray party had arrived. A flap of the tent was jerked back and a boisterous greeting flung in: the pair were clearly in full cry. I could see they were very tired, but resolute and optimistic. They pulled off their snow covered clothes, and while they sipped their tea, told me what they had done during the day. This celebrated partnership, which had conquered all the finest and most dangerous of our Alpine faces, was today living up to its reputation.

"It's not exactly a picnic," said Terray.

"You said it!" agreed Lachenal vehemently. "There are pitches which are easily Grade Five."[15]

"Grade Five!" I was horrified. "How on earth do you think Sherpas can climb pitches of that grade?"

"They are only sections here and there."

"We can fix ropes and by pulling and pushing the Sherpas we'll manage all right."

"Apart from these pitches what's the ridge like?"

"It's certainly very long," said Terray, "and the farther you go the more difficult it becomes."

"And beyond the point you got to I suppose it becomes impossible!"

"I don't really think so," said Terray. "We stopped at about eleven o'clock this morning, after climbing since dawn up to somewhere near 18,000 feet. A bit higher up the ridge steepens again and becomes snowy. After that we couldn't see any more, but I think, and Lachenal agrees with me, that it must run up into the upper plateau of Annapurna a few hundred yards higher up."

"Perhaps," I remarked skeptically.

"Listen, Maurice, it's quite simple. All we have to do," proposed Terray, "is to go there in strength. Tomorrow we'll all set to work and move Base Camp to the summit of the grassy saddle and then begin the assault."

"And we'll have saved several days of indecision," added Lachenal.

"And perhaps we'll spoil all our chances," I replied. "If the attack upon the spur should be unsuccessful we'd have to move Base Camp again and come down into the valley and then start up once more. It's out of the question. I've no intention of hazarding the whole strength of the Expedition on a route we know so little about. Let's push on further with the reconnaissance you have already made; tomorrow let's go beyond the point where you stopped—on until we are certain that it's practicable right up to the summit. We won't make the final decision until then."

"You *are* an obstinate old devil!"

Lachenal and Terray stormed away at me. They thought we ought to decide to attack at once, and kept on insisting that this was the right route. I knew my friends well and had my doubts of their wild enthusiasm; they were in a very excitable state after their day's climbing. I was responsible for the party and it was up to me to be prudent: I stuck to my decision. Tomorrow morning we would all go up the spur, taking light camping gear, and we would only return after we had made sure. Base Camp would remain where it was for the moment; our explorations would be on the scale of a strong reconnaissance party. While my friends got things ready for the next day, I wrote a note for the rearguard:

18 May, 1950

Dear Noyelle,

I am now at the Base Camp. Terray and Lachenal have just come back from the spur, and are fairly hopeful about it. We are keeping to the same plan: we remain a strong reconnaissance party. At the moment the weather is bad, and this threatens to delay operations.

Provisions: *I'm afraid I may be a bit short. Please send up at once three Base Camp containers, three high-altitude containers, and one container of "heavy"[16] tins.*

Equipment: *10 rock-pitons, 10 ice-pitons, 300 feet of nylon line and three fifty-foot, full weight ropes. Two high-altitude units.*

Porters: *Pay off the porters of the first party and give them all the same* baksheesh. *Pay off the second party too: full* baksheesh *to those who have a note for you. The two old boys half* baksheesh, *and nothing to the others as they didn't do well.*

Future provisions: *After the dispatch of what I have asked for, could you, unless you hear to the contrary, send up three more Base Camp containers, and three high-altitude containers?*

Ichac and Oudot: *For the moment, there's nothing to tell them; bad weather has so far prevented me from seeing Annapurna. As soon as there is any news I will send it.*

Greetings from us all,

Maurice.

On May 14, the day on which we had held our council of war, after we had made the decision to turn our attention towards Annapurna, Ichac had told me he wanted to pay a visit to the village of Muktinath with Oudot. I said goodbye to them on the 15th, before leaving for Annapurna. They set off next morning accompanied by the Sirdar Ang-Tharkey, for whom the village of Muktinath was the holy of holies. A fervent believer, zealous in all his religious practices, he took this as a unique opportunity for him to go on a pilgrimage which so many of his brethren had had to renounce. All day long the little party ascended by the right bank of the Gandaki and by the end of the afternoon they came in sight of a large group of buildings: white houses, red temples, the whole dominated by a ruined Tibetan fortress. Ang-Tharkey cried excitedly: "Muktinath!"

But as Ichac and Oudot approached this marvelous city the fine buildings turned out to be dirty and dilapidated. At the end of the village were a few bedaubed *chortens*. Where, then, were the temples, the monasteries and the multitudes of Lamas? Over to the east Ichac saw some rather newer buildings protected by zinc roofs. Making some inquiries, he discovered that Muktinath consisted of only five or six buildings, and that this was Chahar. It couldn't be helped, the pilgrimage would have to be put off until the following morning. They found shelter for the night in a ruined castle, made a quick meal and went to bed before the interested gaze of fifty natives.

Next day at the crack of dawn they started up towards the holy place. After leaving their horses at the door of the first building, they passed by a rock on which there was a vague imprint, something like the shape of a foot.

"Buddha, Sahib!" Ang-Tharkey cried out, throwing himself on the ground.

They passed by a first temple, rather like the one at Tukucha, and came to the sacred fountains: water from the stream ran along a horizontal conduit and fed some sixty spouts in the form of cows or dragons. In the center of the square was a Nepalese shrine. Some pilgrims came to fill up their vessels and drink. Ang-Tharkey, carrying one of the Expedition's water-bottles, made a tour of every fountain, consequently our two friends were not able to use this bottle for the rest of the trip.

A little way to the south they visited another temple guarded by a dozen maidens, dressed in colored robes. A stone was lifted and Ichac and Oudot were shown two narrow apertures. Along them came the sound of the flowing water, and in them flickered the blue flame of a natural gas which burned perpetually. The vestals sang and danced; the sahibs offered their contributions; Ang-Tharkey showed himself particularly generous with the Expedition's cash.

Early next afternoon the pilgrims were back at Tukucha where Noyelle was awaiting them impatiently, for he, too, was very keen to go to Muktinath. His turn came next day, with G. B. Rana. Then on May 20 at nine-thirty Angawa and Dawatondu arrived, bringing the message written at the Base Camp near the spur, after Lachenal and Terray had returned from their reconnaissance.

Chapter VIII

The Spur

We were up and doing before dawn on May 19, in our provisional Base Camp at the foot of the spur. It was still pitch dark. The Sherpas couldn't make out what this untimely commotion was all about. On other expeditions they had never left before sunrise! Still half asleep they prepared *nesthé* and *tonimalt* while Rébuffat, Terray and Schatz packed their sacks.

"How many ice-pitons?"

"Have you got your vitascorbol?"

"How much does your flask hold?"

Then the climbers went off one by one across the moraine and disappeared into the night. I was not long in following, my eyes still heavy with sleep, and I stumbled over the loose stones which I could hardly see in the dark. I made for the foot of the spur. The clink of ice-axe on rock soon told me the others were not far away; we had one more moraine to cross. We were all heavily laden with equipment for three camps and several days' food. The Sherpas would carry the loads up as high as they could and then go back to the Base Camp as quickly as possible so as not to use up the high-altitude provisions. It was daylight when we reached the snow—it was hard, and my "vibram" soles held nicely. Our progress was slow, and somewhat labored, but we gained height steadily.

Was it really going to be fine? Since leaving Tukucha I had barely seen a glimpse of blue sky, and at the risk of slipping on the hard snow of this steep slope, I kept on turning round to admire the view. We were completely overwhelmed by the Great Barrier whose average height I estimated at nearly 23,000 feet. Its defenses culminated in a gigantic and inaccessible keep, right in the center, and its precipitous walls rose 10,000 feet above the camp. The rock was smooth and offered no irregularity, no line of weakness on which the trained eye of a mountaineer might hope to trace out a possible route. Annapurna was a giant fortress and we were still only on the outer defenses.

We were in a savage and desolate *cirque* of mountains never before seen by man. No animal or plant could exist here. In the pure morning light this absence of all life, this utter destitution of nature, seemed only to intensify our own strength. How could we expect anyone else to understand the peculiar exhilaration that we drew from this barrenness, when man's natural tendency is to be attracted to everything in nature that is lush and fruitful?

We were nearly as high as Mont Blanc and it was extremely cold. Everybody was out of breath and labored at his own pace. When we reached the saddle the sun had risen, and whereas a moment ago those stupendous walls had been dark and ominous, now they glowed with light. We had to make for the foot of our actual ridge, and Terray, who had come with us in spite of his previous day's exhaustion, pointed out the line of attack. We took the ropes out of our sacks, and tied on. The previous day's party had left a rope fixed here, all ready for us, and we started climbing up rock which, though limestone, was relatively firm. Sarki was on my rope; Rébuffat followed with Adjiba, Terray with Aila and Schatz.

If the solution of the problem lay up the spur, we must reach it quickly, and we determined to go all out. The plan was that as soon as the ground became too difficult for the Sherpas they would put down their loads and go down again, while the four sahibs would go on and pitch a tent as high as possible; there Rébuffat and I would sleep. Terray and Schatz would go back to the shoulder, where Lachenal would join Terray in the evening, after resting from his climb of the day before. As for Schatz, he would return to Base Camp and come up again the following day with Couzy, and so make a third assault party; they would organize their camp on the shoulder.

The first step was soon accomplished: we sent back the Sherpas who lost a great deal of time on this difficult rock. I noticed, however, how quickly they adapted themselves to terrain, though up till now they had had little actual experience. Sarki in particular, I thought, would be capable of leading a party on very difficult rock. After they had gone we gained height rapidly: we surveyed, as from an airplane, the continuation of our spur, which from here looked rather attractive. We could also see the glaciers flowing down on both sides of our ridge. The clouds, as usual, were low down, obscuring any view of the mountains around us.

The ridge narrowed and put us in mind of our own splendid Chamonix *aiguilles*. The rock was good, and if it had not been for our loads and for the height it would have been a really enjoyable climb.

Soon it became very cold and started to snow; we were certainly above 18,000 feet. I looked up to the ridge and tried to spot a site for the tent. For the moment we could see nothing but some treacherous-looking ledges, and these were few and far between. The weather was threatening and we had to come to some decision, particularly as it was getting late and Schatz and Terray wanted to go back. We were holding on with our hands to a blade-thin little rock ridge, while our feet dangled against the rock. The feeling of space was considerable—I couldn't remember anything quite so steep in the Alps. The few rocks sticking out from the slope were covered with ice. I could not understand how snow could ever lie on these slopes and I realized why avalanches were so frequent.

After this delicate crossing we came to a small triangular snow-covered shelf. The weather had now turned really bad, and at once we decided to pitch our tent here. Setting to work quickly, we hurled the snow off each side of the ridge, starting avalanches. Ice-covered rocks went the same way. But even after this clearing of the decks there was hardly room for two of us to sit down. We tried to pry up some rocks embedded in the ice, hacking away in turn, or using our axes as levers. Terray angrily grabbed my axe and struck such furious blows that the rock seemed likely to split—alas, it was the axe that gave way; the blade was literally bent double. Fortunately he succeeded in straightening it again. The site now looked more promising, and Terray and Schatz could leave us.

In five minutes they had disappeared from sight. I was worried about them—climbing at this height in fresh snow is highly dangerous.

Rébuffat and I were now alone. We went on working away at our emplacement for all we were worth—at least as quickly as our want of breath would allow us. We pried up an enormous stone and placed it carefully on the edge of the slope to extend the surface of our narrow ledge. We consolidated the whole with snow, leveled it and then at last began to get the tent up. We fastened it in front to pitons hammered into the rock, and at the back of our ice-axes driven in up to the hilt. We fixed the guy-ropes to stones instead of to pegs. The careful Rébuffat made a little wall on the edge of the precipice to protect himself from the wind, and prudently put in a good strong piton for us to belay ourselves to. To this piton we remained roped all night.

Snow fell relentlessly, with never a break; the cold became unbearable. Had there ever been such an airy camp as this, we wondered, or one which had been wrested from the mountains with such difficulty? Tea cheered us up a little. We hadn't much appetite, but dutifully swallowed the *vitascorbol* and B_2 vitamins advised by Dr. Oudot. The wind howled, the tent shook; our thoughts went round and round in circles. For a long time we couldn't get to sleep.

At dawn it was still snowing slightly; the rocks had quite a thick covering of powder snow which discouraged any hope of being able to go on. We decided to wait for better weather, and if it didn't improve we would go down at noon, leaving everything in place for our return to the attack. The most difficult pitch was directly above our tent. It consisted of a block split at the top by a little crack which had to be reached—but heaven knew how—for everything was covered with snow. Rébuffat thought it was hopeless and was all for going down at once. But I wanted to exhaust every possibility and so avoid any future regrets. If the weather improved the snow might melt quickly and allow reasonable progress.

"They're coming! Listen, that's their ice-axes."

Lachenal and Terray appeared on the ridge.

"What the hell are you doing here?" they asked. "Are you boys resting?"

"Can't you see the snow?"

"We've seen it just as much as you have. More than you have, for we've been climbing since dawn to get here."

"A couple of sissies!" growled Lachenal.

"We'd be crazy to go on," retorted Rébuffat. "I've no desire to come off here."

"We'll show you who's coming off," cried Lachenal. And without waiting another minute he flung himself at this dangerous pitch which he had climbed two days before. He began a traverse to the left on particularly treacherous snow; it was just lying loose on the slope, but when he stepped on it, it packed and clung to the rock. At the very end of this ledge was a crack up which he climbed for about ten feet. Every hold was covered with ice. I glanced at Terray, to whom he was roped, and saw that he had him well belayed. Lachenal now set to work on a gigantic open corner; he cleared a tiny crack which he tried to use. His feet slipped and only by a miracle did his hands hold. He came down a notch, hammered in a piton which wobbled and inspired no confidence, but he stepped onto it without any hesitation. How on earth was he to get any higher? He took his ice-axe, which was all wet, jammed it an inch or so in the crack and pulled on it hard to see if it held. The axe moved up and down in the crack, but by jerking it he succeeded in jamming it firmly. Then he hung on by both arms to the shaft of the axe. He took his foot off the piton and made a desperate effort to gain a few inches. I wasn't at all happy: it seemed to me that it was wrong to take such risks in the present conditions. I kept close to Terray in case it should be necessary to hold Lachenal on the rope. I hardly had time to say a word before Lachenal was up. He had surmounted the difficult stretch in a really masterly fashion. Without losing a second Terray followed and fixed a second piton and some nylon line.

Closing the tent and shouldering our packs, Rébuffat and I started up too, and a few moments later joined the others roped together on a comfortable stance protected by a great shelter stone. Here of course was where we ought to have pitched our camp, but the foul weather of the previous day had made it impossible. Today we were still surrounded by clouds, but through some rifts I was able to see, over on my left, the final ice-fall of the north Annapurna glacier of which I had so far had only a very poor view.

We held a brief consultation. The only one to take an optimistic view of the route up the spur was Lionel Terray. Lachenal, having made such a to-do when he joined us, was now of the opinion that we should never finish with this endless ridge. Rébuffat was pessimistic. As for myself, I had come to the conclusion that in all probability the spur would not prove to be the way up Annapurna. For even if we should discover that the route itself led to Annapurna, it would be out of the question to bring the whole Expedition up this way. Obviously, the route was so long and difficult that, in the event of prolonged bad weather, or the premature arrival of the monsoon, or any injury to a climber which involved carrying him down, our situation could become highly dangerous.

Much the same reasoning had already made me give up Dhaulagiri. Lionel Terray was so confident, so enthusiastic, that no arguments in favor of caution had the slightest effect on him. I found it hard to discourage so much perseverance, and in particular that burning desire, which I could so well understand, to make an all-out assault on the mountain. On the other hand I did not wish to delay future operations by even one single day.

As I looked once more at the glacier, and the enormous ice-fall down below, I felt in my bones that if there were a way up Annapurna, that was where it lay. So another plan began to take shape in my mind. Rébuffat and Lachenal, who had not the least wish to continue up the spur, would go back as quickly as possible to the temporary Base Camp. They would then take a Sherpa with them, and attempt to force a way—which to all appearances would be found along the right bank—up the glacier to the plateau which, we guessed, probably lay beyond the ice-fall on the north face. If they were successful they would have to send us word at once. Meanwhile Terray and I would continue up the spur to set our minds finally at rest over the possibilities of this present route.

So Lachenal and Rébuffat left us, taking with them instructions for Couzy and Schatz to come up the following day either to back us up, or to help us get everything off the spur.

Terray and I put the tent up. I looked forward to spending a night for the first time high up with him. The weather was very poor. Our aim was to take as little with us as possible and to press on with all speed in order to settle once and for all the question of the spur.

We slept like logs, but Terray, who always wakes on the dot, was up and moving soon after dawn. Snugly installed in my sleeping-bag I played at being the Bara Sahib: Terray made the tea, opened tins and served me my breakfast in bed. We stepped out into the fresh snow which had been falling thickly for two days. Here we felt the height badly and we were still very cold. Although we were carrying very little, it was a tremendous strain at first, but we gritted our teeth and went on, for we did not want to lose a minute.

After an easy chimney we came out again upon the ridge which gradually became so narrow that we could not walk in balance along it. So we followed the crest hanging on by our hands, as though we were traversing an immense horizontal bar, with our feet dangling against the steep sides. We progressed like this over a precipice of some six or seven thousand feet. Gradually we approached the famous snow ridge which Lachenal and Terray had told us about. Their remarks had been so contradictory that I had every reason to be anxious about this obstacle. In fact, as we came nearer, it showed itself to be very high and very steep. Without hesitating a minute Terray went ahead; I followed a short distance behind him. The slope began with an elegant crescent moon, then it did indeed become excessively steep. Soon I felt not only snow under my crampons but hard ice lying just beneath. While the first man cut steps with tremendous blows, I stuck ice-pitons into the slope to belay him. Luckily the thin layer of snow was extremely hard, and it was not necessary to make very large steps. By skirting round to the left we were able to avoid a steep ice wall. I hammered in an ice-piton regularly every rope's length, and Terray did the same, and as I came up I collected the pitons. We had to be very economical since we were carrying only a limited supply of them. Our noses were right up against the slope. Often hand-holds as well as foot-holds had to be cut in the ice. We now came to the first rock gendarmes or rock towers of the ridge—they were overhanging. What a series of disappointments!

Terray traversed boldly to the right to reach a crack in the rock, where he put in a couple of pitons. He belayed himself securely, then, leaning over backwards above those plunging ice-slopes, he brought me up. We were in shadow now, and shivering with cold. In turn I belayed Terray who continued his traverse to the right to avoid a rocky projection. The going was pretty tricky, and the general feel of the climb not too good. Soon we were again together, this time in the sun, but the situation was most uncomfortable and indeed precarious.

The few rays of warmth had been enough to turn the hard snow into a treacherous mush. The last slopes, of bare ice, gave us some trouble; and then we found ourselves at the top of the ridge, at about 20,000 feet. The weather was now brilliantly fine, and I took some photographs. There in front of us seemingly only a stone's throw away was Annapurna.

Our spur continued towards the summit of Annapurna, but the jagged ice ridge, that looked like a cluster of cauliflowers, was scarcely any nearer to us now than when we had started up the spur—the clearness of the atmosphere entirely falsified distances. Terray and I thought over the difficulties that lay ahead, which we were now in a position to appreciate; we realized that it would take several days' climbing to complete the route, even at the same pace we had kept up so far. Nature was too powerful, and the obstacles with which she confronted us were out of all proportion to our resources. No long discussion was necessary. Even if no other obstacle cropped up to hinder our progress—we were thinking of the possibility of a gap in the ridge—it would have been madness to launch an expedition on this route.

No Alpine climb had ever presented us with the number of difficulties we had encountered here. Never, we felt sure, in the Himalaya had men engaged in such acrobatics. With all my heart I hoped that the Annapurna glacier would give up its secret to Lachenal and Rébuffat. From our present situation it looked quite feasible and we had a good view of the plateau which they aimed to reach. Should they be forced to retreat, our last hope would be gone. Would all this sweat, all this struggle, all this pain, result only in some secondary achievement? If so, we should be bitterly disappointed.

Without further delay—for we knew the hardest part still lay before us—we began the descent. Cautiously we moved down in turn, placing pitons whenever possible, for the rock was far from good. It was scorchingly hot in the sun, but in the shadow the cold was intense. We traversed across the slope, then started on the great ice ridge. This time the snow no longer held—it was loose and treacherous; we would rather have been on bare ice. Terray started off; I belayed him with the pitons, but the limited number we had with us forced me to take most of them out. So I had to go down by myself, with no belay, under the watchful eye of Terray, who knew very well that if I slipped I should inevitably drag him off too. When it was his turn I watched him go down face outwards with slow, carefully studied movements so that he should always be in perfect balance. He told me later that twice he had begun to slip and twice been able to pull himself up. My technique was different: I went down face to the slope, using my hands as much as my feet. With my right foot I felt the ice, searching for a good hold, and putting my foot in position without being able to see what I was doing; my left foot held, in spite of the soft snow, by the two front points of my crampons. With my left hand I pressed the wet snow against the ice, using this as a sort of little hold; with my right hand I used my ice-axe as an anchor, with the pick stuck a few millimeters into the rock-hard ice. When my right foot was in position and my balance re-established on three points of contact, such as they were, it was the turn of the left foot to repeat the operation. It was an extraordinary reptilian progress, a kind of balancing trick, in which I held the mountain very gently without jolting it either by speed or movement.

"Hello, you up there!" It was Schatz's voice. He was coming up to help us. Terray, who was nearer to him, called out that we were giving up.

"Hi Schatz, take the tent down, we're going back to Base Camp."

Schatz heard, and watched our progress from a little way off. The clouds were now all around us, and the mist was down and everything melted into a gray sameness. We put in pitons, judged the distance still left to go, and fixed our spare rope. I watched the piton as Terray went down first on the doubled rope; it curved and bent over at each jerk, but came back to its original position, and the ice was so hard that I didn't really worry much. Then in my turn I fixed the rope round myself in the usual way and quickly joined Terray who had prepared a landing-place for me with his ice-axe. I brought down the doubled rope by pulling on one of the ends, and soon we reached the rocks. We couldn't conceal our relief as we took off our crampons. A second later we started on the traverse of the rock ridge with such enthusiasm and such a strong desire to get down, at least as far as the saddle by nightfall, that what had taken us half an hour up in the morning now took only a few minutes.

A race against time began. Terray and I tore along the easy bits of the ridge, sliding down chimneys and shooting down couloirs. In spite of the cold we were soon sweating hard. In record time we reached our morning camp and found Schatz and Sarki had just finished taking the tent down. While we swallowed beef in tomato sauce, and nougat, and sipped the excellent tea which Terray had just made, we summed up in jerky sentences the significance of the enterprise. Those thrilling and inspiring moments—yet so exhausting—had led only to a useless victory on a minor spur of the mountain. Nevertheless, as Terray declared later, nothing would ever equal those first desperate days when he put forth every ounce of his courage, strength and resolution.

The cloud ceiling was low, but we hoped the weather would become more settled. We soon reached the pitch where we had left the nylon line, and one after the other we went down into space and then re-assembled again on the narrow platform where Rébuffat and I had spent the night before last. The four of us carried two entire high-altitude outfits over difficult and dangerous ground, but this did not slow up our pace. Sarki was terrified at our speed, but was not long in adopting a rhythm as rapid as that of the Sahibs. There was thick snow on the spur and we had to take all kinds of precautions. As soon as we were over the difficult pitches we raced on again, for all of us were keyed up by the rhythm of action. The saddle was getting visibly nearer, we negotiated the last pitches, and then ran down the grassy slopes now covered with fresh snow.

Soon we all reached the advanced camp which had been established during the assault on the shoulder of the spur. We came down terrain in a few hours what it had taken us two days to get up. The Base Camp on the moraine in the bed of the valley was plainly visible—the yellow of the tents stood out distinctly against the uniform gray of the surrounding stones. The rain, or rather the wet snow, which had been falling a few minutes earlier, had now turned to a light drizzle. Terray and I glanced at each other in agreement; in a second we had collected from the two Base Camp tents as much equipment as we could, made up our sacks and sprung off down the slopes. Schatz and Sarki tried to keep up with us, but we had apparently been transformed into human projectiles, hurtling down in spite of our sacks which threatened to throw us off balance. We controlled our speed by jumping against tufts of grass and any irregularity of the ground. Traversing left we reached a tongue of snow lying in the bed of a little valley: without hesitation we both glissaded down, describing some magnificent slaloms. By this elegant and rapid method we gained the moraine a few minutes later.

Schatz must have been wondering why we went at such a rate—to tell the truth there was no reason at all. Instead of taking a quarter of an hour we might just as well have come down quietly in an hour. It was all due to the exhilaration produced by this splendid day of hard climbing.

At Base Camp we were greeted with sensational news. Lachenal and Rébuffat had sent back their Sherpa with a note: the right bank of the glacier was practicable; they guaranteed to reach the plateau which they had so far not been able to see. On the other hand they had been able to see nothing of the upper part of Annapurna.

From the point Terray and I had reached on the spur, at a height of about 20,000 feet, I had been able to see the whole of the section which had remained invisible to them. I knew that the plateau was level and would present no difficulties.

For the first time during the Expedition, we had real grounds for hope. Were our perseverance and our faith at last to be rewarded? In a few hours the fate of the expedition would be decided.

For the moment we dried ourselves—all our clothes were soaked with rain, melting snow and sweat. Schatz arrived with Sarki and plans for the next day were immediately drawn up.

"I've spotted my own little route," said Schatz. "Give me two Sherpas and . . ."

"Two Sherpas," cut in Terray. "And what next?"

"Two high-altitude units and three days' provisions."

"The Chief wants his own expedition," said Couzy, using the nickname given to Schatz in Alpine circles on account of his passion for organization.

"Give him a chance to speak: what's your idea?"

"To go up the glacier by an easy ridge which I've spotted, and which would avoid the seracs on the right."

"He's right," I said. "Supposing Lachenal and Rébuffat don't succeed, what would you do next? You'd be extremely glad to have an alternative route."

At dawn next day Schatz went off, full of hope. He had been one of the discoverers of the route along the Miristi with Couzy and Oudot, and he now looked forward to being in the lead again, and opening up the decisive route to the top of Annapurna. Terray and I, as well as Sarki, were worn out with our recent exertions, and we gave ourselves the next morning off. Early in the afternoon we would set off to rejoin the advance party, under the guidance of Adjiba. This time I had great hopes and it took all my good sense to force myself to "waste" those few very precious hours.

"Couzy, you are going to have a thankless job. . . ."

"What's that?"

"You will have to pack up the advanced camp on the spur, move the present Base Camp and establish a permanent Base Camp where I tell you—that's to say at the farthest point we can get the porters up to."

"It certainly doesn't sound much fun, but if the job's really got to be done . . ."

"Yes, it has to be done, and unfortunately you'll have only one Sherpa."

"It doesn't sound like a picnic."

"You'll have to carry loads yourself . . ."

For several days, Jean Couzy, the youngest of the party, would, in spite of all his ardor and enthusiasm, be condemned to stay low to carry out an essential but unspectacular job. He did it to perfection and without a single word of complaint, although he knew that, when the final attack was launched, he would not be sufficiently acclimatized and so would lose the chance of being on it. It is this admirable spirit of self-denial which determines the strength of a team.

In spite of the wretched weather we had a very pleasant evening for we were warmed by our hopes. Conversation flowed easily, and we vied with each other in good humor. The hour of decision was drawing near.

The rain beat with deafening noise on the taut canvas of the tents, but we fell happily asleep, beautifully warm in our sleeping-bags. Drugged by sleep I heard cries, the clanking of pitons, hushed voices, the sound of a stove, the noise of a can being opened, stones rolling over: it was Schatz getting ready with Pansy and Aila. While it was still dark, he came to my tent.

"I'm off, Maurice," he whispered.

"What's the weather like?"

"The sky is full of stars."

"Good luck, Marcel."

"Thanks, goodbye."

For a while I heard the noise of stones as the others moved off. How wonderful it is to stay in the warmth when other people are at work! How pleasant just to be able to dream, with no sense of time, when you know that in a few hours the pleasant idleness will give place to action. Since the beginning of the Expedition I had never had a moment's quiet; this morning I had the chance to take things easy, and I thoroughly appreciated it.

Slowly I got up and went round to the other tents: Terray, who had become possessed with the demon of orderliness, was sorting, tidying, selecting and organizing: on the eve of the critical time ahead he did not want to be caught unprepared. Before becoming immersed myself in this work I took a long look at the mountains; the sun was already high, the temperature warm. It was a good day.

But everything comes to an end—even the best moments. I had one big worry. We were getting short of food, and I was anxious to make a list of what remained. We collected our provisions together; then, squatting in the tent, I sorted things into different categories, spread them out, counted up and calculated. With these figures in my head, my mind was now at ease. Early in the afternoon we set off carrying enormous sacks. I felt in grand form; the morning off had completely rested me after the last eight days of uninterrupted action. The fine weather held.

The tiresome and monotonous moraines stretched out for miles, and several times one of us slipped on the stones which were treacherously covered with hard black ice. Presently we saw a man coming to meet us: it was Adjiba bringing wonderful news. Lachenal and Rébuffat had reached the glacier plateau! Rébuffat added in his note that the way lay over rocks on the right bank which were easy to climb. So the great ice-fall of the north Annapurna glacier had been overcome. With hope in our hearts, we hurried on. The temperature was fairly comfortable and the nearby rocks reflected the warmth. The walls of the Great Barrier, in whose direction we were going, gradually came nearer. They were smooth and unclimbable, a salty somber gray. The moraine on the true right bank of the glacier, as so often happens, offered a quick easy route. Adjiba was guiding us now, and by mid-afternoon we came to a sort of flattening of the moraine which spread out and abutted against the Great Barrier.

We now had to climb up the walls of the right bank. I decided that this place would be where the porters must stop. I made a quick sketch to indicate as near as possible the future site of the Base Camp. It was getting late and we wanted to make the plateau that evening. After leading us along at a good pace, Adjiba brought us to the foot of the Great Barrier. A system of ledges cut by chimneys extending into couloirs enabled us to reach the top of the ice-fall of the Annapurna glacier. We were very nearly exhausted by this march at high altitude and our sacks grew heavier and heavier. Dusk had fallen when at last we came to the foot of a big wall of ice where the first party had pitched their tent at a height of about 16,700 feet; this was to be the future Camp I.

Everyone welcomed us in the highest spirits. We could see nothing at this time of night, but they told us:

"There's not a shadow of doubt; we ought to be able to get up Annapurna."

Chapter IX

Annapurna

AN ASTONISHING SIGHT GREETED ME NEXT MORNING. LACHENAL AND RÉBUFFAT were sitting outside on a dry rock, with their eyes riveted on Annapurna. A sudden shout brought me out of my tent: "I've found the route!" cried Lachenal. I went up to him, blinking in the glare. For the first time Annapurna was beginning to reveal its secrets. The huge north face with all its rivers of ice shone and sparkled in the light. Never had I seen a mountain so impressive in all its proportions. It was a world both dazzling and menacing; the eye was lost in its immensities. But for once, we were not being confronted with vertical walls, jagged ridges and hanging glaciers which put an end to all hopes of climbing.

"You see," explained Lachenal, "the problem . . . is to get to that sickle-shaped glacier high up on the mountain. To reach the foot of it without danger of avalanches, we'll have to go up well over on the left."[17]

"But how the hell would you get to the foot of your route?" interrupted Rébuffat. "On the other side of the plateau that we're on there's a glacier which is a mass of crevasses and quite impossible to cross."

"Look. . . ."

We looked hard. But I am bound to admit I felt almost incapable of following Lachenal's explanations. I was carried away on a wave of enthusiasm, for at last our mountain was there before our eyes.

This May the twenty-third was surely the Expedition's greatest day so far!

"Look," insisted Lachenal, his knitted cap all askew, "we can avoid the crevassed section by skirting round to the left. After that we'll only have to climb the ice-falls opposite, and then make gradually over to the right towards the Sickle."

The sound of an ice-axe distracted our attention for a moment: it was Adjiba breaking up ice to melt into water.

"Your route isn't direct enough, Lachenal," I told him. "We'd be certain to sink up to our waists in the snow: the route must be the shortest possible, direct to the summit."

"And what about avalanches?" queried Rébuffat.

"You run a risk from them on the right as well as on the left. So you may as well choose the shortest way."

"And there's the couloir too," said Lachenal.

"If we cross it high enough up, the danger won't be very great. Anyway, look at the avalanche tracks over on the left on your route."

"There's something in that," admitted Lachenal.

"So why not go straight up in line with the summit, skirt round the seracs and crevasses, slant over to the left to reach the Sickle, and from there go straight up to the top?"

Rébuffat struck me as being not very optimistic. Standing there, in the old close-fitting jersey that he always wore on his Alpine climbs, he seemed more than ever to deserve the name the Sherpas had given him of Lamba Sahib, or "long man."

"But," continued Lachenal, "we could go straight up under the ice cliff and then traverse left and reach the same spot . . ."

"But cutting across to the left is certainly more direct."

"That should be possible," agreed Lachenal, letting himself be won over.

Rébuffat's resistance yielded bit by bit.

"Lionel! Come and have a look . . ."

Terray was bending over a container and sorting out provisions in his usual serious manner. He raised his head: it was adorned with a red skiing bonnet, and he sported a flowing beard. I asked him frankly what *his* route was. He had already examined the mountain and come to his own conclusion:

"My dear Maurice," he said, pursing up his lips in the special way that marked a great occasion, "it's perfectly clear to me. Above the avalanche cone of the great couloir, just in line with the summit . . ." and he went on to describe the route he had worked out.

So here we were, all in complete agreement.

"Let's get going," Terray kept crying in great excitement. Lachenal, no less excited, came and yelled in my ear:

"A hundred to nothing! That's the odds on our success!"

And even the more cautious Rébuffat admitted that "It's the least difficult proposition and the most reasonable."

The weather was magnificent; never had the mountains looked more beautiful. Our optimism was tremendous, perhaps we were over-optimistic for the gigantic scope of the face set us problems that we had never had to cope with in the Alps. And above all, time was short. If we were to succeed not a moment must be lost. The arrival of the monsoon was announced for about June 5. *We had just twelve days left.* We'd have to move fast, very fast indeed. I was haunted by this idea. To do so we would have to lengthen out the intervals between the successive camps, organize a shuttle service to bring up the maximum number of loads in the minimum time, acclimatize ourselves,[18] and, finally, maintain communications with the rear. This last point worried me. Our party was organized on the scale of a reconnaissance and the total supply at our disposal was only five days' food and a limited amount of equipment.

How could I possibly keep track of the thousand and one questions that buzzed round in my head? The rest of the party were all highly excited and talked away noisily while the Sherpas moved about the tents as usual. There were only two of them here and we could not possibly begin operations with just these two. So the Sahibs would have to set off alone and carry their own loads; in this way we should be able to get Camp II pitched the next day. When I asked the others' opinion they enthusiastically agreed to make this extra effort, which would save us at least two days. Adjiba would go back to the Base Camp and show the people there the way up to Camp I, which would have to be entirely re-equipped since we were going to take everything up with us for Camp II. For Sarki there was an all-important job: he would have to carry the order of attack to all the members of the Expedition.

I took a large sheet of paper and wrote out:

Special message by Sarki, from Camp I to Tukucha. Urgent. May 23, 1950

Camp I: Annapurna glacier.
Have decided to attack Annapurna.
Victory is ours if we all make up our minds not to lose a single day, not even a single hour!

Individual Instructions:

Couzy: *Move Base Camp as rapidly as possible and reorganize it, about two hours farther on from present site, on a very big and very comfortable site just below an avalanche cone. Bring everything up. Send all high-altitude units to Camp I, as well as all possible food, wireless sets, Gaston's and my rucksacks, and Lionel's camp boots. (Give Sarki 15 rupees: you'll find them at the bottom of my sleeping-sack which you must bring up to me).*

Schatz: *If Schatz comes down again from his ridge, organize Camp I, because Biscante, Lionel, Gaston and myself will take everything on to Camp II. The site is marked by a large cairn. It is just on the edge of the glacier. Bring up all possible food and equipment here.*

Matha: *Come up quickly. Have got small camera with me. Bring films and send them up to me. Porters can get up to Base Camp; you can leave reserves there.*

Oudot: *Come as quickly as possible to Camp I with essential medical supplies; leave further stuff (especially surgical equipment) at Base Camp.*

Noyelle: *Most important, without losing a* single hour, *send up to Base Camp: 10 high-altitude containers, 6 valley containers, all high-altitude camping units, the last walkie-talkie, one can of alcohol, 2 gallons of gasoline, one 100 foot 8 mm. rope, two 50-foot 9 mm. ropes, 650 feet of 5 mm. line, 15 ice-pitons, 5 rock-pitons, 10 snap-links, all the head lamps, 2 hanging lamps plus reserve batteries. The Austrian* cacolet[19] *1 pair skis, 2 pairs ski-sticks, Dufour sledge, everybody's no. 2 rucksack, Emerson set with wires, 3 pairs spare Tricouni gaiters, 1 pair* Ours *trousers, 2 valley tents (there will be 3 at Base Camp and 2 at Camp I), 4 pairs boots: 1 size 10, 2 size 9, 1 size 8.*

As the valley camping units have got disorganized (sleeping-bags and air mattresses left at Tukucha), bring up what's necessary to outfit them again.

All reserves of gloves and socks—Tsampa or rice for the Sherpas. Pack up safely what's left over. Prepare 10 high-altitude containers and 6 valley containers for future use. A Sherpa could see to bringing those up later. Come along. Your headquarters will be at Base Camp. G.B. is free to do what he likes.

Matha: *Send a wire to Devies: "Camp I at 16,700 feet. Following reconnaissance have decided attack by north Annapurna glacier. Route entirely snow and ice. Weather favorable. All in fine form. Very hopeful. Greetings.*

Herzog."

MAIN ANNAPURNA RANGE

1. Summit of Annapurna, 26,493 ft.
2. East peak.
3. The White Table.
4. The Black Rock.
5. Buttresses of the Great Barrier.
6. North Annapurna Glacier.
7. Route of attempt on north-west spur.
8. Subsidiary peak of north-west spur.
9. Summit of north-west spur.
10. Cauliflower Ridge.
11. Camp I, about 16,750 feet.
12. Camp II, about 19,350 feet.
13. Camp III, about 21,650 feet.
14. Camp IV, about 23,500 feet
15. Camp V, about 24,600 feet.

The reconnaissance was now being transformed into a definite assault. This order of the day would delight the whole Expedition, but I was worried to think that it would take four days for my message to reach Tukucha. I explained as best I could to Sarki:

"Annapurna," I said pointing to the mountain. "*Atcha now!*"[20]

"Yes, Sahib."

"All Sahibs go now," I said in English continuing to point to Annapurna.

"Yes, Sahib."

"Like this," I said, making as if to run, "very quickly to Tukucha for all Sahibs: Couzy Sahib, Doctor Sahib, Noyelle Sahib."

Sarki's face was solemn. He had read in my eyes that this was not just an ordinary order; he had understood what I expected of him. He knew we had little food with us and not much equipment, and that if the Sahibs had decided to go up the mountain they must be able to rely upon help from the rear.

Sarki was the most active and the strongest of all our Sherpas, and this mission he was about to undertake was of the greatest importance. He stood in front of me, his stomach protruding as though he had a tendency to dropsy, his legs wide apart. His typically Mongolian face was adorned with a blue balaclava surmounted by his dark glasses.

"Off you go, Sarki! Good luck! It is very important . . ." and I shook him by the hand. He didn't lose a second; snatched up his things, briefly explained the essential points to Adjiba in his clipped guttural voice, and a few minutes later we saw them go off under the great ice cliff which sparkled in the light, then disappear over the moraine.

After a moment's silence I turned round to gaze again on Annapurna, all bathed in light. There wasn't much shadow around us. A few minutes ago we had been shivering, now we had to take off our eiderdown jackets, sweaters and shirts. Dhaulagiri towered in the far distance, nearer at hand were the Nilgiris, and I thought of all that had gone before—the Dambush Khola, the Hidden Valley, the Great Ice Lake, Manangbhot. We were very far from everything that we'd foreseen: "a light expedition"— "nylon"—as we called it, a really fast expedition. We wanted to apply Alpine methods to a Himalayan enterprise—that was the basic strategy of all the plans we'd made in Paris. The danger, we had decided in Paris, lay in avalanches, so we must stick to ridges. And why arrange a route up the mountain fit for Sherpas? The Sahibs would undertake everything: no Sherpas; hence no need for complications. How wrong could we be!

Ridges were out of the question. Sherpas? We weren't exactly sorry to have them with us. Lightness? Rapidity? The heights are so great that the numbers of intermediate camps will always be needed. And then we hadn't paid sufficient attention to the question of exploration: you arrive in a district, you're burning with impatience to attack something—yes, but in which direction?

All four of us, Lachenal, Rébuffat, Terray and myself, got our things ready and filled our sacks with as much as we could possibly carry in the way of equipment, food, tents, and sleeping-bags, leaving behind only one container with a few accessories which we did not need at once. We shared out the equipment: as usual, some preferred the heavier but less bulky loads, with others it was the opposite. It worked out at an average of about forty-five pounds apiece. At this height, where the least exertion is an effort, we felt crushed beneath our burdens. The straps cut into our shoulders and it seemed a physical impossibility to walk for more than five minutes. All the same we somehow struggled on, for although our packs were far too heavy, we reflected on all the time we were saving.

So the four Sahibs, in single file, and well spaced out on the rope, climbed heavily up through the snow of the great plateau at the foot of Annapurna. With the sun vertically above us, the glacier basin was like a furnace, with every ray reflected back from the surface of the snow. Walking soon became a dull agony. We sweated and suffocated. Then we stopped, split open some tubes of anti-sunburn cream and applied the paste thickly to our sweating faces. Lachenal and Rébuffat, who seemed to suffer even more than Terray and myself, made themselves white Ku Klux Klan cowls out of the cotton lining of my sleeping-bag. They assured me that this was admirable protection against sunstroke, but I wasn't convinced; they seemed to be stifling in them. Terray and I preferred to rely on the cream.

There wasn't a single breath of air in this furnace and we longed for the first slopes. Crushed beneath our loads, we had to summon up all our resolution to overcome our difficulty in breathing and our lassitude. We climbed up the *rognon,* a rocky outcrop in the middle of the glacier, under huge overhanging seracs which threatened us with a forest of icicles that turned the sun's rays into a rainbow of color. Terray and I took turns at making the trail: the other two seemed utterly worn out. As we approached the 20,000-foot level, our breathing was short and uneven.

"We're not Sherpas!" said Lachenal bitterly.

"We didn't come to the Himalaya to be beasts of burden," growled Rébuffat.

Terray was stung to answer.

"A climber ought to be able to carry his gear," he said. "We're as good as the Sherpas, aren't we?"

Lachenal was bent over his ice-axe, Rébuffat had flopped down on his rucksack. Their faces were scarlet and running with sweat; they didn't usually show their feelings, but now they were really angry.

"If we wear ourselves out now with this ridiculous porterage, how the hell can we manage in a few days' time? It isn't the Sherpas who'll be making a safe route through the seracs."

At this, Terray saw red:

"And you call yourselves Chamonix guides! You're just damn amateurs, that's what you are."

"The more you're put upon, the more you like it," flung back Lachenal. "You'll tell me next that you're positively enjoying this job."

"When I have to carry a load, I get on with it."

I tried to restore peace.

"I know it's hell but it's saving us two days. If the Expedition succeeds it'll perhaps be on account of what we're doing today."

Rébuffat spoke again:

"You and Terray can manage your loads, we just can't."

"You're supermen," went on Lachenal, "real supermen, and we're just poor weaklings."

After this outburst, which seemed to relieve him, we went on. The "supermen" took turns at making the trail. We were extremely tired, and our legs barely held us up as with slow, uneven steps we tried to wrest a few yards from the mountain. Each step was automatic, eyes glued to the heels of the man in front. We had to resist the temptation to stop or relax our effort. Everyone knew in his heart that Terray's hard words were justified even if not strictly necessary.

For some minutes we had heard yodeling behind us: it could only be Schatz. The route he'd planned joined ours here. Had he discovered the perfect way up? Anyhow it was an excellent excuse for a good halt: we stuck our ice-axes in up to the hilt and wedged our sacks behind them to make comfortable seats. We opened some cans and seized our water bottles, but each sip was rationed for we had only a limited supply.

Schatz came up with his two Sherpas.

"There you are! God, I'm tired!"

There were certainly signs of considerable fatigue on his face. No doubt we looked much the same, but he had been alone with his Sherpas.

"Well, how did you make out?"

"The route's no good. If yours is at all reasonable, mine is out."

"Too difficult?"

"Yes, and dangerous. Instead of being able to traverse easily from the top of the little spur to the plateau, we came to a secondary glacier, very steep and with magnificent seracs. We pitched our tent last night as best we could on a microscopic site. Then, this morning, we had to pass beneath a wall of seracs on the point of crashing down, and finally go up a very steep snow slope which I wouldn't like to descend at any price . . ."

"And then?"

"Look here, isn't that enough for one man? Then I caught sight of you, so I wound in and out between the seracs to join your tracks. But you're making me talk, when I'm dying of hunger."

While he hastily swallowed a laboriously prepared lunch, the mist came down on us—forerunner of the usual daily storm.

"Let's go," said Terray.

As we went up visibility decreased. Everything was blurred in the mist, and snow began to fall. The trail that Terray and I made by guess-work was certainly not very logical, but what did it matter? All we had to do that evening was to pitch Camp II somewhere towards the center of the plateau, out of danger from avalanches. It was snowing heavily now and we took our thick capes out of our sacks. With Terray behind me, I could manage to steer some sort of a course. I must not turn round in a circle as I had once done in similar circumstances. As far as we could judge we had now reached the center of the plateau. We decided to pitch the camp where we stood for that night, at any rate.

In ones and twos Sahibs and Sherpas arrived at the site and put down their loads. We took hasty stock of the situation: it would not be wise to let the Sherpas go back by themselves to Camp I. So Terray, who was in good form, proposed to accompany them. It was late and still snowing very hard. Terray was in a hurry to leave, for the tracks of our ascent were already almost obliterated. He intended to bivouac at Camp I in Sarki's sleeping-bag, after sending the Sherpas on down to Base Camp which was easy to reach. These men would then be available for carrying up more loads.

Our poor little Camp II was completely lost among the snow and ice. We were deafened by the continuous roar of avalanches and could not determine their whereabouts—for that night we would have to put up with only relative security. Amid flurries of snow and gusts of wind we got the tents up, fixed in the pegs and constructed some sort of level platform; an hour later we were all warm and snug inside.

I was with Schatz in the experimental tent that had served as a model for the construction of the other fourteen. It was slightly larger and Schatz assured me that with our heads at the back we should be ideally comfortable. Maybe . . . All the same I had never spent such a bad night, and I would not for anything have repeated this miserable experience during which I was half suffocated. I prefer to have my head near the opening of the tent and so be able to adjust the ventilation. In other respects Schatz was a perfect companion. Snug in my sleeping-bag I watched him do the cooking; he served me with a substantial dinner where I lay. Sleeping-pills soon brought our conversation to an end.

While we were thus making the best of the situation, Terray, bivouacking down at Camp I, was kept awake for part of the night by a violent wind. The thickly falling snow covered him up completely, so he shut himself right into the cowl of his cape, at the risk of being suffocated. After several hours he relaxed and slept the sleep of exhaustion with his head resting on the stones.

When we woke at nine o'clock in Camp II, at 19,350 feet, it was already very hot, and the tents were suffused with golden light. But it was hard work to get our frozen boots on—they were just like blocks of wood. In the future I put them at the bottom of my sleeping-bag. I poked my head out—the sky was blue and the view magnificent: a wonderful chain of peaks and ridges stood out round us at a height of 23,000 feet. Quite close above us was that jagged ridge which we called "Cauliflower Ridge." It was a continuation of the north-west spur on which we had spent ourselves to no purpose. We could now see its whole length; we had, in fact, only climbed about a tenth of it! And to our surprise there was an enormous gap in the center cutting off all possibility of progress. So we had no more regrets on that route.

Shining in the distance was a mountain of crystal—Dhaulagiri; and nearer to us were the proud and inaccessible Nilgiris. To the right, towering above our lilliputian camp, was the Great Barrier with its flanks falling directly to the basin of the upper Miristi Khola. To the extreme right, a great swollen glacier and a beautiful peak—the triangular peak or Black Rock that we had seen from the East Tilicho pass. I turned round: an enormous ice face bristling with seracs and seamed with crevasses sparkled in the sun. Far above, so high that one had to tilt one's head backwards to see it, was Annapurna, resplendent, dominating everything as a goddess should.

I inspected the face we had to attack with some anxiety. It was all so disproportionate, on such a different scale from our puny resources. What was to be our plan of campaign? I had to estimate the party's fitness, take into account the rather sketchy equipment we had at our disposal up here, and allow for dangers and difficulties and, above all, the time factor. There were such hundreds of things to bear in mind. But I had made up my mind to push on actively establishing camps, whatever the weather, short of an actual blizzard. It could all be reduced to a mathematical formula; to pile up the maximum weight per distance during the day, at the same time taking care to conserve the physical form of the climbers for the final assault. On this last stage to the top, deterioration would be bound to set in: at that moment we must be able to call up all our reserves of energy and resolution, without losing sight of the needs of the descent.

By morning we had forgotten the previous day's weariness and were all ready to take advantage of the fine weather to go up and establish Camp III. Over the gaiters which we wore above our boots, we adjusted the extra-lightweight crampons, which from now on we used almost continuously. We took one tent with us, leaving the other where it was, with some food. We each carried about twenty-two pounds. Before leaving camp we took a last look at the whole of the ice face, all unknown ground. Before we started out we tried to pick out in advance a route between the many ice walls blocking the way, for once among them we should be hemmed in and unable to see more than fifty yards ahead.

We roped up in the same order in which we had camped—Lachenal and Rébuffat together, and Schatz and I on the second rope. It was nearly ten o'clock—high time to start. After carefully closing the one remaining tent at Camp II we steered towards the snow chute at the foot of the great central couloir which descends from the slopes of the summit. On the section of the plateau between us and the couloir there were few crevasses, so our route was straightforward. When we put our feet in the snow they were numbed by the cold, yet the air was so warm that we soon took off our eiderdown jackets. The gigantic wall of snow and ice seemed to tower higher and higher above us. On the left a ridge of bare ice, typically Himalayan in its formation, surprised me by its transparent blueness which was intensified by the lateral position of the sun. On the right the Cauliflower Ridge, immaculately white, proudly displayed its tracery and seemed to taunt us: "If ever you climb this high . . ." In this strange world where everything tends toward the vertical, one's notion of balance is quite peculiar: all these vistas of chaos render one's first impressions unreliable.

After we had been going for an hour we had got only as far as the first slopes of the snow chute. But what worried me was what came next: thousands of tons of a titanic flood seemed to be frozen in indescribable confusion. The nearer we got to the wall, the steeper appeared the average angle. Seracs crashed down with hideous din, and the rumbling of avalanches put us all on edge. For the moment there was nothing coming down the couloir. For some minutes we should be exposed to danger, for though we would cross it at a point where it narrowed—it was never very wide—every block that fell from the upper slopes would inevitably hurtle down this funnel. Lachenal crossed first. In turn, each of us followed in his tracks under the watchful eyes of the others waiting on the edge. Above us an enormous roof of ice, that turned a livid green as soon as the sun disappeared, constituted some slight protection. But would it be enough if an avalanche came down?

All went well, the danger zone was passed and we arrived out of breath on the opposite side. The place was scarcely suitable for a halt, for the slope was so steep that the snow no longer held firm, and we did not stop. The first party rapidly cut some tiny steps barely sufficient for two spikes of our crampons. The ice was smooth and compact, like glass, and split off with a sharp noise beneath the axe. The chips broke off cleanly, went flying down into space and disappeared at high speed, each time starting up little avalanches. We continued to move over to the right under the protection of the seracs, and a rickety snow-bridge brought us to a snowy platform where we were at last able to stop. The fine weather held, for the time being, and we were cheered by the sight of a few healthy-looking clouds.

At our feet lay the plateau with Camp II which we now saw in its true dimension: we only managed to pick out the microscopic tent by following the tracks of our ascent. Higher up, the next part of the route was not very encouraging, and a hundred and fifty feet or so above our heads the way was barred by a huge vertical wall of ice. There was not a hope either to the left or to the right. If we were to be held up like this so early in the climb . . .

Schatz and I boldly went to the attack. We sank in up to our waist, and the ice beneath the snow made us slide irresistibly down the slope. I seized hold of one foot with both hands and using the other knee as a fulcrum I brought my foot out several inches above the snow. Then I planted my ice-axe as high up as I could and pulled on it to free the other foot left behind. I slipped and came back to my original position.

My heart thumped; I was weak for want of breath. Finally we had to clear a trough; this one hundred and fifty feet took us an hour. We were now so close to the wall of ice that we shivered in spite of the heat. I examined the obstacle: a snow-covered ledge led up to a great overhang of ice. This proud colossus, smooth and etched by little avalanches, could be surmounted by cutting steps up it—a practical route after all. I told the second party that it would take at least two hours to reach the top of the overhang and that, during this time, they might as well skirt along the wall in search of an easier way.

For a second I took off my dark glasses, but I could not stand the dazzling glare all around us. Far away below, the green of the lower slopes gave a momentary relief to my eyes. My glasses were steamed with sweat and melted snow; I rubbed them with my handkerchief, then glanced at my waist to make sure the knot of my rope was all right, counted the number of ice-pitons and checked that I had my piton-hammer. A glance at Schatz to satisfy myself that he was firmly placed, then:

"I'm starting. A bit of slack, please."

"Go ahead," replied Schatz, letting the rope out round his firmly planted ice-axe.

Unaccustomed effort at this height is terribly hard work and each blow of the axe made me pant. First I cleared the ledge; the snow was hard and compact, but at last I had a stance at my disposal about a foot wide and three feet long on which I was obliged to crouch as my head bumped against the overhanging ice. I still had to advance horizontally for a couple of yards. I moved along inch by inch; the ledge became narrower and narrower, the wall above pushed me out further and further until I was nearly overbalanced. I finished by crawling. I stopped to rest, lying on my stomach and clutching the shaft of the axe with which I held myself in. I now had to attack the ice on the roof. With one hand, and with nothing to lean against I could not hit very hard. The splinters of ice showered down on to Schatz who stood stoically watching my every movement, and ready to stop a possible fall. First I broke down the end of the little gutter in which I was penned. A few nicks chipped in the ice upside down served as a hand-hold for my left hand. Holding on thus with my left hand I pulled myself up very, very slowly, scraping up against the overhanging ice, with a drop underneath. I could feel Schatz's eyes on me. With my right hand now free I gripped my axe and made a better hold for my left hand on the bare ice of the roof itself. Then having driven in my axe I made a lightning grab for the hold. Now gripping firmly with my left hand, I withdrew the axe and with the utmost difficulty made two steps very high up for my feet. These were for use after I had got over the overhang, to enable me to remain a few seconds in position against the wall and to help me up. I let myself down again to my original position on the ledge, breathing hard, like a steam-engine this time. I dug my ice-axe in up to the hilt and while I clung to it Schatz came up, wriggling serpent-like along the ledge. Soon he was touching me, behind. As soon as I had gone up three feet he would take my place, belay me, and pass his axe up to me.

My turn to move now. I raised myself up and put my foot on the axe which sank in, but all the same I managed to reach the upper hold with my left hand. I was completely out of balance. I used my piton-hammer, which I had taken out of its holster, as an anchor, though its security was purely illusory. Schatz made the next move as planned, took my place underneath, belayed me and passed me his axe. Without turning round I grabbed it and with a great swing dug the pick in hard a couple of feet higher up. There wasn't a second to be lost—my feet scrabbled in the air and I pulled up on my left hand-hold and upon Schatz's axe dug in the ice. It seemed an eternity; I had to fight every inch of the way. My right knee reached the level of the lower of the two foot-holds, groped for it, found a lodgment—a terrific relief. With another spurt of energy I got my boot up to where my knee had been, but was I going to be able to heave my leg high enough to get the points of my crampon in? I was almost there—the crampon came up with hideous slowness, one point, two, just another heave to get them right in . . . I was up!

Careful not to make a wrong move or to lose my balance I pulled on the axe, holding the shaft against the ice the whole time so that the pick should not suddenly jerk out. I found something for my left foot. I stretched out, pulled up once more, and there I was in the two steps prudently prepared in advance.

"Gosh! I'm up! What a brute!"

Schatz, who had been desperately anxious, was waiting for this.

"Well done, Maurice!"

"Don't move! A yard of slack!"

Again, without a moment's rest, for it was a thoroughly unhealthy place, I hacked away harder than ever to make big steps in the good hard ice. A couple of yards further on the slope eased and I came to snow. I cut a large step where I could stand on both feet, and called out to the invisible Schatz:

"Wait a bit, yet. Give me ten feet of slack and I'll put in a piton."

"O.K.!" The reply reached me through the wind which had just begun to rise.

My heart was thumping as though it would burst; my breath came in irregular gasps, and great drops of sweat poured off me. Before going on I leaned on my axe and shut my eyes a second. Then I began cutting again; the ice became granulated and the work was not so hard. I was now above the overhang, with another yard to go to reach a good stance. With my axe I cleared a flat space in the ice in which to place the piton. Chips flew up: I wondered what Schatz was thinking, still lying on his stomach on the ledge.

"Ready in a minute!"

Hanging from my waist was a spike, a kind of giant fishhook, as long as a man's forearm and provided with inverted teeth. Using my hammer I drove this ice-piton in, with all my strength. The ice was so soft here that after a few blows it was in position. Would it hold? It would become firmer as it froze in. I now turned my attention to the spare rope—it was nylon, white and dry and clean. I opened my knife and cut off a six-foot length—enough to make a decent loop which I fixed to the piton. All this would remain fixed in place. The sixty-foot length threaded through the loop would run down the slope and hang freely out above the overhang. I tugged to test the piton. All was well.

It was my privilege to be the first to try it out. I hung onto the rope and regained my comfortable step, below and a bit to the right.

"Hello, Schatz. You can come up."

"O.K. I'll tell you when I'm starting."

Schatz made his preparations. He put on his rucksack which he had shoved under the overhang and secured his axe to his wrist by a special bit of line which the others had made particular fun of. His voice rang out in the climber's familiar call: "I'm coming!" I held him on a tight rope.

Schatz took hold of the fixed rope. I heard a jabbering, and a dirty cap appeared, then a dark face twisted into a grimace. He wasn't exactly handsome at that moment! He found a hold for a crampon, then drove his axe in, took fresh hold on the rope, pulled himself up, and there he was beside me. The obstacle had been overcome!

Suddenly it grew cold and clouds darkened the air. We got into our anoraks and long capes. But what were the others up to? We hallooed at them.

"We're over here," came back the answer, in the tones of people who have been disturbed. They were sitting at their ease on the lower slopes.

Their reconnaissance had come to nothing. Neither to the left nor to the right was there any possibility of turning the wall. The only solution was the way we had found. And so they were philosophically waiting to see what happened next. In a quarter of an hour they rejoined us.

The slow painful advance began again, zigzagging through a wild sea of ice. The weather, too, was wild. Every step, every yard gained on the mountain cost us such an effort that it left us trembling. I was seriously worried: if we had to go on struggling over this sort of ground for long, we should never win through. The others were no more optimistic than I was.

If only these heavy daytime snowfalls would stop, the snow would then freeze at night, and over this firmer ground we should be able to make reasonable progress. But for the past few days every afternoon there had been a storm bringing with it twelve to eighteen inches of snow daily. So that every day our work had to begin all over again. Now we hoped that our tracks would at least leave a foundation for future use. This was our last remaining hope—would it, too, prove illusory?

Through the snowflakes I could see Schatz's gray shadow battling through the powder snow as he went ahead to relieve me. The wind continued to blow, we could not see more than fifty feet, and the angle of the slope was horribly steep. There wasn't the vestige of a site on which we could pitch the tent. In any case it would be preferable to have Camp III higher up: the aneroid registered 21,650 feet, though later on we found out that we were only at 21,000 feet. It seemed to us a tremendous height.

It snowed without a stop and clearing the snow was a terribly exhausting job. But anyway we were on the move. We really were making progress towards the summit, and it gave me tremendous satisfaction. We stowed the tent, equipment and food beneath a serac, shaped like a crescent moon. To mark the cache for the others following later, we hollowed out a niche in the wall and stuck in a red flask, jamming it well in.

"They'll be able to spot that from a good way off," I said to Schatz.

Once again I noticed how much easier it was going down. Lachenal and Rébuffat went first now and had already disappeared into the mist. The snow fell thicker than ever. I was in front of Schatz and I let myself drop over a very awkward little wall of ice. Unfortunately I hadn't made sure of the length of the rope between us, so Schatz felt a strong pull which he wasn't at all expecting, and he shot down the slope. He hurtled past me, yelling. By good luck the thick snow which we had been cursing slowed him up and then stopped him, deadening his fall. Getting up with great difficulty he came back towards me, rather stunned, and swaying in a drunken sort of way, but not hurt. He now went ahead and I held him on a short rope as we retraced our tracks in the storm. Lachenal and Rébuffat waited for us before crossing the couloir. They were worried about Schatz's unsteady balance and they kept very close to him, following his movements with a watchful eye. For the second time we crossed the terminal chute of the great couloir without any incident. In the days to come, many parties had to cross and recross this dangerous place, but everyone escaped the avalanches.

It grew warmer, and we continued to sink in as much as ever. We failed to spot Camp II which was hidden in the clouds. We went by guesswork, though here and there we came upon the tracks of our ascent which were now barely visible. The wind grew stronger, the snow stuck to our glasses and lashed our faces; we tightened the hoods of our anoraks and went along bent double beneath the squalls. A glissade, a few footprints, a large crevasse—we thought we must be quite close to the camp. We bore to the right and saw, a few paces off, a tent covered with snow: in actual fact we only spotted it because some of the fabric was showing. What were we to do? We couldn't all spend the night here, there just wasn't room. And if we went down we would be available to carry more loads up.

We went on again. It was getting late, and as we descended towards the plateau visibility became worse. There was a thick mist, but by keeping in single file we were able to steer an approximately straight course. We knew that near Camp I, we had to cross a dangerous crevassed section. There was only one way through and this was marked with cairns, but we just couldn't find the first one. Rébuffat thought we should go lower down on the left; Lachenal, higher on the right. As for me, I thought we were on the right route. But on no account did I want the party to separate. Finally we decided to try Rébuffat's way, though we weren't altogether convinced. Actually, by bearing to the left we did reach the great line of seracs which ought to lead us straight to Camp I.

The mist grew thicker and thicker. We were going along between two crevasses which suddenly converged: impossible to advance a step further. Back we had to go and turn the whole crevassed section by traversing right round it. All at once we felt absolutely exhausted—this last petty difficulty on the glacier took the stuffing out of us. We knew we couldn't be far from the camp, so we bawled, "Hello! Hello!"

In a few seconds we heard, faint but distinct, "Over here!"

"I told you we ought to have gone to the right," snapped Lachenal.

Soon a shadow appeared—it was Terray. He explained that there wasn't room for all of us at the camp; there was very little equipment and the food would have to be saved up for the higher camps. I decided at once that Lachenal, Rébuffat and myself would take advantage of the last of the daylight to go down to Base Camp, while Schatz, who had not yet recovered from his fall, would remain here to recuperate a bit.

Terray described his last night's bivouac, while Lachenal listened disapprovingly. We then told our story and described the serac under which we had dumped the equipment.

"Early tomorrow morning I'll go up with Pansy and Aila," said Terray, "and at the same time Adjiba will move up and down between Base Camp and Camp I." Adjiba who was extremely strong had become a specialist on this particular job: twice a day he made this journey, bringing up hundreds of pounds of supplies to Camp I. It was unrewarding and unspectacular work but it had to be done and was of the utmost value. Individual efforts like these would give the Expedition its greatest chance of success.

So, leaving Schatz, Terray, Pansy and Aila, we made off down the slopes with Adjiba. We glissaded down the screes, braking as best we could, dashed along the ledges, and in a few minutes had descended a thousand feet or more. Then reaching the *névé,* we found to our great joy not only merely one tent pitched at Base Camp, but several. Ichac and Oudot had just arrived with the Sherpas and a number of porters. There were sleeping-bags for all and food in plenty. There was even one of the big green tents which would be much appreciated by the porters, for it was still snowing.

Victory was in sight! Contact had been established between the rearguard and the advance party.

Chapter X

The Sickle

IT WAS NOW THE EVENING OF THE 24TH, AND SARKI HAD LEFT WITH THE ALL important order of the day on the morning of the 23rd. Ichac told me that he had met our messenger careering down the gullies of the Miristi Khola, when he himself was coming up to meet us. He and Oudot were delighted to learn that we had established camps up to nearly 21,700 feet[21] in such record time. That evening at Base Camp there was a general feeling of gaiety, and how delightful it was to relax in optimism and creature comfort! We had a delicious meal: chicken in aspic and a bottle of rum. (Terray was later to complain bitterly that we might have waited for him for this feast.) But in the end our physical exhaustion—as well as these other excesses—got the better of us.

We rose late next morning; we were pretty stiff after all our exertions, but in the warm sun we soon began to show signs of life. I decided to go and wash, and even to shave. It was wonderful to feel clean again and to move about at ease in camp boots. I was able to see things more clearly; plans for the coming struggle were beginning to take shape. This was uppermost in all our minds—as was quite clear from the way the others, field glasses in hand, discussed the problems of the assault. As for myself, I had made my decisions, but there was still the question of supplies to be dealt with. I had every confidence in Noyelle, who had prepared the "mobilization" at Tukucha a long time in advance, and after a series of calculations I felt quite reassured. There was no danger on that score—all our strength could be concentrated in the spearhead of the attack. So I decided to leave that afternoon with Rébuffat for Camp I, without hurrying, and to take a number of loads with us. We were determined not to come down again unless victorious. I wrote my last letter to Lucien Devies.

Base Camp May 25, 1950

My dear Devies,

A final note before the attack. Everything is going well. Base Camp is three to four days from Tukucha and this doesn't help matters. The change-over from a strong reconnaissance to a full-scale attack might have proved extremely difficult at this distance from our starting point. Yesterday I went up to 21,700 feet. The route lies entirely over snow and ice. Objective dangers are comparatively small. Camps are situated as follows: Base Camp on the right bank of the North Annapurna glacier at 14,500 feet. Camp I, also on the right bank, on the edge of a large plateau very like the upper Argentière plateau, at 16,750 feet. Camp II on a glacier that descends directly from the summit of Annapurna, on a little plateau at 19,350 feet. In due course I expect to pitch Camp III at about 21,700 feet, Camp IV at about 24,600 on what we call the "Sickle" glacier. (You will see this at once on Matha's drawings and sketch-map.) We may set up a Camp V—it all depends on the lay of the land.

The weather is fine in the mornings and bad in the evenings. It snows a lot, which is a fearful nuisance, for we sink in terribly. Everybody's feeling fine. In a few minutes I am going up to Camp I. During the next few days we shall make the final assault. We are all very hopeful. Conditions are difficult high up, but if we get to the top we shall be so overjoyed we'll forget all that. I haven't time for more as there's a lot to be done, as you can imagine. Matha will explain the situation in more detail.

Yours ever,

Maurice.

While I was writing, the porters and the Sherpas had finished striking camp under Couzy's directions. After our meal, the weather began to cloud over, and by three-thirty it was snowing. I thought of Terray who had left Camp I early that morning with two high-altitude units, plus twenty pounds of food, intending to carry on up to Camp III and spend the night there. When we left at about five o'clock it was snowing hard, but nevertheless we went up rapidly and reached Camp I by nightfall. Quickly we pitched one of the valley tents in which we all three slept. Rébuffat complained again of his sunburn, and of his lips, which were very sore.

The alarm watch rang at six-thirty. "Sherpas . . . Sherpas!" But they were in no hurry and preparations dragged on. Through the glasses we picked out three black dots on the mountain a bit above and to the left of the highest point we ourselves had reached. No doubt that's Camp III, we thought. We left at about ten o'clock for Camp II. Rébuffat and Dawatondu on one rope—this Sherpa had been passed on to us by Ichac with various warning injunctions[22]—and Lachenal, Angawa and I on another. It was appallingly hot on the great plateau, and Lachenal suffered terribly. He plodded along in a daze, streaming with sweat, and when anyone spoke to him he looked up with dull and anguished eyes. Rébuffat had stomach pains which got worse and worse so that in the end we had to take turns carrying his sack. Progress was very difficult. At the end Lachenal was practically dragging himself along; the last hundred yards to Camp II were a drawn-out agony for him. He had stuck a bit of adhesive tape on to his terribly burned lips, which gave them a slight protection. It was the only light colored patch on his brown face, and it looked very odd.

At Camp II we found Terray, Pansy and Aila who had just come down. Terray was highly excited. "There's no time to lose," he said. "Yesterday I went up to 22,000 feet and I couldn't find the equipment you left—it must have been completely buried under the snow. At the point we got to there was no sign of a platform. So Pansy and Aila and I made one with our axes, but it's far from level, and right in the middle of a slope. The three of us spent the night in this tiny shelter with avalanches coming down all round us."

He imitated the sound of the snow cascading down a few inches away from him. Then he laughed and went on:

"The Sherpas weren't very happy and neither was I! After such a night we weren't fit for anything but coming down, so here we are. I'm going back to Camp I to recuperate."

"Right," I said. "Couzy and Schatz are coming up with Ichac and Oudot to Camp I, so you'll be able to rest in comfort. Also this will mean you can make an extra journey up, with a load—these darned loads are always on my mind."

"I left our stuff at 22,000 feet," Terray continued, "probably further to the left than the point you reached. Our place is in the middle of a slope, fifty yards to the right of a line of seracs."

He did up his sack, hailed the Sherpas, threw them each a loop of rope, and then, bidding us farewell in his deep voice, off he went.

We were now alone at Camp II. Neither Lachenal's nor Rébuffat's morale was very high; they were not feeling too good. Moreover Terray's remarks about deep snow hadn't exactly encouraged them—they had

108

already had a taste of it on the first trip. I realized that I must not push them too hard next day if I wanted to be able to count on them later. There were two Sherpas available, as well as equipment and the food that we had brought up. Why shouldn't I go on, and try to establish Camp III, and even perhaps Camp IV, while the other two were resting? If I were to stay above Camp II for more than a day, then they, along with Schatz and Couzy, who would have arrived by that time, would in their turn be able to carry stuff up to the higher camps. In view of the way things were going, and the fact that it was already May 26, the four Sahibs would have to move up a stage—from Camp II to Camp III—and continue their slow progress up, without further descents, from camp to camp, right up to the very top. Meanwhile Terray would come up again, in fighting trim, and it should be possible for me to carry another load, in this way all the camps would be established in the least possible time.

For once the weather was fine in the afternoon. While the other two slept soundly in their tents, I went over all the equipment and got things ready for next morning.

At dawn I began to roll out the Sherpas, Dawatondu and Angawa. We had to get off early so as to take advantage of the hardness of the snow after the night frost; the sun had not yet touched the camp when we left. I retraced Terray's descending tracks up towards the terminal chute of the couloir. I had the camera and hoped to be able to get some pictures. In the couloir I made Dawatondu go first to see if he could cut steps reasonably well, but when we reached the pitch with the fixed rope there was no further question: the Sahib had to do his stuff. This reminded me of the story Terray had told me the night before: at this same point he had been on the rope with Pansy and Aila, with Pansy leading. As they got near to the wall a look of terror spread over Pansy's face and he just firmly dug his ice-axe in the snow. Terray, the "strong man" as the Sherpas called him, said: "Carry on, Pansy, your turn." And Pansy answered with a broad grin, "No thank you, for Sahib only!"

Terray found it useless to press the point.

Dawatondu felt the same way as Pansy, but this time I wanted to take a few shots with the movie camera so I pushed Angawa into the lead. He was shaking with fright as he passed in front of me, but proceeded to lead up, since the Bara Sahib had willed it so. I held him firmly on the end of my rope, and while he grappled with the pitch I manipulated the camera as best I could lying awkwardly on the ice ledge, hardly able to lift my head on account of the overhang. Angawa's efforts soon came to an end

Annapurna seen from Camp I. Routes between Camps II and IVA. The camps are shown as black dots.

and in spite of the security of the rope I had not the heart to ask him to go on, so I took his place and went ahead. It was considerably easier with the fixed line, and in a few seconds I had hoisted myself up to the little stance on the right, twenty-five feet above. There I fixed a belay and brought up Dawatondu, who found the going pretty difficult—the idea of climbing up ice had never entered his head. I felt that the prestige of the Sahibs was rising rapidly! Dawatondu arrived, puffing like a grampus, his face screwed up with effort. I showed him how to bring Angawa up on the rope, while I took a shot of the proceedings. It all went off very well.

We sorted ourselves out and went on. But while we had been busy, time had slipped by; the sun was now directly overhead and beating down so fiercely on the slopes that we were wallowing in slush. It was most exhausting work and by now Terray's tracks were barely visible. Anyway, as they now went off to the left and I wanted to pick up the equipment we had dumped on the first trip, I continued straight up. Soon afterwards I recognized the serac shaped like a crescent moon. I poked round with my ice-axe for a while and finally located some compact objects: the stuff was there. We cleared away the snow, and sure enough we found the tent, quite complete, with the food and equipment which Lachenal, Rébuffat and myself had taken up three days before. We lifted the lot, and tried to rejoin Terray's tracks over on the left. They were fifty yards away, but it took us nearly an hour to reach them, for we had to make a regular trough, sinking in up to our waists in the snow. At last we reached the track at the foot of a very steep wall of bare and shining ice. The steps cut by Terray had already almost melted away and I had to re-cut the whole pitch. To make it easier for the Sherpas I drove in a big ice-piton at the top of the wall and fixed a long nylon line to it. Then I went up a few steps higher so as to be able to belay them well. I saw my Sherpas, one after the other, make wonderful pendulums, yell as they rebounded on their backsides, and then roar with laughter at the whole experience.

We were now above the whole area of alternate ice walls and snow slopes. Lifting my head and looking upwards I saw an even snow slope in the middle of which I could pick out Terray's tracks. On the left was the great central couloir, very steep and looking as if it was waiting to swallow up anything and everything that fell from the upper slopes. The air was luminous, and the light was tinged with the most delicate blue. On the other side of the couloir, ridges of bare ice refracted the light-like prisms and sparkled with rainbow hues. The weather was still set fine—not a single cloud—and the air was dry. I felt in splendid form and as if, somehow, I had found a perfect balance within myself—was this, I wondered, the essence of happiness.

But after all we had still a long way to go. Like ants getting over an enormous obstacle we climbed up without appearing to make any progress. The slope was very steep, and also the snow began to ball up under our feet, which made me keep an extra watchful eye on the Sherpas. Every other yard I stopped to get my breath. Behind me I could feel the two Sherpas oppressed by the tremendous effort required. From time to time I looked up to gauge the distance we had to go. Suddenly I spotted a patch of bright yellow—undoubtedly Terray's tent. After an eternity of ploughing through the thick, treacherous snow we at last reached his highest point. The food and equipment were buried in the snow, but they were carefully wrapped in a *pied d'éléphant*—a nylon bag into which you put both legs, to protect them from the cold. I was very pleased to have got so far, but the site puzzled me. There could be no question of re-establishing Camp III on the slope itself. To the right there was a deep drop, to the left a cataract of seracs, on the far side of which ran the central couloir, and fifty yards above us, a very broken up area began. Looking at the seracs on the left I noticed that the crevasses between them were all blocked with fresh snow. An idea had come into my head: why not put the camp right there in a crevasse? Given the height, and the lay of the ground, they would be completely blocked up. Moreover the neighboring seracs would form a splendid protection against avalanches. And so "Why not" became "Let's go and take a look."

With my two Sherpas I traversed across and reached the edge of the blocked-in crevasse. Well belayed, I ventured on it—my first steps were very cautious. I drove my ice-axe in right up to the hilt and found that the snow was well consolidated. I went forward now with more confidence and made a little platform on which I turned round, taking a few steps in each direction, then I started dancing about and finally jumping. It held! Once the hard crust had been removed, here and there, and the surface levelled, it would make an ideal site—there would easily be room for two tents facing each other. Without losing a minute the two Sherpas pitched the tents and prepared tea. That was enough for one day: we had achieved our object of establishing a permanent Camp III. The others would not be able to see the site from below; no doubt they would be wondering where we had got to.

While the Sherpas fixed up our bivouac I pushed on a little towards the central couloir at the far end of our crevasse, as we should have to go that way next day. I had made up my mind that we must endeavor to establish Camp IV the following day. I had plenty of time to look at the surrounding peaks, to observe the remarkable Cauliflower Ridge with its bizarre formation, to admire the distant Dhaulagiri, and to let my mind and my eyes wander over the desert land of Tibet, hardly more than a dozen miles away from us.

A cold and violent wind came up, but no disquieting clouds appeared— it would be fine tomorrow for sure. With this optimistic prophecy I went inside the tent—a nice tent all to myself, with two air mattresses and two sleeping-bags. I was waited upon like a king by the Sherpas. They brought me tea and then I dealt around aspirin and sleeping-tablets and the whole drug store that Oudot has insisted on. It was not long before I dozed off.

In the morning we had to step lively. I took down one tent, packed up as much food as possible, shared out the loads and, after a quick breakfast, we started. I took the lead and made a detour towards the central couloir. We skirted along the foot of the serac that protected our camp and climbed up a sort of gable of bare ice which the Sherpas didn't much appreciate. It wasn't possible to go any higher and we had to resign ourselves to crossing the couloir. It was, however, relatively narrow at this height, as if it had been squeezed in by the batteries of seracs on either side. It could scarcely have been more than a couple of hundred feet across. If one of us went over quickly while the others kept a lookout, they would be able to give warning of any avalanche. In my opinion it was reasonably safe. Leaving Dawatondu on the left bank I began to cross. The slope was exceedingly steep, falling straight down beneath my feet, and we could not get a grip on the snow, which had been hardened by successive avalanches. First, with the blade of my axe I had to cut little steps for the points of my crampons; then when I moved I stuck the pick into the ice above me as an anchor, and held on to it with both hands. I went as quickly as I could; a glance up every now and then had its uses, if only for one's morale. Looking down, on the other hand, was not to be recommended, for the sight of those colossal precipices might have shaken even the most confident climber. The traverse was quickly completed and I allowed myself a few moments to get my breath before bringing over the Sherpas.

"Dawatondu!"

"Yes, sir," he replied in a voice which sounded rather queer. He smelled danger, the old fox! Without wasting a minute and in spite of his load he came over like a whirlwind to reach safety. Angawa followed, but he was younger and didn't move so well, and took much longer than Dawatondu. Whew! Here we were, safe and sound across that terrible couloir! From my present position I could see just what had been threatening us. The couloir ran up for about a thousand feet to merge into a very steep snow slope—a gathering-ground for avalanches. Above was the rock wall and then the Sickle glacier from which a few dozen tons of superfluous ice split off from time to time.

Our situation was critical; before me stretched a broken-up area lying at a very steep angle. From here onwards the route, as planned from Camp I, consisted in slanting up to the left and then back to the right as far as the top of the central couloir at the point where the great bergschrund, separating this couloir from the steep snow slope above, was blocked with snow and where, in all probability, there would be a way across. But straight ahead of me were enormous seracs. I could either skirt round them by descending slightly and then traversing to the left, or else I could climb up the true right hand edge of the couloir and reach the upper slopes that way. I chose the latter alternative, since there was practically no danger of avalanches at this early hour. Moreover, by going rapidly up on the extreme edge of the couloir we gained the necessary hundred yards or so. We then bore over to the left and once more sank into deep snow with which we were unfortunately all too familiar. But at any rate we were out of danger.

After a few minutes' rest we started off again; we had to keep traversing to the left and gaining height at every possible opportunity. But the slope was steep and I had only limited confidence in my Sherpas' balance. They were not accustomed to such difficult ground and if one of them had slipped we should all three have shot out into space; so I kept a watchful eye on them. The first traverses were accomplished without incident. I did my best to pack the snow at each step in order to make a safe and comfortable track. One stretch over bare ice needed particular attention. Three blows of the axe and the ice chips flew—there was just room for two points of my crampons and on I went. But Dawatondu thought differently and began to enlarge the steps behind me, but desperately slowly. At last he arrived—I took his rope and belayed Angawa who in his turn started off. He did not seem very confident—he lifted his left foot, failed to fix his crampon points properly into the ice, the toe of his boot slipped, he banged his knee, lost his balance, and there he was sliding away down the slope. Luckily I had been watching him like a hawk: the loop of rope tightened round my axe, the rope stretched taut and then held fast. Angawa got off with a fright—and in future he would have confidence in the rope.

We continued over this soft snow lying on hard ice. The setting was wonderful—everything was a transparent blue, even our shadows, and there was not a cloud in the sky. On our left was the Sickle ridge, quite close, apparently almost within reach, dripping bare ice and shining in the sun—a real Diamond Mountain.

My two Sherpas were exhausted and Dawatondu was very near to regretting those escapades which had made it necessary for him to come up such a height in so short a time. (From Choya, about 8,000 feet, he had come up without a day's break to 23,000 feet.) We had some difficulty in climbing over a serac by a tricky piece of step-cutting during which I had my turn of being very frightened. After having cut three good steps, and a good hold for the left hand, I suddenly heard a dull sound; the ice made a loud cracking noise as if the whole serac were about to collapse. I held my breath but nothing happened: no doubt it was the ice settling deep down. So I was able to go on. After half an hour of cutting I came out on the upper slopes and could distinctly see the great bergschrund running horizontally right around the sloping plateau, and the enormous wall of the Sickle.

"It's your turn, Dawatondu."

I pointed out the line we had to follow, which was now rather easier. There was a fairly steep snow slope, then a hundred yards or so of moderately steep ice up which we should have to cut steps, another snow slope, and then we should be at the bergschrund.

This time I decided to take it easy; I let the others go ahead to do the work and took my place at the end of the rope. But the Sherpas lacked our technique and were very slow. Dawatondu cut a great many steps very close together and much too big. Just the same, we gained ground and soon came to the gaping bergschrund, very deep, but so long that the depth was not noticeable. There was no break in it for more than half a mile, except at the cone of avalanche snow. Certainly the place wasn't safe, but we had no alternative but to pass that way.

I took the lead again, climbed up the rib leading to the avalanche cone and began to go straight up it. Dawatondu belayed me from below and this was no easy job—I slipped down as fast as I climbed up. The snow was soft and my worst fear was that it might collapse just where it bridged the bergschrund. When I reached the top of the avalanche cone, I stretched out my axe as high up as I could to drive it into the slope. There was a dull sound—the avalanche! I swung my axe and it stuck in—I was saved; with some difficulty I pulled myself up on it out of the snow which was sliding down everywhere and swishing between my legs. I tried to get my crampons onto the wall and just managed it; quickly I cut a few steps and at last reached an area which was less trying to the nerves.

It was now the Sherpas' turn and I held them firmly. They had no professional pride to prevent them from pulling on the rope and they did so, vigorously—my arms were nearly pulled out of their sockets. My little party was now assembled on the upper plateau. A great wave of content flowed through me: the technical difficulties seemed to be over. We didn't know whether we should find good snow higher up, or an ice slope, but at any rate, there would be no walls or couloirs.

"Let's go!" This time we went right over to the left towards the Sickle, plainly visible from here. The glacier, which lay on a bed of reddish-colored rocks, stopped dead at the edge of space, and the great cliff, a huge drop of nearly seven hundred feet, plunged vertically down towards us—a most impressive sight.

Fortunately the handle of the Sickle offered a more accessible route and it was there we should have to go. Once again, ploughing through snow up to our waists and stopping at every step to get our breath, we approached the wall and after an hour of this exhausting going got to the foot of it. We had gone a long way since morning, and debated whether it was wise to increase still further the distance between Camps III and IV. I thought not, we should have to be capable of doing this lap in one day without undue fatigue, and so I decided to establish the camp where we were. There was hardly any suitable site; the whole place seemed to be swept by avalanches. There was just one small serac which would give protection to a few square yards below. It made an ideal wind screen and our tents would be completely sheltered from avalanches. The three of us began to cut away at the ice with a will to make a comfortable platform. Soon the camp was in order—tent pitched and food stored away—and we could allow ourselves a good rest.

The Sherpas had frightful headaches. I looked at the altimeter which showed 24,600 feet and thought the figure higher than it should have been. Aneroid barometers tend to exaggerate height and, reckoning from the summit, and the position of the other camps, I judged that we were at about 23,500 feet. I gave Dawatondu and Angawa aspirin, and offered them some food, but they made it clear that they couldn't touch a thing. I was forced to consume a can of tuna fish before their eyes and the very sight of it made them feel sick. Looking all about me, I felt an exhilarating sense of domination, and complete confidence in our victory. I was almost at the height of the Great Barrier. Beneath me I could see the Cauliflower Ridge which had taunted us for so long, and then far down, right at the bottom, the plateau with Camp II so far that we could not even pick out the black dots of the other members of the Expedition.

"Let's go!" My two Sherpas needed no pressing—for once they were ready immediately. We shut the tent carefully, hoping we should find it again in good order in spite of the cascades of snow, and then plunged downwards. The return journey was made without incident and incomparably faster than our climb up. We descended the walls face inwards and the Sherpas went very well, safeguarded by me. About an hour and a half later we reached Camp III and found our friends in occupation.

I was delighted to be able to tell them that Annapurna was practically in the bag! The quick descent had rather gone to my head. The four others were lying in the two tents and hardly bothered to get up when we arrived. What could be the matter?

Couzy and Schatz, coming up the day before from Camp I, had picked up Lachenal and Rébuffat on their way. After a night's rest at Camp II they had left in the morning and come up here to Camp III. As usual the snow had held them up a lot. Couzy, still insufficiently acclimatized, suffered from bad headaches. Schatz was morose, Rébuffat felt he wasn't well enough to go any further, and Lachenal had no appetite. I vainly tried to rouse them, telling them that we were practically there. I could tell they had not yet found their form again, but I judged that the night's rest would do them all good. As for myself, there was no point in my waiting any longer. There wasn't any room, and anyway we should have to carry another load. I hoped that, with Terray's convoy, we should be able to bring up everything necessary to equip the route, and that the next journey up would lead to victory.

But time was pressing—I was dismayed to see that it was already May 28 and the monsoon, according to the latest reports, would reach us about June 5. That gave us barely a week to bring everything to a successful conclusion.

This time the Sherpas went much quicker; they had greatly benefited by the lessons learned during the last few days and their technique had improved. At the overhanging pitch they grasped the fixed line without hesitation, let themselves slide down rapidly, and upon arrival gave an easy wave of the hand to indicate that the rope was free for the next man. My job was made much easier and I was well pleased to see the plateau on which Camp II stood getting quickly closer.

But for some time Dawatondu had been complaining of a strange pain, which he found it difficult to locate precisely. He indicated the whole of that part of his anatomy between his chest and his thighs. Was it excess of methylated alcohol, altitude, or simply a kind of prudent precaution in view of the operations ahead? He groaned continuously and Angawa had to support him, but it was impossible to make out what this sly old fellow was about. As we reached camp, snow began to fall. We were welcomed by shouts from Terray.

Chapter XI

Camp II

THE MINUTE I ARRIVED, TERRAY GAVE ME SOME BOILING HOT TEA. I WAS NOT allowed to get a word in: he forced me to eat; indeed he practically stuffed the food down my throat. In the other tents the Sherpas were very busy looking after Dawatondu, who was putting up a continuously good performance as an invalid. And as for me, after this very substantial meal I wasn't in the least worried by the fact that I was tired; this seemed a perfectly natural result of our exertions. At last Terray allowed me to speak and I gave him particulars of the present position of the camps.

"By now most of the equipment is already on the spot. We've got to do one more carry to establish Camp V, which will be the taking-off point for the final attack; we've got it all figured. This time there's a very good chance."

Terray had apparently completely recovered down at Camp I, from which he had just come, but he still looked worried.

"Yes, everything will be all right if only the weather holds. The weather reports on the radio are very bad: the monsoon has reached Calcutta, and it will be here in a few days."

"Anyway I'm feeling in good condition," I said. "I'm certain, from the way I've been going at 23,000 feet, that I'll do fine at 26,000 and without oxygen too."

But Terray was not so optimistic.

"If we have to plough along as we've been doing so far, it will be a labor of Hercules and we shall end by running into trouble."

He asked me what I thought of the condition of the climbers up at Camp III. I had to admit it wasn't promising. The four I had left up there had struck me as being in a bad way, both in their physical condition and in their morale.

"On the other hand, Lionel, I'm not in the least anxious about us two," I said. "What's more, the route is now equipped right up to the glacier. With the four Sherpas we've got here, you and I can now go steadily on up to the top."

"We'll have to give it the works," replied Terray, enunciating the phrase as though he had just invented it.

118

"Listen, I'm absolutely certain—unless there is some unforeseeable catastrophe—we'll succeed. Even admitting that the four at Camp III remain in poor form, which I don't think likely—particularly the ones who are better acclimatized—we ought to be able to make it. I think we ought to stay here all tomorrow to give ourselves a rest. We'll have plenty of time to make our preparations, and the day after tomorrow we'll be fresh as paint and able to go on up from camp to camp. Then of the four who come down here tomorrow, the two strongest after resting a day will go up again to back us up. The other two, who will have had the advantage of an extra day's rest, will have plenty of time to follow on, one camp behind. Both these teams will bring up more equipment, and help the first summit party to come down."

"There's not a minute to lose," Terray replied obstinately. "Your plan's all very fine, but it makes me waste time. What will I do all day tomorrow? I'm already rested. It'll be better if I go on up and so gain a stage that might well turn the scale . . ."

"I don't deny that, but if you go tomorrow we won't be together any more; we'll be out of step, and for the moment we're the only two who are really fit—and two men are needed for the work above 23,000 feet. I'm positive that together we'll bring it off."

"Let's be practical, Maurice," he argued. "However you look at it we lose a day that way. It can't be helped if I'm not in the first party to reach the summit—I'll be in the second, that's all. But if only one party gets there it may be because of the load that I'm going to carry up."

I hardly knew what to do. Terray's unselfishness did not surprise me—I had appreciated it for years—but at this moment it seemed to me that his heroism had in it a certain disregard for reality. Terray thought only of doing his duty. But I could not help wondering if there might not be an element of selfishness in my wish to have him as a partner the day after tomorrow. With Terray's example of self-sacrifice before me, this notion worried me and made me hesitate.

"Well, I suppose I must say yes," I said, regretfully; "on the face of it, you're right, but I am sure a chance like this will never come again."

Terray seemed uncertain. Then I had an idea.

"If you insist on going up tomorrow, Lionel, why don't you go up just to Camp III, with a high-altitude unit which the others can then take on further up, and come back here yourself the same evening? We'll stay a day longer so that you've time to recuperate and then we can start. We'll both go up with lightly loaded Sherpas who will then be able to take turns at making the tracks, leading for short spells. As we go up we can strike Camp IV, and establish Camp V if necessary, and then we'll carry right on to the top."

I had seized on this solution, for I was positive that it would enlist Terray's support, impatient as he was to ensure the continuity of the load-carrying.

"All right, if that's what you want," he said, to my deep relief.

We spent a very cheerful evening. I appreciated the great comfort of Camp II with its valley tents, electric lighting, reserve containers, camp boots, water in plenty. It had been entirely reorganized by Terray after an avalanche had blown down the tents: it was in a well-sheltered position behind a crevasse wide enough to swallow up even the largest avalanches.

We were warm in our sleeping-bags, while outside the snow was falling thick and fast.

By the dim light of the hanging lamp I could barely see the smoke curling up from our cigarettes, and Terray's face was hidden in the shadows. We kept coming back to our plan of attack, and wondered how soon Noyelle would arrive from Tukucha with our main supplies of food and equipment. But we were tired, and Terray economical as ever soon put out the light. In a few minutes we sank into oblivion.

In the dark somebody knocked against me, I heard a steady muttering—a hand brushed my face and the light went on. "Time to get up," said Terray.

He put his boots on and quickly went out to wake his Sherpas. All through the Expedition he remained faithful to his tactics of the early start. And he was certainly right, for the snow is far better during the first hours of daylight. But it needed resolution, and only he seemed to have it. I shut my eyes again and reflected with deep satisfaction that while others were sweating their guts out, I should be warm and snug and pampered by the Sherpas. At the first streaks of dawn I heard a deep: "Goodbye, then, Maurice."

"See you tomorrow—good luck!"

Terray closed the tent carefully. He was an invaluable man. I know of no one in France who comes nearer to being the ideal member of an expedition.

The hours went by and the sun lit up my tent and warmed it. The camp was silent as the grave. My two Sherpas were recuperating too. But it was getting late and from my sleeping-bag I called out:

"Angawa! *Cana! Cana!*"

I heard muffled sounds, then: "Yes, sir!" and I guessed that preparations were somehow getting under way.

With depressing slowness I extricated myself from my bedding, took my frozen boots and began tapping them before putting them on. I put on my eiderdown jacket, my cap and glasses and was then ready to go outside. The weather was magnificent; the valley down below was filled with a splendid sea of clouds. Above, everything was perfectly clear. There had been a heavy fall of snow during the night and I thought that Terray would be finding the going very bad. Looking through the glasses I followed his tracks and soon picked up his party just at the first ice wall. He and his Sherpas were battling their way up and must have been breathless with the struggle. I examined the neighborhood of Camp III and saw two black specks leave it and come *down*. But they ought all to have been continuing *up* to Camp IV; I was afraid that their physical condition must have taken the heart out of them.

Heavy clouds appeared in the Miristi Khola valley, and their unusual color bothered me; I had gloomy forebodings about the outcome of the day. Could these clouds be the forerunner of the monsoon?

Dawatondu was feeling worse and worse and I decided to send him down in the first party returning to Camp I. For the moment he lay in his sleeping-bag, moaning and holding his stomach with both hands.

Snow began to fall again; I went into my tent and lay on my air mattress day-dreaming. Before long I heard shouts. I thought it was sure to be Lachenal and I shouted back. There was such a maze of tracks on the plateau that a shout might well be useful. A few minutes later he arrived with Couzy.

"No use going on," said Lachenal, "my stomach was all inside out."

"And I had the most appalling headaches," said Couzy. "Even with aspirin and sleeping tablets I couldn't sleep."

"If only you could have heard him," Lachenal began again. "He moaned all night."

"It's the altitude," I said. "You were perfectly right to come down. What about the others? Will they go up again with Lionel?"

"We weren't feeling enterprising up there," explained Lachenal, "particularly after all the snow that fell during the night. I can't really tell you, but I think they were waiting for Lionel before deciding."

We went inside the tent. Lachenal visibly relished the comfort it offered. Couzy's headache had disappeared as he came down. It commonly happens—as soon as you descend a few hundred yards all the ills due to the altitude vanish away. While the two of them were changing and getting dry, I went off to find out from Angawa what there was for lunch. There must be no hesitation about killing the fatted calf to raise my friends' morale! In spite of their exertions they had scarcely eaten a thing since the day before yesterday.

We managed a very substantial meal, and to my great satisfaction, Lachenal and Couzy did full justice to it; then we lay down and chatted in a more cheerful frame of mind. As we were taking it easy, Angawa poked his panic-stricken little face through the opening of the tent and cried out:

"Bara Sahib! Other Sahibs come!"

Then, after a moment's silence:

"Bara Sahib, hear!"

And indeed I heard someone calling.

As it was still snowing steadily I quickly put on my gaiters and anorak and went out. I couldn't see more than ten yards. From time to time I thought I heard shouts. It was certainly a Sahib, for the Sherpas could make themselves understood over great distances. The voice did not come from the direction of Camp III, but from a point much nearer the Cauliflower Ridge. There were two possibilities: either it was someone coming from Camp III who had gone off to the left and who now found himself among the crevasses, or else it was someone from Camp I who had gone up too high. Anyway they were in no danger, because there's never any mistaking a cry of "Help!" in the mountains. I gave an answering shout, and in spite of the distance the man heard; he appeared to move to the left—he had understood. His shouts came nearer and I was able to give directions.

"Keep left, always to the left, beside the big crevasse."

I went on repeating this until he answered that he had understood.

A quarter of an hour later a reeling white ghost appeared. I had difficulty in recognizing it as Schatz.

"Where's Rébuffat?"

"I came down alone."

"Alone? You're crazy! In this weather and over that ground?" I felt the blood rushing to my face.

"Sorry, old man," said Schatz, "I couldn't do anything else. I felt completely done in at Camp III. I was quite incapable of helping Lionel tomorrow, and just a useless mouth to feed, so I decided to come down."

I was really angry. It was, I think, the first time since the beginning of the Expedition, that I had been angry like this.

"And so, you, practically a sick man, go and run useless risks! Just imagine, a simple slip, like the other day . . . and suppose Angawa hadn't heard your shouts . . ."

However, it was over and done with. The thing now was to help Schatz forget the strain of his lone descent. Hot tea and a good meal brought the color back to his face. And then he, too, became infected by the pervasive optimism of the camp and began to see the future in a rosier light.

"Did Terray reach Camp III all right?" I asked him.

"The deep snow slowed him up a lot. When Rébuffat and I were coming down we ran into him in the mist. He was in such tremendous form that we went back with him."

"How was it that Rébuffat didn't come down with you afterwards?"

"I'll explain; we talked it all over. Lionel said that Camp IV ought, properly, to be organized by the four who had slept at Camp III the night before—Couzy, Lachenal, Rébuffat and myself. Even though two had gone down, the job ought to be done."

"So you decided to go up with him?"

"Exactly."

As usual Terray had put efficiency before everything else. He considered it his plain duty to do so. But Schatz went on:

"As I was so tired, I told Lionel that rather than peter out next day on the slope, it would be better for me to go down to recuperate. Later, I could make a rope with Couzy."

"So tomorrow Terray and Rébuffat will be going right up?"

"Yes, if it's fine enough."

Would they really be able to go on? Perhaps they were now to be given the real, longed-for chance.

Outside, the Sherpas were talking excitedly. What was going on now? I put my head out and saw Adjiba who had just come up from Camp I, with a number of porters. Behind him was a coolie whom Ichac had dubbed "the Chinee." Later we learned that his real name was Pandy. He had come up to Camp II easily, in spite of the technical difficulties; he was honorary Sherpa. To celebrate this promotion, we made him a present of a very magnificent nylon waistcoat which he wore with great pride. Adjiba handed me two notes which I read aloud in the tent:

Camp I May 29, 1950

Marcel Ichac to Maurice Herzog.

Ang-Tharkey arrived at 12:10. There are twenty-two loads at Base Camp.

Available to carry loads between Base Camp and Camp I— the Chinee, and a young gigolo brought up by Ang-Tharkey. Ang-Tharkey is going down again to Base Camp to meet Noyelle and his fifteen coolies and try to keep some of them on, to ferry loads.

Send Adjiba back as soon as possible with a list of things urgently required (high-altitude tents?).

Do you need us to convoy Sherpas between Camps II and III, and if so when?

Marcel Ichac.

Splendid news! With Noyelle coming up we were certain now of being provisioned, and supported by the main bulk of our equipment. Everyone was in great spirits in the camp.

The second note was a message in which Noyelle acknowledged receipt of my order of the day and announced his arrival in force. This note was dispatched from Tukucha on the 25th, the day after Sarki's arrival there. Good old Sarki! He had taken barely thirty-six hours to cover a distance which normally took four or five days; he had served us well and at the proper time the leader would know how to show his gratitude.

These happy events called for the opening of a bottle of rum, but there was no time. Adjiba would have to go down again immediately to get on with the load-carrying. I wrote a note at once to the Sahibs at the lower camps.

Camp II May 29, 1950

Herzog to Noyelle, Matha and all other Sahibs.

Congratulations to Noyelle for the speed with which he got going everything dispatched. It means a lot to us all. Yesterday Camp IV was established at 23,500 feet on the upper part of the handle of the Sickle. At this moment Terray, Rébuffat and two Sherpas are at Camp III (21,650 feet).

Our immediate objective is to pitch Camp V before the final assault which will be carried out by parties in succession.

For Matha: urgent: Sarki, Adjiba, Foutharkey and the Chinee to come up tomorrow very early with an extra valley tent and two lots of bedding (mattress and sleeping-bag), plus a gasoline stove and a quart of fuel (a large Coleman), also films for the move camera (I have taken a certain number which I'm sending back), also some more medical supplies, sleeping tablets, aspirin—the equivalent of ten tubes; ten tubes of rosat *cream, tubes of anti-frostbite ointment (8), five tubes of anti-sunburn cream;* Tschamba-Fii,[23] *four pairs of Tricouni gaiters and one extra high-altitude unit.*

Complete the loads with food: put in some saucisson *and a bottle of cognac.*

From Lachenal's sack get stockings, socks (three pairs), camp boots, a shirt and pair of pants.

We'll be calling you on the walkie-talkie at eight o'clock this evening.

Couzy and Schatz will go down tomorrow and will give further instructions.

Important: *send all this off very early, as I shall be waiting to go up with Sarki, Foutharkey, and Lachenal to Camp III. Given good weather, we have high hopes.*

Maurice Herzog.

Adjiba and the Chinee had brought up a high-altitude unit, food and a walkie-talkie. In the evening, at eight o'clock as arranged, we intended to try to establish communication—at long last. This would make things much easier.

I was well satisfied with the way Noyelle was doing his job—he was showing the stuff he was made of. Without him there would have been no hope of getting up before the monsoon. I went off to have a look at Dawatondu whom I wished to send down as soon as possible. But I found a very sick man—really, he looked almost at death's door—and I hadn't the heart to send him down in weather like this. He would have to go tomorrow.

Adjiba didn't waste a minute. This time he had no load and he disappeared rapidly with his great ungainly strides, followed by the Chinee trotting along behind him. In a few minutes they had vanished into the mist.

I set up the walkie-talkie. From time to time I pressed the button.

"Hello, Maurice speaking. Can you hear me, Matha?"

All I heard was crackling. After a while I made out some wild Indian music—it almost set me dancing up there, at nearly 20,000 feet, in the heart of the Himalaya.

"Hello, Herzog speaking. Are you receiving, Matha?"

Still no answer.

At eight-fifteen, in accordance with our previous arrangements, I shut off. This matter of radio communications on expeditions could certainly stand improvement. I went back into the tent, a little depressed by this failure and found the others nearly asleep.

Next morning was fine, the light was brilliant and the sun was already beating down on the tent. I felt well rested and soon had a look outside. It must have been a cold night: the snow crystals sparkled in the sun like so many diamonds. Our plan was simple: we would have to wait for the convoy from Camp I, which should not be long in arriving, and set off immediately with fresh loads for Camp III. Couzy and Schatz were still not feeling very fit: while Couzy preferred to remain here to recuperate, Schatz was definitely in favor of going lower down; he decided to descend to Camp I. He would escort Dawatondu who was still, after three days, in bad shape. Lachenal was a new man—I saw this by the way he got out of his sleeping-bag; he went off to see what the Sherpas were doing, and looked up for signs of Terray. His morale seemed much better—would his physical fitness come back too? If so we should both be able to leave, and constitute the second party.

"What on earth can Adjiba be doing?" I said impatiently. "I particularly asked them at Camp I to send him off early so that we ourselves should have time to leave Camp II today." We took turns looking through the glasses.

"Look!" I cried. "You can spot Rébuffat and Terray, moving along with their Sherpas."

"They're going very slowly."

"The snow's deep and it's tough going."

Bluish mist—a very good sign—rose up from the depths of the Miristi Khola before being dispersed by the sun. We took some photographs of ourselves and of the mountains around us.

"Midday, and still no Adjiba!"

At lunch we began a discussion about Chamonix guides, and Lachenal aired his views on his profession. The hours went by, and while Schatz got ready to go down with Dawatondu, it became obvious to me that it was too late for us to go up to Camp III that day.

"Salaam, Bara Sahib!"

"Salaam!"

It was six o'clock when Ang-Tharkey, Foutharkey and Sarki arrived and I was very glad indeed to see them. They had brought up heavy loads with equipment, food, and, most welcome—a second valley tent for Camp II. Before the light faded we had a look through the glasses at Camp IV;

126

we saw no movement. No doubt the party had already settled in for the night—the lack of activity was a good sign. Tomorrow they would go on to establish Camp V.

Ang-Tharkey was wreathed in smiles; he, too, seemed pleased to see us. His little trip to Muktinath had been a great joy to him and he was still feeling the thrill of his pilgrimage. Now that I had him with me I felt much less anxious; with his great Himalayan experience, Ang-Tharkey knew what to do and what not to do, and he had no hesitation about taking the initiative; his authority over the Sherpas took a weight off my shoulders. Ang-Tharkey opened the loads and handed me a note from Ichac, Noyelle and Oudot:

May 30, 1950

1. *Impossible to get the Sherpas off first thing this morning, since we didn't get your note until late yesterday and the Sherpas and equipment were at Base Camp.*
2. *We are sending you Ang-Tharkey, Sarki and Foutharkey. They are bringing up everything you asked for (complete); fix up about bedding with the Sherpas.*
3. *Tomorrow we'll send up a food convoy, perhaps accompanied by one of us, to Camp II.*
4. *Leave any messages at Camp II.*
5. *If you require one of us to escort Sherpas carrying food to Camp III, let us know.*
6. *Radio: heard nothing. Try again at 17 hr. 19 hr. 20 hr. We've got a big receiver set.*
7. *We are in the midst of temporary disturbances caused by the monsoon. The monsoon itself is advancing over Calcutta. It is ahead of time.*
8. *G. B. Rana has gone down to Base Camp. Send us news. A runner will leave here tomorrow. G.B. will go back to Tukucha.*
9. *What are you doing about the return journey. The coolie situation will be critical: it takes eight days between giving the order here and the arrival of a first batch—only twenty at a time.*

Good hunting!

F.D.N., Ichac, Oudot.

P.S. from Ichac: For taking movie shots in color: when the light is full strength you can go up to F.11.

It was too late for a radio message at 17 hrs., but I would try at 19 hrs., this time, I hoped, with more success. The news about the monsoon worried me. It would be heartbreaking to be stopped by its sudden arrival now that we were nearing our goal. If it had already struck Calcutta it would be only a few days before reaching us here. I tried to establish radio communication with Camp I, but with no success. To give the people at Camp I the latest news, I decided to answer their note at the last possible moment before leaving.

The sunset was magnificent; the precipices of the Nilgiris and of Annapurna turned from gold to orange, and orange to purple; the sky was pure and clear and it was very cold—all excellent signs. Were these few days of fine weather to be our last chance? The Nilgiris were now in shadow and the upper rocks of Annapurna had turned to old rose. When the rest of the mountain was already plunged in darkness one last point—the summit—held the light for a few seconds longer.

We passed an uneventful night: there were only a few avalanches since there had been no snow during the day. At six o'clock we climbed out of our sleeping-bags; the weather was perfect. Lachenal struck me as being in excellent form—he seemed to have got over his bad humor and to be making a splendid comeback.

"So you've got your socks and your shirt?" I asked, while he was packing his rucksack. This extra little bit of comfort had put him in good humor. We were both convinced that his journey up would bring us victory.

While the Sherpas made up the loads, I quickly wrote a note for Camp I:

May 31, 1950

To all Sahibs:

I am about to leave for Camp III with Lachenal. We intend to push on right to the top, weather permitting. Schatz and Couzy will form the third contingent. Will Ichac dispatch the following telegram to Devies:

ATTACKING ANNAPURNA STOP DIFFICULT ROUTE OVER SNOW AND ICE BUT ALLOWING RAPID PROGRESS STOP OBJECTIVE DANGERS FROM AVALANCHES AND SERACS SLIGHT STOP CAMP I/16,750 II/19,350 III/21,650 IV/23,500 ESTABLISHED STOP HOPING FOR VICTORY HEALTH AND MORALE OF ALL PERFECT MAURICE HERZOG.

Food: *a small quantity has been taken up. Couzy at Camp II will give directions for its dispatch up to Camp III.*

Radio: *have been able to hear very little. Look into it with Schatz who has gone down.*

Monsoon: *keep me well posted.*

Return: *an advance guard will go to Tukucha and see to recruiting coolies.*

Movies: *I'll do my utmost to take a movie camera to the summit.*

M. Herzog.

That we were all optimistic was apparent in our preparations. I noticed that each of us paid great attention to the contents of his own little medical supply and to the spare films for cameras and the movie camera. Surreptitiously I put the little French flag, made specially by Schatz, into my sack as well as the pennants which I was so anxious to take up. Everything was ready.

We left the camp and, having gone around the big crevasse, made straight for the great avalanche cone. The snow held well and it was neither too cold nor too soft, but just right. Our morale rocketed up.

Suddenly:

"Maurice, what's happening?"

"They're coming down!"

It was only too true. To our great disappointment we made out four black specks coming down the track towards us.

Chapter XII

The Assault

WHY HAD THEY GIVEN UP? WE COULD NOT UNDERSTAND IT. LACHENAL, WHO was moving at a fair pace and appeared to be going much more easily than during the last few days, was the first up the avalanche cone and across the couloir. It was the third time I had been over this route and I knew it well by now, but again as I went to meet them I found it both difficult and dangerous. On the little platform beneath the ice wall where we had left a fixed rope, we came upon Terray and Rébuffat.

"What's happened?" I asked Terray.

He seemed disheartened. "We'd have been crazy to go on. What with the wind and this hellish snow it took us more than seven hours yesterday to get from Camp III to Camp IV."

"Did you find the tent?"

"Sure, but we had to straighten the poles which had been bent over by the avalanche. We got the other tent up in a tearing wind. Rébuffat felt his feet beginning to freeze."

"I thought I'd had it," put in Gaston. "Fortunately, Lionel rubbed me and flogged me with an end of rope, and at last got the blood circulating again."

"This morning," Terray went on, "the cold was worse than in Canada and the wind even stronger. I figured it out like this: if yesterday, when we were quite fit, we only covered just over a thousand feet in seven hours, we wouldn't have a hope of climbing the last four thousand feet under present conditions. I know we must do all we can, up to the limit, but I'm beginning to have doubts about our success."

Although Lachenal and I protested vigorously, the other two did not seem to be affected by our enthusiasm. Terray, for all his strength, had only just managed to cope with the snow (which covered the tracks afresh every day) and the slopes which had to be mastered yard by yard, and with the deterioration of mind and body brought on by altitude. But he did not care to dwell on all these obstacles—he had no wish to undermine our solid morale.

"We're going up," I said without the least hesitation. "When we come down it'll mean the top's been reached—it's all or nothing."

And I felt that Lachenal was as determined as myself. The other two wished us good luck, but I read doubt in their faces. Now it was up to us.

We set to on the slope; Sarki, Ang-Tharkey, Lachenal and myself took it in turns to go ahead to improve the tracks fortunately left by Terray and Rébuffat on their way down. The going wasn't too bad, but all the same Ang-Tharkey was amazed at the difficulty of the ground.

Pansy had already told him that neither on Kanchenjunga nor on Everest had they ever struggled with such difficult terrain. It was the first time these Sherpas had done any climbing on ice, and been obliged to get up vertical walls. But all went well, we pushed on steadily, and found the going much easier than the previous times, which showed just how vital acclimatization is on Himalayan expeditions. It was now burningly hot, and by the time we reached Camp III we were sweating. What a truly magnificent camp this was, lost in the very heart of the mountains in a tiny snow-blocked crevasse! How sung and comfortable it appeared!

We had to conserve our strength: there would be no going further today. Most of the time we just lay in our sacks, and the Sherpas handed us our meals through the entrance of the other tent. The weather was fine. This time everything was in our favor and we would get to the top.

It took the Sherpas a long time to make tea because of the decreased heating power of the stoves at this height. A few cigarettes, followed by the ration of pills, which both Sahibs and Sherpas obediently swallowed, and before dark everybody at Camp III was already asleep.

In the morning we waited placidly for the sun, since the day's program consisted of going only as far as Camp IV, which would take us barely four hours. But we should also have to move that camp again and re-pitch it right on the Sickle glacier. We each set about getting our things ready, and I took a few movie shots. Down below, the plateau on which Camp II was pitched appeared to have become a regular village. Big valley tents and high-altitude tents stood side by side and it looked altogether like an advanced Base Camp.

"Lionel and Gaston must be resting now," said Lachenal.

We decided to move off, taking advantage of the relatively good state of the snow, and we reached the site of Camp IV more rapidly than we had expected. On the way I took more movie shots, in particular of the bergschrund by the plateau on which the camp was situated. The weather was still very fine. Ang-Tharkey and Sarki had gone splendidly, one of them on Lachenal's rope, the other on mine. It was still early and we should therefore be able to move Camp IV right up on the Sickle glacier. We were pleased about this, for beyond this camp there would be no further technical difficulties to keep us back. We quickly took down one tent, which we ourselves would be carrying, as well as food and equipment.

"In less than an hour we ought to be up the big ice slope leading to the edge of the Sickle," I said to Lachenal, "it's not all that long." Ang-Tharkey and Sarki would come back to the present camp where we were leaving the other tent. The following morning they would have to dismantle it and carry it up to the new Camp IV. From there we would start out for the next one—Camp V.

Laden like donkeys, we sank up to our waists in new snow on the first few yards of the great ice slope. But shortly there was far less snow, and very soon only a thin layer of loose snow lying on ice. The angle was comparable with that of the steepest Alpine slopes. Now and again we cut a few steps, but most of the time we just went straight up on our crampons—though cramponing at this height was not exactly restful and we puffed away like steam-engines.

The Sherpas were not at all happy. They were not expert on this sort of ground, but as they were afraid of getting left behind they made all possible speed. After a couple of hundred yards of this exhausting work we came to the edge of the Sickle. Lachenal, who was leading, had a look around up there, and I did the same down below. Our choice fell upon an inviting site at the base of a serac just where we had emerged from the ice slope. It was an ideal place, protected from the wind both by the serac itself and by a little ice ridge which formed a natural screen. Lachenal was delighted:

"Once we've fixed things up we'll be as snug as in my own little chalet at Chamonix."

We set to work at once and the tent was soon in position. As it was already late afternoon I packed Ang-Tharkey and Sarki off to the lower camp, none too happy at the prospect of going down such a difficult slope. But I knew that Ang-Tharkey would not hesitate to cut extra steps and, if necessary, to make a staircase the whole way.

"Good night, sir!"

We shook hands warmly and our two Sherpas disappeared down the slope. Meanwhile we arranged our shelter. Mist closed around us and an icy wind got up, stinging our faces with blown snow. Neither of us had much appetite, but we forced ourselves to eat, and when the tea was ready I set out in a row the collection of pills that Oudot had strictly ordered us to swallow. For all Lachenal's assertions, we were only relatively comfortable. We put our boots into our sleeping-bags to prevent them from freezing, and settled ourselves in for an excellent night.

SUMMIT 26,493

EAST PEAK

CAMP V

CAMP IV A

CAMP IV

✚ Position of the crevasse

Route of the final assault on Annapurna from Camp IV to the summit.

When dawn came I poked my head anxiously through the opening of the tent: the sun was rising and it was fine and cold. It looked as if the monsoon would not arrive that day and I felt much relieved, for the latest news had worried me. We were embarked upon a race against time. As soon as Ang-Tharkey and Sarki arrived we shared out the loads and made up our sacks. We were shivering and could not leave our serac quick enough. Leaving one tent where it was, we set out; the other was for Camp V.

A traverse to the left across the Sickle glacier enabled us to avoid an area of broken-up seracs. In this way we reached the base of a wide valley of large, steep snow fields with few obstacles in the way. Nobody said anything—every one of us was tense with effort, and the loads weighed us down. We thought of what lay ahead. For me, the main question was the monsoon: it was now June 2, and we could not reasonably hope for more than four days of fine weather. That would just give us time, but there was not a moment to lose. Now that we had only this great snow field before us, we held the advantage; there were no technical obstacles—or at least hardly any. Not for a single moment did either Lachenal or myself entertain the slightest doubt about our victory.

We stopped frequently and ate a bit of candy or nougat for which we always had a great craving. Looking back down the mountain the sight was enough to make one dizzy; the plateau of Camp II was a mere pocket handkerchief, and the great Annapurna glacier, which took an hour to cross, was reduced to a small tongue of ice. In the distance, over the top of the Great Barrier, we could distinctly see Tibet; on the extreme left Dhaulagiri was partially hidden by the great rock wall of Annapurna. Our zigzagging upward tracks were visible the whole way.

The jagged ice ridge at the summit produced a curious effect—a snow-laden wind blew through it as if through the teeth of a comb. Mist straggled right across the sky over our heads. One of the buttresses of Annapurna towered above us, in rose-red rock—it was the shape of a bird's beak and looked like the *Bec d'Oiseau* on the Grepon in the Mont Blanc massif. A thin rib of rock in the shape of a spearhead ran up to it.

"We're pretty sure," I told Lachenal, "to be able to find a place somewhere on that rib big enough for our 'coffin.'"

Lachenal agreed: "We'll use as many pitons as necessary, and anyhow we shall be on dry ground."

With dogged perseverance he and I took turns in making the trail. The two Sherpas got terribly winded and we kept stopping to regain our breath. Two or three times we made long traverses to avoid the seracs and one particularly long crevasse. Often we sank in the snow and each step seemed an eternity. Although we progressed upwards the rib always appeared to remain just as far off.

"Enough to take the heart out of you," complained Lachenal.

Gradually the difficulties lessened, the snow became firmer and we did not sink so far. We had the feeling that we were climbing on an enormous roof: the slope was constant, and though it was at an angle of about forty degrees we were able to crampon up it. Every ten yards we halted, in cold so intense that our feet grew numb. But we could not afford any unnecessary delay: "On to Camp V!" became for us a kind of refrain. The going became terribly exhausting, for the surface crust of the snow broke through beneath our crampons and again we sank in at each step.

With a final spurt of energy we gained the rib of rock.

"Hell!"

What a disappointment! Those fine, clear-colored rocks were plastered with ice—there were no ledges, no holds. We should have to pitch camp right on the slope.

The Sherpas joined us: we were at 24,600 feet and the height laid them out completely. They couldn't speak a word and made signs that their heads were hurting. But we all had to set to work. With our axes we made a level space. In order to accomplish this on such a steep slope we had to move great quantities of snow. Every thirty seconds I had to rest; I felt as though I were suffocating, my breathing was out of control, and my heart pounding away. Yet the Sherpas, who were not in such good shape as we were, managed to carry on for five minutes without a break. An hour later the shelf was ready: it was close to the rib and we were able to anchor the tent to the two pitons which Lachenal drove into cracks in the rock.

I had a brief conversation with Ang-Tharkey in pidgin-English.

"Tomorrow morning Lachenal Sahib and Bara Sahib go to the summit of Annapurna."

"Yes, sir."

"You are the Sirdar and the most experienced of all the Sherpas. I should be very glad if you will come with us."

"Thank you, sir."

"We must have the victory *together.* Will you come?"

At that moment I felt it my duty to take into consideration the Sherpas' very understandable feelings. After a pause Ang-Tharkey replied. He was grateful for the choice of action I had given him, but he held back:

"Thank you, very much, Bara Sahib, but my feet are beginning to freeze . . ."

"I see."

". . . and I prefer to go down to Camp IV."

"Of course, Ang-Tharkey, it's as you like. In that case go down at once as it is late."

"Thank you, sir."

In a second their sacks were packed and, just as they were setting off, they turned around and I could guess their anxiety at leaving us alone.

"Salaam, sir. Good luck!"

"Salaam—and be careful!"

A few minutes later two black dots were on their way down the slope we had just come up. How strangely their minds worked. Here were these men, proverbial for their trustworthiness and devotion, who quite certainly enjoyed going high on the mountains; and yet, when on the point of reaping the victory from their labors, they prudently held back. But I don't doubt that our attitude struck them as even more strange.

Not a word did Lachenal and I speak. Our silence had something heavy and obsessive about it. This time we would not turn back.

It would be a grim night. The site was dangerous and the ground unstable. Under the action of the wind the snow slid down the length of the slope and piled up above our shelter. We hoped it would not weigh too much on the tent. The pitons driven into the limestone, the axes driven right into the snow, gave us only moral support and we had no illusions. We said nothing but we both feared that the edge of the platform would collapse and carry the tent away.

Our minds worked slowly during this last night before the final assault. I had great difficulty in concentrating and I couldn't get up an interest in anything. Conversation languished. With great effort, and only because we urged each other on, we managed to make some tea on the stove and swallow our pills with military discipline. It was impossible to swallow any food down at all.

A fierce wind sprang up and the nylon fabric of the tent flapped noisily. Several times we feared that the wind would blow the tent away, and at each gust we clung to the poles as a drowning man clings to a plank. It began to snow; the storm howled and moaned around us. The air was fraught with terror, and in the end we became terrified too.

Every movement demanded a tremendous effort of will. There was no question of undressing. Pushing our boots to the bottom of our wonderful sleeping-bags we tucked ourselves in. Good old Pierre Allain! How we blessed him that night! And away flew our thoughts to the friend who had designed our marvelous equipment.

Lachenal settled himself on the outer side of the tent while I curled up against the slope. It wasn't pleasant for either of us. Lachenal, on the edge of the precarious platform, felt as though he were slipping off into space, while I was threatened with suffocation under the snow which slid down and piled up persistently on the roof of the tent.

"It's made of nylon, and it's elastic," I tried to reassure Lachenal, "otherwise the fabric would give way. Hell! I've forgotten to put my camera inside my sleeping-bag."

I stretched out a hand for the precious object and slid it down beside me to the bottom of my sack which was already cluttered up with my boots.

What a night! Lachenal slid further and further towards the edge, and I felt more and more suffocated. We looked at the time repeatedly. The situation was beginning to be alarming. I could no longer breathe. The weight of the snow was literally crushing me. Like a boxer on guard I held both arms to my chest and so made a small space which allowed me to expand my lungs. The noise of the wind was ear splitting, and every onslaught was accompanied by a high-pitched whistling. The tent poles bent over dangerously, while with the strength of desperation we tried to hold them in place. Why the tent was not blown down, I don't know. Our very worst Alpine bivouacs were nothing compared with this unequal and exhausting struggle.

We were worn out and utterly weary, but the storm saw to it that we were kept wide awake.

Rébuffat and Terray, skeptical about the success of our attempt, went down towards Camp II. When they arrived there they found Couzy and Schatz who gave them the latest news. Then they dropped with fatigue and so, no doubt, did Pansy and Aila, for they disappeared into the Sherpas' tent and were seen no more that day. Couzy and Schatz, in excellent trim, were pleased to be on a rope together again. Early the following morning they left Camp II, and as arranged, they followed us up, one camp behind.

At Camp II Terray gradually recovered. He felt that the final attack was imminent and set about his preparations with his usual meticulous care. Rébuffat was busy writing. Early in the afternoon sleet began to fall.

"Hello, everybody!"

The white ghost who had just come in was Ichac!

"The others are coming up."

Oudot and Noyelle then appeared, shaking the snow off inside the tent with the cheerful carelessness of people coming from outside. It was five-thirty.

"What, it's you!" exclaimed Ichac. "We were expecting to see Schatz and Couzy."

"No—it's only us."

And Terray went on to explain how they had had to retrace their steps the day before without having been able to establish Camp V because of Rébuffat's feet showing signs of frostbite.

"We'll be off again tomorrow morning," said Terray.

Outside the sleet had turned to snow. Oudot was impatient to find out to what extent oxygen would be of use. Displaying his usual authority, he insisted upon our liaison officer Noyelle going around with a mask on. His face became a snout connected by a tube to cylinders of duralumin full of compressed oxygen. He might have been exploring the moon! Poor Noyelle, with his ridiculous hat pulled down over his nose and ears—he was the only one unable to appreciate the comic figure he cut.

After the tests everyone collected in the tent and Ichac took some flashlight photographs.

"Right now I'm going to establish a record for the highest flashlight shot."

As a matter of fact this camp was not far off 20,000 feet high, and it was unlikely that many flashlights had been taken on Himalayan expeditions.

After dinner the sky cleared and the stars shone and the Great Barrier was clothed in a mantle of white, lit up by the moon. The latest news on the radio was alarming: the monsoon had reached the north of Bengal and, moreover, considerable disturbances were forecast from the west.

The following morning—June 2—the sky was brilliant, it was going to be a glorious day. As usual Lionel Terray had timed his departure for an early hour. He left camp with Rébuffat and two Sherpas at six o'clock, before the sun was up. (At Camp IV we were still sleeping soundly.) Ichac took some telephotos of them as they went up the avalanche cone.

Now, the whole mountain was inhabited, and as the hours went by activity increased. An onlooker would have seen an astonishing sight. At Camp II men were swarming round the settlement of tents. A little higher up Terray and Rébuffat with their two Sherpas, Pansy and Aila, were cutting fresh steps up the first slopes. Above, at Camp III, Schatz and Couzy, accompanied by Angawa and Foutharkey, were preparing to cross the great couloir. And finally Lachenal and myself, with Ang-Tharkey and Sarki, were once again ploughing through snow on the slope of the Sickle glacier.

During the afternoon clouds appeared along the bed of the Miristi Khola, and even on the plateau by Camp II. Through a rent in them Ichac was able to see, at the foot of the spear-shaped rib, a new black speck which he guessed must be Camp V. Would the final assault be made the following morning? That would be decided by the weather.

The mist grew thicker and calls for help were heard. Noyelle and Ichac went out to see who it was and found Angawa and Foutharkey wandering in the mist. Having only one tent at Camp IV—the other was at Camp V— Couzy and Schatz had had to send their two Sherpas down.

The rest of the equipment for Camp IV was to be brought up the following day by the Rébuffat-Terray party who would strike Camp III and take it up with them. And the group at Camp II would move up the day after and reestablish Camp III.

At Camp IV morale was good. Rébuffat and Terray had just arrived and everyone was in good form. Terray meditated upon the unpredictable nature of conditions in the Himalaya: four days ago he and Rébuffat had climbed to Camp III with the greatest difficulty, taking seven hours to crawl up. This time they had successfully carried out an ambitious program of which it would be hard to find the equivalent in the history of Himalayan climbing: leaving Camp II at dawn they had succeeded in reaching Camp III at about eleven o'clock in the morning; they had struck this camp and then carried everything on up to Camp IV, in this way gaining one precious day. Although there were only four of them they carried two high-altitude units as well as twenty-two pounds of food. Rébuffat, like Lachenal, had made a magnificent comeback.

There were two people who were mighty pleased to see them, and these were Couzy and Schatz. Otherwise, the next day these two would have had to carry up a complete camp themselves, and they had not found this prospect particularly attractive. Thanks to aspirin and sleeping tablets and thanks also to a sense of tremendous well-being caused partly by good physical condition and partly by the imminence of a happy outcome, everybody passed an excellent night.

Chapter XIII

The Third of June

ON THE THIRD OF JUNE, 1950, THE FIRST LIGHT OF DAWN FOUND US STILL clinging to the tent poles at Camp V. Gradually the wind abated, and with daylight, died away altogether. I made desperate attempts to push back the soft, icy stuff which stifled me, but every movement became an act of heroism. My mental powers were numbed: thinking was an effort, and we did not exchange a single word.

What a repellent place it was! To everyone who reached it, Camp V became one of the worst memories of their lives. We had only one thought—to get away. We should have waited for the first rays of the sun, but at half-past five we felt we couldn't stick it any longer.

"Let's go, Biscante," I muttered. "Can't stay here a minute longer."

"Yes, let's go," repeated Lachenal.

Which of us would have the energy to make tea? Although our minds worked slowly we were quite able to envisage all the movements that would be necessary—and neither of us could face up to it. It couldn't be helped—we would just have to go without. It was quite hard enough work to get ourselves and our boots out of our sleeping-bags—and the boots were frozen stiff so that we got them on only with the greatest difficulty. Every movement made us terribly breathless. We felt as if we were being stifled. Our gaiters were stiff as a board, and I succeeded in lacing mine up; Lachenal couldn't manage his.

"No need for the rope, eh, Biscante?"

"No need," replied Lachenal laconically.

That was two pounds saved. I pushed a tube of condensed milk, some nougat and a pair of socks into my sack; one never knew, the socks might come in useful—they might even do as Balaclavas. For the time being I stuffed them with first-aid equipment. The camera was loaded with a black and white film; I had a color film in reserve. I pulled the movie-camera out from the bottom of my sleeping-bag, wound it up and tried letting it run without film. There was a little click, then it stopped and jammed.

"Bad luck after bringing it so far," said Lachenal.

In spite of our photographer, Ichac's, precautions taken to lubricate it with special grease, the intense cold, even inside the sleeping-bag, had frozen it. I left it at the camp rather sadly: I had looked forward to taking it to the top. I had used it up to 24,600 feet.

We went outside and put on our crampons, which we kept on all day. We wore as many clothes as possible; our sacks were very light. At six o'clock we started off. It was brilliantly fine, but also very cold. Our super-lightweight crampons bit deep into the steep slopes of ice and hard snow up which lay the first stage of our climb.

Later the slope became slightly less steep and more uniform. Sometimes the hard crust bore our weight, but at others we broke through and sank into soft powder snow which made progress exhausting. We took turns in making the track and often stopped without any word having passed between us. Each of us lived in a closed and private world of his own. I was suspicious of my mental processes; my mind was working very slowly and I was perfectly aware of the low state of my intelligence. It was easiest just to stick to one thought at a time—safest, too. The cold was penetrating; for all our special eiderdown clothing we felt as if we'd nothing on. Whenever we halted, we stamped our feet hard. Lachenal went as far as to take off one boot which was a bit tight; he was in terror of frostbite.

"I don't want to be like Lambert," he said. Raymond Lambert, a Geneva guide, had to have all his toes amputated after an eventful climb during which he got his feet frostbitten.[24] While Lachenal rubbed himself hard, I looked at the summits all around us; already we overtopped them all except the distant Dhaulagiri. The complicated structure of these mountains, with which our many laborious explorations had made us familiar, was now spread out plainly at our feet.

The going was incredibly exhausting, and every step was a struggle of mind over matter. We came out into the sunlight, and by way of marking the occasion made yet another halt. Lachenal continued to complain of his feet. "I can't feel anything. I think I'm beginning to get frostbite." And once again he undid his boot.

I began to be seriously worried. I realized very well the risk we were running; I knew from experience how insidiously and quickly frostbite can set in if one is not extremely careful. Nor was Lachenal under any illusions. "We're in danger of having frozen feet. Do you think it's worth it?"

This was most disturbing. It was my responsibility as leader to think of the others. There was no doubt about frostbite being a very real danger. Did Annapurna justify such risks? That was the question I asked myself; it continued to worry me.

Lachenal had laced his boots up again, and once more we continued to force our way through the exhausting snow. The whole of the Sickle glacier was now in view, bathed in light. We still had a long way to go to cross it, and then there was that rock band—would we find a gap in it?

My feet, like Lachenal's, were very cold and I continued to wriggle my toes, even when we were moving. I could not feel them, but that was nothing new in the mountains, and if I kept on moving them it would keep the circulation going.

Lachenal appeared to me as a sort of specter—he was alone in his world, I in mine. But—and this was odd enough—any effort was slightly *less* exhausting than lower down. Perhaps it was hope lending us wings. Even through dark glasses the snow was blinding—the sun beating straight down on the ice. We looked down upon precipitous ridges which dropped away into space, and upon tiny glaciers far, far below. Familiar peaks soared arrow-like into the sky. Suddenly Lachenal grabbed me:

"If I go back, what will you do?"

A whole sequence of pictures flashed through my head: the days of marching in sweltering heat, the hard pitches we had overcome, the tremendous efforts we had all made to lay siege to the mountain, the daily heroism of all my friends in establishing the camps. Now we were nearing our goal. In an hour or two, perhaps, victory would be ours. Must we give up? Impossible! My whole being revolted against the idea. I had made up my mind, irrevocably. Today we were consecrating an ideal, and no sacrifice was too great. I heard my voice clearly:

"I should go on by myself."

I would go alone. If he wished to go down it was not for me to stop him. He must make his own choice freely.

"Then I'll follow you."

The die was cast. I was no longer anxious. Nothing could stop us now from getting to the top. The psychological atmosphere changed with these few words, and we went forward now as brothers.

I felt as though I were plunging into something new and quite abnormal. I had the strangest and most vivid impressions, such as I had never before known in the mountains. There was something unnatural in the way I saw Lachenal and everything around us. I smiled to myself at the paltriness of our efforts, for I could stand apart and watch myself making these efforts. But all sense of exertion was gone, as though there were no longer any gravity. This diaphanous landscape, this quintessence of purity—these were not the mountains I knew: they were the mountains of my dreams.

The snow, sprinkled over every rock and gleaming in the sun, was of a radiant beauty that touched me to the heart. I had never seen such complete transparency, and I was living in a world of crystal. Sounds were indistinct, the atmosphere like cotton wool.

An astonishing happiness welled up in me, but I could not define it. Everything was so new, so utterly unprecedented. It was not in the least like anything I had known in the Alps, where one feels buoyed up by the presence of others—by people of whom one is vaguely aware, or even by the dwellings one can see in the far distance.

This was quite different. An enormous gulf was between me and the world. This was a different universe—withered, desert, lifeless; a fantastic universe where the presence of man was not foreseen, perhaps not desired. We were braving an interdict, overstepping a boundary, and yet we had no fear as we continued upward. I thought of the famous ladder of St. Theresa of Avila. Something clutched at my heart.

Did Lachenal share these feelings? The summit ridge drew nearer, and we reached the foot of the ultimate rock band. The slope was very steep and the snow interspersed with rocks.

"Couloir!"

A finger pointed. The whispered word from one to another indicated the key to the rocks—the last line of defense.

"What luck!"

The couloir up the rocks though steep was feasible.

The sky was a deep sapphire blue. With a great effort we edged over to the right, avoiding the rocks; we preferred to keep to the snow on account of our crampons and it was not long before we set foot in the couloir. It was fairly steep, and we had a minute's hesitation. Should we have enough strength left to overcome this final obstacle?

Fortunately the snow was hard, and by kicking steps we were able to manage, thanks to our crampons. A false move would have been fatal. There was no need to make handholds—our axes, driven in as far as possible, served us for an anchor.

Lachenal went splendidly. What a wonderful contrast to the early days! It was a hard struggle here, but he kept going. Lifting our eyes occasionally from the slope, we saw the couloir opening out on to . . . well, we didn't quite know, probably a ridge. But where was the top—left or right? Stopping at every step, leaning on our axes we tried to recover our breath and to calm down our racing hearts, which were thumping as though they would burst. We knew we were there now—that nothing could stop us. No need to exchange looks—each of us would have read the same determination in the other's eyes. A slight detour to the left, a few more steps—the summit ridge came gradually nearer—a few rocks to avoid. We dragged ourselves up. Could we possibly be there?

Yes!

A fierce and savage wind tore at us.

We were on top of Annapurna! 8,075 meters, 26,493 feet.

Our hearts overflowed with an unspeakable happiness.

"If only the others could know . . ."

If only everyone could know!

The summit was a corniced crest of ice, and the precipices on the far side which plunged vertically down beneath us, were terrifying, unfathomable. There could be few other mountains in the world like this. Clouds floated halfway down, concealing the gentle, fertile valley of Pokhara, 23,000 feet below. Above us there was nothing!

Our mission was accomplished. But at the same time we had accomplished something infinitely greater. How wonderful life would now become! What an inconceivable experience it is to attain one's ideal and, at the very same moment, to fulfill oneself. I was stirred to the depths of my being. Never had I felt happiness like this—so intense and yet so pure. That brown rock, the highest of them all, that ridge of ice—were these the goals of a lifetime? Or were they, rather, the limits of man's pride?

"Well, what about going down?"

Lachenal shook me. What were his own feelings? Did he simply think he had finished another climb, as in the Alps? Did he think one could just go down again like that, with nothing more to it?

"One minute, I must take some photographs."

"Hurry up!"

I fumbled feverishly in my sack, pulled out the camera, took out the little French flag which was right at the bottom, and the pennants. Useless gestures, no doubt, but something more than symbols—eloquent tokens of affection and goodwill. I tied the strips of material—stained by sweat and by the food in the sacks—to the shaft of my ice-axe, the only flagstaff at hand. Then I focused my camera on Lachenal.

"Now, will you take me?"

"Hand it over—hurry up!" said Lachenal.

He took several pictures and then handed me back the camera. I loaded a color-film and we repeated the process to be certain of bringing back records to be cherished in the future.

"Are you mad?" asked Lachenal. "We haven't a minute to lose: we must go down at once."

And in fact a glance round showed me that the weather was no longer gloriously fine as it had been in the morning. Lachenal was becoming impatient.

"We must go down!"

He was right. His was the reaction of the mountaineer who knows his own domain. But I just could not accustom myself to the idea that we had won our victory. It seemed inconceivable that we should have trodden those summit snows.

It was impossible to build a cairn; there were no stones; everything was frozen. Lachenal stamped his feet; he felt them freezing. I felt mine freezing too, but paid little attention. The highest mountain to be climbed by man lay under our feet! The names of our predecessors on these heights raced through my mind: Mummery, Mallory and Irvine, Bauer, Welzenbach, Tilman, Shipton. How many of them were dead—how many had found on these mountains what, to them, was the finest end of all?

My joy was touched with humility. It was not just one party that had climbed Annapurna today, but a whole expedition. I thought of all the others in the camps perched on the slopes at our feet, and I knew it was because of their efforts and their sacrifices that we had succeeded. There are times when the most complicated actions are suddenly summed up, distilled, and strike you with illuminating clarity: so it was with this irresistible upward surge which had landed us two here.

Pictures passed through my mind—the Chamonix valley, where I had spent the most marvelous moments of my childhood; Mont Blanc, which so tremendously impressed me! I was a child when I first saw "the Mont Blanc people" coming home, and to me there was a queer look about them; a strange light shone in their eyes.

"Come on, straight down," called Lachenal.

He had already done up his sack and started going down. I took out my pocket aneroid: 8,500 meters. I smiled. I swallowed a little condensed milk and left the tube behind—the only trace of our passage. I did up my sack, put on my gloves and my glasses, seized my ice-axe; one look around and I, too, hurried down the slope. Before disappearing into the couloir I gave one last look at the summit which would henceforth be all our joy and all our consolation.

Lachenal was already far below; he had reached the foot of the couloir. I hurried down in his tracks. I went as fast as I could, but it was dangerous going. At every step one had to take care that the snow did not break away beneath one's weight. Lachenal, going faster than I thought he was capable of, was now on the long traverse. It was my turn to cross the area of mixed rock and snow. At last I reached the foot of the rock-band. I had hurried and I was out of breath. I undid my sack. What had I been going to do? I couldn't say.

"My gloves!"

Before I had time to bend over, I saw them slide and roll. They went further and further straight down the slope. I remained where I was, quite stunned. I watched them rolling down slowly, with no appearance of stopping. The movement of those gloves was engraved in my sight as something irredeemable, against which I was powerless. The consequences might be most serious. What was I to do?

"Quickly, down to Camp V."

Rébuffat and Terray would be there. My concern dissolved like magic. I now had a fixed objective again: to reach the camp. Never for a minute did it occur to me to use as gloves the socks which I always carry in reserve for just such a mishap as this.

On I went, trying to catch up with Lachenal. It had been two o'clock when we reached the summit; we had started out at six in the morning, but I had to admit that I had lost all sense of time. I felt as if I were running, whereas in actual fact I was walking normally, perhaps rather slowly, and I had to keep stopping to get my breath. The sky was now covered with clouds, everything had become gray and dirty-looking. An icy wind sprang up, boding no good. We must push on! But where was Lachenal? I spotted him a couple of hundred yards away, looking as if he was never going to stop. And I had thought he was in indifferent form!

The clouds grew thicker and came right down over us; the wind blew stronger, but I did not suffer from the cold. Perhaps the descent had restored my circulation. Should I be able to find the tents in the mist? I watched the rib ending in the beak-like point which overlooked the camp. It was gradually swallowed up by the clouds, but I was able to make out the spearhead rib lower down. If the mist should thicken I would make straight for that rib and follow it down, and in this way I should be bound to come upon the tent.

Lachenal disappeared from time to time, and then the mist was so thick that I lost sight of him altogether. I kept going at the same speed, as fast as my breathing would allow.

The slope was now steeper; a few patches of bare ice followed the smooth stretches of snow. A good sign—I was nearing the camp. How difficult to find one's way in thick mist! I kept the course which I had set by the steepest angle of the slope. The ground was broken; with my crampons I went straight down walls of bare ice. There were some patches ahead—a few more steps. It was the camp all right, but there were *two tents!*

So Rébuffat and Terray had come up. What a mercy! I should be able to tell them that we had been successful, that we were returning from the top. How thrilled they would be!

I got there, dropping down from above. The platform had been extended, and the two tents were facing each other. I tripped over one of the guy-ropes of the first tent; there was movement inside, they had heard me. Rébuffat and Terray put their heads out.

"We've made it. We're back from Annapurna!"

Chapter XIV

The Crevasse

RÉBUFFAT AND TERRAY RECEIVED THE NEWS WITH GREAT EXCITEMENT.

"But what about Biscante?" asked Terray anxiously.

"He won't be long. He was just in front of me! What a day—started out at six this morning—didn't stop . . . got up at last."

Words failed me. I had so much to say. The sight of familiar faces dispelled the strange feeling that I had experienced since morning, and I became, once more, just a mountaineer.

Terray, who was speechless with delight, wrung my hands. Then the smile vanished from his face: "Maurice—your hands!" There was an uneasy silence. I had forgotten that I had lost my gloves: my fingers were violet and white and hard as wood. The other two stared at them in dismay—they realized the full seriousness of the injury. But, still blissfully floating on a sea of joy remote from reality, I leaned over towards Terray and said confidentially, "You're in such splendid form, and you've done so marvelously, it's absolutely tragic you didn't come up there with us!"

"What I did was for the Expedition, my dear Maurice, and anyway you've got up and that's a victory for the whole lot of us."

I nearly burst with happiness. How could I tell him all that his answer meant to me? The rapture I had felt on the summit, which might have seemed a purely personal, egotistical emotion, had been transformed by his words into a complete and perfect joy with no shadow upon it. His answer proved that this victory was not just one man's achievement, a matter for personal pride; no—and Terray was the first to understand this—it was a victory for us all, a victory for mankind itself.

"Hi! Help! Help!"

"Biscante!" exclaimed the others.

Still half intoxicated and remote from reality I had heard nothing. Terray felt a chill at his heart, and his thoughts flew to his partner on so many unforgettable climbs; together they had so often skirted death, and won so many splendid victories. Putting his head out, and seeing Lachenal clinging to the slope a hundred yards lower down, he dressed in frantic haste.

Out he went. But the slope was bare now; Lachenal had disappeared. Terray was horribly frightened, and he could only utter unintelligible cries.

At Tansing, April 11th, 1950. Standing, left to right: Lachenal, Couzy, Schatz, Oudot, Terray, Herzog, Noyelle, and the Sherpas, Pansy, Sarki, Adjiba, Aila, Dawatondu. Sitting: Rébuffat, Ichac, and the Sherpas, Foutharkey, Ang-Tharkey and Angawa.

Dhaulagiri and Tukucha Peak from the east.

The brave Sherpas who bore the burdens of the expedition. Clockwise from upper left: "The Red Porter," Dawatondu, Ang-Tharkey, Manangbhot.

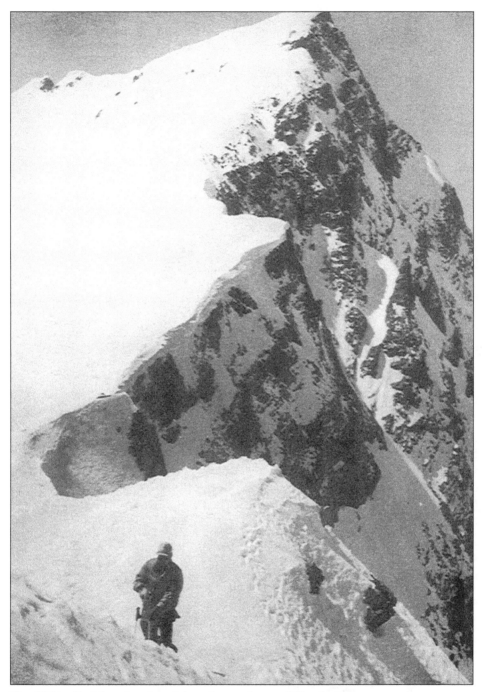

The "White Peak" at the edge of the arête southeast of Dhaulagiri.

Fifteen thousand feet up, above the Dambush Khola, Herzog catches sight of Annapurna, barely visible in the clouds behind the Nilgiris, on the right of the photograph.

The Great Ice Lake on the Tilicho pass, with Ganga Purna in the background.

Village and valley of Manangbhot.

Annapurna, showing the ice cliffs of the Sickle glacier and the couloir by which Herzog and Lachenal finally reached the summit. The avalanche in the center of the photograph hides Camp II.

Herzog, first on the rope, climbing the northwest spur of Annapurna.

Sherpas at Camp II examining the Cauliflower Ridge in the left background.

The Sherpas at Camp III prepare tea while Lionel Terray searches the horizon.

A Sherpa crosses the ice slope below Camp IV at about 23,000 feet.

Victory! Maurice Herzog is photographed by Louis Lachenal holding up the tricolor on the top of Annapurna.

Terray, snow-blinded, returning to Camp II supported by Ang-Tharkey, with Schatz holding the rope. Right, behind them, Lachenal is helped by two Sherpas, and higher up the two dots are Couzy and his Sherpa.

Rébuffat being taken down on a sledge from Camp I by Schatz and four Sherpas.

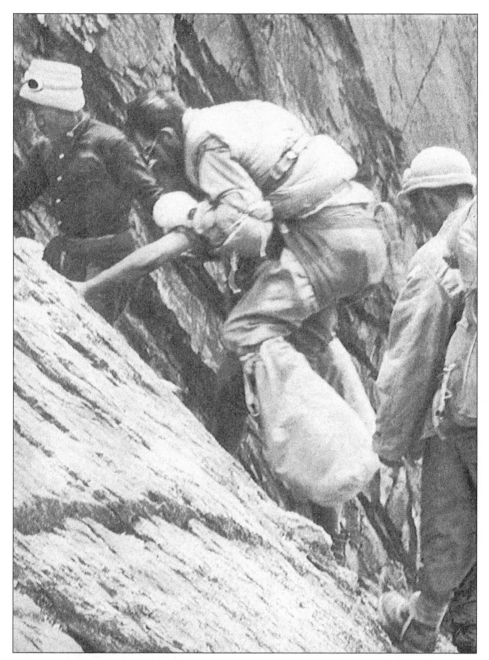

Sarki (left) helps the porter who is carrying Herzog in the *cacolet* down toward the Base Camp.

But the victory is ours . . .

In the night, Doctor Oudot operates again on Maurice Herzog.

On the tenth of June, enveloped by a monsoon, the wounded are carried from the Base Camp on the backs of the porters.

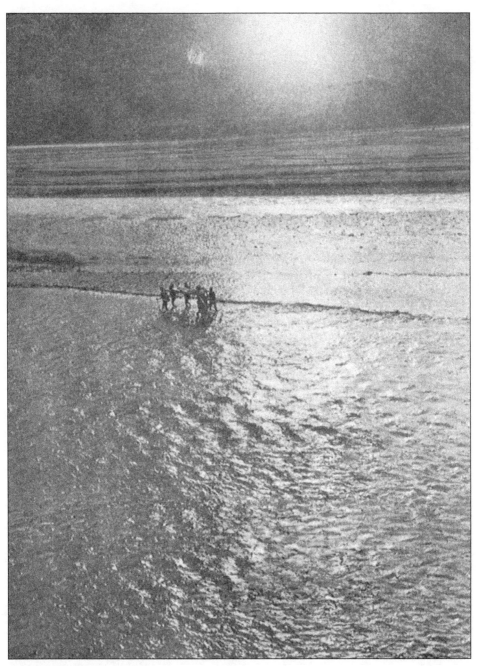

Bearing the stretcher through the paddy fields.

Schatz shows Herzog the beautiful sabre with its silver scabbard that the *Suba* of Tukucha has sent him.

And the Maharajah said to Maurice Herzog, "You are a brave man, and we welcome you here as a brave man."

It was a ghastly moment for him. A violent wind sent the mist tearing by. Under the stress of emotion Terray had not realized how it falsified distances.

"Biscante! Biscante!"

He had spotted him, through a rift in the mist, lying on the slope much lower down than he had thought. Terray set his teeth, and glissaded down like a madman. How would he be able to brake without crampons, on the wind-hardened snow? But Terray was a first-class skier, and with a jump turn he stopped beside Lachenal, who was suffering from concussion after his tremendous fall. In a state of collapse, with no ice-axe, balaclava, or gloves, and only one crampon, he gazed vacantly around him.

"My feet are frost-bitten. Take me down . . . take me down, so that Oudot can see to me."

"It can't be done," said Terray sorrowfully. "Can't you see we're in the middle of a storm . . . It'll be dark soon."

But Lachenal was obsessed by the fear of amputation. With a gesture of despair he tore the axe out of Terray's hands and tried to force his way down; but soon saw the futility of his action and resolved to climb up to the camp. While Terray cut steps without stopping, Lachenal, ravaged and exhausted as he was, dragged himself along on all fours.

Meanwhile I had gone into Rébuffat's tent. He was appalled at the sight of my hands and, as rather incoherently I told him what we had done, he took a piece of rope and began flicking my fingers. Then he took off my boots with great difficulty for my feet were swollen, and beat my feet and rubbed me. We soon heard Terray giving Lachenal the same treatment in the other tent.

For our comrades it was a tragic moment: Annapurna was conquered, and the first eight-thousander had been climbed. Every one of us had been ready to sacrifice everything for this. Yet, as they looked at our feet and hands, what can Terray and Rébuffat have felt?

Outside the storm howled and the snow was still falling. The mist grew thick and darkness came. As on the previous night we had to cling to the poles to prevent the tents being carried away by the wind. The only two air-mattresses were given to Lachenal and myself while Terray and Rébuffat both sat on ropes, rucksacks, and provisions to keep themselves off the snow. They rubbed, slapped and beat us with a rope. Sometimes the blows fell on the living flesh, and howls arose from both tents. Rébuffat persevered; it was essential to continue painful as it was. Gradually life returned to my feet as well as to my hands, and circulation started again. Lachenal, too, found that feeling was returning.

Now Terray summoned up the energy to prepare some hot drinks. He called to Rébuffat that he would pass him a mug, so two hands stretched out towards each other between the two tents and were instantly covered with snow. The liquid was boiling though scarcely more than 60° centigrade (140° Fahrenheit). I swallowed it greedily and felt infinitely better.

The night was absolute hell. Frightful onslaughts of wind battered us incessantly, while the never-ceasing snow piled up on the tents.

Now and again I heard voices from next door—it was Terray massaging Lachenal with admirable perseverance, only stopping to ply him with hot drinks. In our tent Rébuffat was quite worn out, but satisfied that warmth was returning to my limbs.

Lying half unconscious I was scarcely aware of the passage of time. There were moments when I was able to see our situation in its true dramatic light, but the rest of the time I was plunged in an inexplicable stupor with no thought for the consequences of our victory.

As the night wore on the snow lay heavier on the tent, and once again I had the frightful feeling of being slowly and silently asphyxiated. I tried, with all the strength of which I was capable, to push off with both forearms the mass that was crushing me. These fearful exertions left me gasping for breath and I fell back into the same exhausted state. It was much worse than the previous night.

"Rébuffat! Gaston! Gaston!"

I recognized Terray's voice.

"Time to be off!"

I heard the sounds without grasping their meaning. Was it light already? I was not in the least surprised that the other two had given up all thought of going to the top, and I did not at all grasp the measure of their sacrifice.

Outside the storm redoubled in violence. The tent shook and the fabric flapped alarmingly. It had usually been fine in the mornings: did this mean the monsoon was upon us? We knew it was not far off—could this be its first onslaught?

"Gaston! Are you ready?" Terray called again.

"One minute," answered Rébuffat. He did not have an easy job: he had to put my boots on and do everything to get me ready. I let myself be handled like a baby. In the other tent Terray finished dressing Lachenal whose feet were still swollen and would not fit into his boots. So Terray gave him his own, which were bigger. To get Lachenal's on to his own feet he had to make slits in them. As a precaution he put a sleeping-bag and some food into his sack and shouted to us to do the same. Were his words lost in the storm? Or were we too intent on leaving this hellish place to listen to his instructions?

Lachenal and Terray were already outside.

"We're going down!" they shouted.

Then Rébuffat tied me on the rope and we went out. There were only two ice-axes for the four of us, so Rébuffat and Terray took them as a matter of course. For a moment as we left the two tents of Camp V, I felt childishly ashamed at leaving all this good equipment behind.

Already the first rope seemed a long way down below us. We were blinded by the squalls of snow and we could not hear each other a yard away. We had both put on our *cagoules,* for it was very cold. The snow was apt to slide and the rope often came in useful.

Ahead of us the other two were losing no time. Lachenal went first and, safeguarded by Terray, he forced the pace in his anxiety to get down. There were no tracks to show us the way, but it was engraved on all our minds—straight down the slope for 400 yards then traverse to the left for 150 to 200 yards to get to Camp IV. The snow was thinning and the wind less violent. Was it going to clear? We hardly dared to hope so. A wall of seracs brought us up short.

"It's to the left," I said, "I remember perfectly."

Somebody else thought it was to the right. We started going down again. The wind had dropped completely, but the snow fell in big flakes. The mist was thick, and, not to lose each other, we walked in line: I was third and I could barely see Lachenal who was first. It was impossible to recognize any of the pitches. We were all experienced enough mountaineers to know that even on familiar ground it is easy to make mistakes in such weather. Distances are deceptive, one cannot tell whether one is going up or down. We kept colliding with hummocks which we had taken for hollows. The mist, the falling snow-flakes, the carpet of snow, all merged into the same whitish tone and confused our vision. The towering outlines of the seracs took on fantastic shapes and seemed to move slowly around us.

Our situation was not desperate, we were certainly not lost. We would have to go lower down; the traverse must begin further on—I remembered the serac which served as a milestone. The snow stuck to our *cagoules,* and turned us into white phantoms noiselessly flitting against a background equally white. We began to sink in dreadfully, and there is nothing worse for bodies already on the edge of exhaustion.

Were we too high or too low? No one could tell. Perhaps we had better try slanting over to the left! The snow was in a dangerous condition, but we did not seem to realize it. We were forced to admit that we were not on the right route, so we retraced our steps and climbed up above the serac which overhung us. No doubt, we decided, we should be on the right level now. With Rébuffat leading, we went back over the way which had cost us such an effort. I followed him jerkily, saying nothing, and determined to go on to the end. If Rébuffat had fallen I could never have held him.

We went doggedly on from one serac to another. Each time we thought we had recognized the right route, and each time there was a fresh disappointment. If only the mist would lift, if only the snow would stop for a second! On the slope it seemed to be growing deeper every minute. Only Terray and Rébuffat were capable of breaking the trail and they relieved each other at regular intervals, without a word and without a second's hesitation.

I admired this determination of Rébuffat's for which he is so justly famed. He did not intend to die! With the strength of desperation and at the price of super-human effort he forged ahead. The slowness of his progress would have dismayed even the most obstinate climber, but he would not give up, and in the end the mountain yielded in face of his perseverance.

Terray, when his turn came, charged madly ahead. He was like a force of nature: at all costs he would break down these prison walls that penned us in. His physical strength was exceptional, his will power no less remarkable. Lachenal gave him considerable trouble. Perhaps he was not quite in his right mind. He said it was no use going on; we must dig a hole in the snow and wait for fine weather. He swore at Terray and called him a madman. Nobody but Terray would have been capable of dealing with him—he just tugged sharply on the rope and Lachenal was forced to follow.

We were well and truly lost.

The weather did not seem likely to improve. A minute ago we had still had ideas about which way to go—now we had none. This way or that . . . We went on at random to allow for the chance of a miracle which appeared increasingly unlikely. The instinct of self-preservation in the two fit members of the party alternated with a hopelessness which made them completely irresponsible. Each in turn did the maddest things: Terray traversed the steep and avalanchy slopes with one crampon badly adjusted. He and Rébuffat performed incredible feats of balance without the least slip.

Camp IV was certainly on the left, on the edge of the Sickle. On that point we were all agreed. But it was very hard to find. The wall of ice that gave it such magnificent protection was now ironical, for it hid the tents from us. In mist like this we should have to be right on top of them before we spotted them.

Perhaps if we called, someone would hear us? Lachenal gave the signal, but snow absorbs sound and his shout seemed to carry only a few yards. All four of us called out together: "One . . . two . . . three . . . Help!"

We got the impression that our united shout carried a long way, so we began again: "One . . . two . . . three . . . Help!" Not a sound in reply!

Now and again Terray took off his boots and rubbed his feet; the sight of our frost-bitten limbs had made him aware of the danger and he had the strength of mind to do something about it. Like Lachenal, he was haunted by the idea of amputation. For me, it was too late: my feet and hands, already affected from yesterday, were beginning to freeze up again.

We had eaten nothing since the day before, and we had been on the go the whole time, but men's resources of energy in face of death are inexhaustible. When the end seems imminent, there still remain reserves, though it needs tremendous will power to call them up.

Time passed, but we had no idea how long. Night was approaching, and we were terrified, though none of us made any complaint. Rébuffat and I found a way that we thought we remembered, but were brought to a halt by the extreme steepness of the slope—the mist turned it into a vertical wall. We were to find next day that at that moment we had been only thirty yards from the camp, and that the wall was the very one that sheltered the tent which would have been our salvation.

"We must find a crevasse."

"We can't stay here all night!"

"A hole—it's the only thing."

"We'll all die in it."

Night had suddenly fallen and it was essential to come to a decision without wasting another minute; if we remained on the slope, we should be dead before morning. We would have to bivouac. What the conditions would be like, we could guess, for we all knew what it meant to bivouac above 23,000 feet.

With his axe Terray began to dig a hole. Lachenal went over to a snow-filled crevasse a few yards further on, then suddenly let out a yell and disappeared before our eyes. We stood helpless: should we, or rather would Terray and Rébuffat, have enough strength for all the maneuvers with the rope that would be needed to get him out? The crevasse was completely blocked up save for the one little hole which Lachenal had fallen through.

"Lachenal!" called Terray.

A voice, muffled by many thicknesses of ice and snow, came up to us. It was impossible to make out what it was saying.

"Lachenal!"

Terray jerked the rope violently; this time we could hear.

"I'm here!"

"Anything broken?"

"No! It'll do for the night! Come along."

This shelter was heaven-sent. None of us would have had the strength to dig a hole big enough to protect the lot of us from the wind. Without hesitation Terray let himself drop into the crevasse, and a loud "Come on!" told us he had arrived safely. In my turn I let myself go: it was a regular toboggan-slide. I shot down a sort of twisting tunnel, very steep, and about thirty feet long. I came out at great speed into the opening beyond and was literally hurled to the bottom of the crevasse. We let Rébuffat know he could come by giving a tug on the rope.

The intense cold of this minute grotto shriveled us up, the enclosing walls of ice were damp and the floor a carpet of fresh snow; by huddling together there was just room for the four of us. Icicles hung from the ceiling and we broke some of them off to make more head room and kept little bits to suck—it was a long time since we had had anything to drink.

That was our shelter for the night. At least we should be protected from the wind, and the temperature would remain fairly even, though the damp was extremely unpleasant. We settled ourselves in the dark as best we could. As always in a bivouac we took off our boots; without this precaution the constriction would cause immediate frost-bite. Terray unrolled the sleeping-bag which he had had the foresight to bring, and settled himself in relative comfort. We put on everything warm that we had, and to avoid contact with the snow I sat on the movie camera. We huddled close up to each other, in our search for a hypothetical position in which the warmth of our bodies could be combined without loss, but we couldn't keep still for a second.

We did not open our mouths—signs were less of an effort than words. Every man withdrew into himself and took refuge in his own inner world. Terray massaged Lachenal's feet; Rébuffat felt his feet freezing too, but he had sufficient strength to rub them himself. I remained motionless, unseeing. My feet and hands went on freezing, but what could be done? I attempted to forget suffering by withdrawing into myself, trying to forget the passing of time, trying not to feel the devouring and numbing cold which insidiously gained upon us.

Terray shared his sleeping-bag with Lachenal, putting his feet and hands inside the precious eiderdown. At the same time he went on rubbing.

Anyhow the frost-bite won't spread further, he was thinking.

None of us could make any movement without upsetting the others, and the positions we had taken up with such care were continually being altered so that we had to start all over again. This kept us busy. Rébuffat persevered with his rubbing and complained of his feet; like Terray he was thinking: We mustn't look beyond tomorrow—afterwards we'll see. But he was not blind to the fact that "afterwards" was one big question-mark.

Terray generously tried to give me part of his sleeping-bag. He had understood the seriousness of my condition, and knew why it was that I said nothing and remained quite passive; he realized that I had abandoned all hope for myself. He massaged me for nearly two hours; his feet, too, might have frozen, but he didn't appear to give the matter a thought. I found new courage simply in contemplating his unselfishness; he was doing so much to help me that it would have been ungrateful of me not to go on struggling to live. Though my heart was like a lump of ice itself, I was astonished to feel no pain. Everything material about me seemed to have dropped away. I seemed to be quite clear in my thoughts and yet I floated in a kind of peaceful happiness. There was still a breath of life in me, but it dwindled steadily as the hours went by. Terray's massage no longer had any effect upon me. All was over, I thought. Wasn't this cavern the most beautiful grave I could hope for? Death caused me no grief, no regret—I smiled at the thought.

After hours of torpor a voice mumbled "Daylight!"

This made some impression on the others. I only felt surprised—I had not thought that daylight would penetrate so far down.

"Too early to start," said Rébuffat.

A ghastly light spread through our grotto and we could just vaguely make out the shapes of each other's heads. A queer noise from a long way off came down to us—a sort of prolonged hiss. The noise increased. Suddenly I was buried, blinded, smothered beneath an avalanche of new snow. The icy snow spread over the cavern, finding its way through every gap in our clothing. I ducked my head between my knees and covered myself with both arms. The snow flowed on and on. There was a terrible silence. We were not completely buried, but there was snow everywhere. We got up, taking care not to bang our heads against the ceiling of ice, and tried to shake ourselves. We were all in our stockinged feet in the snow. The first thing to do was to find our boots.

Rébuffat and Terray began to search, and realized at once that they were blind. Yesterday they had taken off their glasses to lead us down and now they were paying for it. Lachenal was the first to lay hands upon a pair of boots. He tried to put them on, but they were Rébuffat's. Rébuffat attempted to climb up the chute down which we had come yesterday, and which the avalanche had followed in its turn.

"Hi, Gaston! What's the weather like?" called up Terray.

"Can't see a thing. It's blowing hard."

We were still groping for our things. Terray found his boots and put them on awkwardly, unable to see what he was doing. Lachenal helped him, but he was all on edge and fearfully impatient, in striking contrast to my immobility. Terray then went up the icy channel, puffing and blowing, and at last reached the outer world. He was met by terrible gusts of wind that cut right through him and lashed his face.

Bad weather, he said to himself, this time it's the end. We're lost . . . we'll never come through.

At the bottom of the crevasse there were still two of us looking for our boots. Lachenal poked fiercely with an ice-axe. I was calmer and tried to proceed more rationally. We extracted crampons and an axe in turn from the snow, but still no boots.

Well—so this cavern was to be our last resting-place! There was very little room—we were bent double and got in each other's way. Lachenal decided to go out without his boots. He called frantically, hauled himself up on the rope, trying to get a hold or to wiggle his way up, digging his toes into the snow walls. Terray from outside pulled as hard as he could. I watched him go; he gathered speed and disappeared.

When he emerged from the opening he saw the sky was clear and blue, and he began to run like a madman, shrieking, "It's fine, it's fine!"

I set to work again to search the cave. The boots *had* to be found, or Lachenal and I were done for. On all fours, with nothing on my hands or feet I raked the snow, stirring it around this way and that, hoping every second to come upon something hard. I was no longer capable of thinking—I reacted like an animal fighting for its life.

I found one boot! The other was tied to it—a pair! Having ransacked the whole cave I at last found the other pair. But in spite of all my efforts I could not find the movie camera, and gave up in despair. There was no question of putting my boots on—my hands were like lumps of wood and I could hold nothing in my fingers; my feet were very swollen—I should never be able to get boots on them. I twisted the rope around the boots as well as I could and called up the chute:

"Lionel . . . Boots!"

There was no answer, but he must have heard for with a jerk the precious boots shot up. Soon after the rope came down again. My turn. I wound the rope around me. I could not pull it tight so I made a whole series of little knots. Their combined strength, I hoped, would be enough to hold me. I had no strength to shout again; I gave a great tug on the rope, and Terray understood.

At the first step I had to kick a notch in the hard snow for my toes. Further on I expected to be able to get up more easily by wedging myself across the runnel. I wriggled up a few yards like this and then I tried to dig my hands and my feet into the wall. My hands were stiff and hard right up to the wrists and my feet had no feeling up to the ankles, the joints were inflexible and this hampered me greatly.

Somehow or other I succeeded in working my way up, while Terray pulled so hard he nearly choked me. I began to see more distinctly and so knew that I must be nearing the opening. Often I fell back, but I clung on and wedged myself in again as best I could. My heart was bursting and I was forced to rest. A fresh wave of energy enabled me to crawl to the top. I pulled myself out by clutching Terray's legs; he was just about all in and I was in the last stages of exhaustion. Terray was close to me and I whispered:

"Lionel . . . I'm dying!"

He supported me and helped me away from the crevasse. Lachenal and Rébuffat were sitting in the snow a few yards away. The instant Lionel let go of me I sank down and dragged myself along on all fours.

The weather was perfect. Quantities of snow had fallen the day before and the mountains were resplendent. Never had I seen them look so beautiful—our last day would be magnificent.

Rébuffat and Terray were completely blind; as he came along with me Terray knocked into things and I had to direct him. Rébuffat, too, could not move a step without guidance. It was terrifying to be blind when there was danger all around. Lachenal's frozen feet affected his nervous system. His behavior was disquieting—he was possessed by the most fantastic ideas:

"I tell you we must go down . . . down there . . ."

"You've nothing on your feet!"

"Don't worry about that."

"You're off your head. The way's not there . . . it's to the left!"

He was already standing up; he wanted to go straight down to the bottom of the glacier. Terray held him back, made him sit down, and though he couldn't see, helped Lachenal put his boots on.

Behind them I was living in my own private dream. I knew the end was near, but it was the end that all mountaineers wish for—an end in keeping with their ruling passion. I was consciously grateful to the mountains for being so beautiful for me that day, and as awed by their silence as if I had been in church. I was in no pain, and had no worry. My utter calmness was alarming. Terray came staggering towards me, and I told him: "It's all over for me. Go on . . . you have a chance . . . you must take it . . . over to the left . . . that's the way."

I felt better after telling him that. But Terray would have none of it: "We'll help you. If we get away, so will you."

At this moment Lachenal shouted: "Help! Help!"

Obviously he didn't know what he was doing . . . Or did he? He was the only one of the four of us who could see Camp II down below. Perhaps his calls would be heard. They were shrieks of despair, reminding me tragically of some climbers lost in the Mont Blanc massif whom I had endeavored to save. Now it was our turn. The impression was vivid: we were lost.

I joined in with the others: "One . . . two . . . three . . . *Help!* One . . . two . . . three . . . *Help!*" We tried to shout together, but without much success; our voices could not have carried more than ten feet. The noise I made was more of a whisper than a shout. Terray insisted that I should put my boots on, but my hands were dead. Neither Rébuffat nor Terray, who were unable to see, could help much, so I said to Lachenal: "Come and help me to put my boots on."

"Don't be silly, we must go down!"

And off he went once again in the wrong direction, straight down. I was not in the least angry with him; he had been sorely tried by the altitude and by everything he had gone through.

Terray resolutely got out his knife, and with fumbling hands slit the uppers of my boots back and front. Split in two like this I could get them on, but it was not easy and I had to make several attempts. Soon I lost heart—what was the use of it all anyway since I was going to stay where I was? But Terray pulled violently and finally he succeeded. He laced up my now gigantic boots, missing half the hooks. I was ready now. But how was I going to walk with my stiff joints?

"To the left, Lionel!"

"You're crazy, Maurice," said Lachenal, "it's to the right, straight down."

Terray did not know what to think of these conflicting views. He had not given up like me, he was going to fight; but what, at the moment, could he do? The three of them discussed which way to go.

I remained sitting in the snow. Gradually my mind lost grip—why should I struggle? I would just let myself drift. I saw pictures of shady slopes, peaceful paths, there was a scent of resin. It was pleasant—I was going to die in my own mountains. My body had no feeling—everything was frozen.

"Aah . . . aah!"

Was it a groan or a call? I gathered my strength for one cry: "They're coming!" The others heard me and shouted for joy. What a miraculous apparition! "Schatz . . . it's Schatz!"

Barely two hundred yards away Marcel Schatz, waist-deep in snow, was coming slowly towards us like a boat on the surface of the slope. I found this vision of a strong and invincible deliverer inexpressibly moving. I expected everything of him. The shock was violent, and quite shattered me. Death clutched at me and I gave myself up.

When I came to again the wish to live returned and I experienced a violent revulsion of feeling. All was not lost! As Schatz came nearer my eyes never left him for a second—twenty yards—ten yards—he came straight towards me. Why? Without a word he leaned over me, held me close, hugged me, and his warm breath revived me.

I could not make the slightest movement—I was like marble. My heart was overwhelmed by such tremendous feelings and yet my eyes remained dry.

"It is wonderful—what you have done!"

Chapter XV

The Avalanche

I WAS CLEAR-HEADED AND DELIRIOUS BY TURNS, AND HAD THE QUEER FEELING that my eyes were glazed. Schatz looked after me like a mother, and while the others were shouting with joy, he put his rope around me. The sky was blue—the deep blue of extreme altitude, so dark that one can almost see the stars—and we were bathed in the warm rays of the sun. Schatz spoke gently:

"We'll be moving now, Maurice, old man."

I could not help obeying him, and with his assistance succeeded in getting up and standing in balance. He moved on gradually, pulling me after him. I seemed to make contact with the snow by means of two strange stilt-like objects—my legs. I could no longer see the others; I did not dare to turn around for fear of losing my balance, and I was dazzled by the reflection of the sun's rays.

Having walked about a couple of hundred yards, and skirted around an ice wall, suddenly, and without any sort of warning we came upon a tent. We had bivouacked two hundred yards from the camp. Couzy got up as I appeared, and without speaking held me close and embraced me. Terray threw himself down in the tent and took off his boots. His feet, too, were frost-bitten; he massaged them and beat them unmercifully.

The will to live stirred again in me. I tried to take in the situation: there was not much that we could do—but we would do whatever was possible. Our only hope lay in Dr. Oudot; only he could save our feet and hands by the proper treatment. I heartily agreed to Schatz's suggestion that we should go down immediately to the lower Camp IV which the Sherpas had re-established. Terray wanted to remain in the tent, and as he flailed his feet with the energy of despair he cried out:

"Come and fetch me tomorrow if necessary. I want to be whole, or dead!"

Rébuffat's feet were affected too, but he preferred to go down to Oudot immediately. He started the descent with Lachenal and Couzy, while Schatz continued to look after me—for which I was deeply grateful. He took the rope and propelled me gently along the track. The slope suddenly became very steep, and the thin layer of snow adhering to the surface of the ice gave no foothold; I slipped several times, but Schatz, holding me on a tight rope, was able to check me.

Below there was a broad track: no doubt the others had let themselves slide straight down towards the lower Camp IV, but they had started an avalanche which had swept the slope clear of snow, and this hardly made things easier for me. As soon as we drew in sight of the camp the Sherpas came up to meet us. In their eyes I read such kindliness and such pity that I began to realize my dreadful plight. They were busy clearing the tents which the avalanche had covered with snow. Lachenal was in a corner massaging his feet; from time to time Pansy comforted him, saying that the Doctor Sahib would cure him.

I hurried everyone—we must get down—that was our first objective. As for the equipment, well it could not be helped; we simply must get off the mountain before the next onslaught of the monsoon. For those of us with frostbitten limbs it was a matter of hours. I chose Aila and Sarki to escort Rébuffat, Lachenal and myself. I tried to make the two Sherpas understand that they must watch me very closely and hold me on a short rope. For some unknown reason, neither Lachenal nor Rébuffat wished to rope.

While we started down, Schatz, with Ang-Tharkey and Pansy, went up to fetch Terray who had remained on the glacier above. Schatz was master of the situation—none of the others were capable of taking the slightest initiative. After a hard struggle he found Terray:

"You can get ready in a minute," he said.

"I'm beginning to feel my feet again," replied Terray, now more amenable to reason.

"I'm going to have a look in the crevasse. Maurice couldn't find the camera and it's got all the shots he took high up."

Terray made no reply; he had not really understood, and it was only several days later that we fully realized Schatz's heroism. He spent a long time searching the snow at the bottom of the cavern, while Terray began to get anxious. At last he returned triumphantly carrying the camera which contained the views taken from the summit. He also found my ice-axe and various other things, but no movie camera. So our last film shots would stop at 23,000 feet.

The descent began—Ang-Tharkey was magnificent, going first and cutting comfortable steps for Terray. Schatz, coming down last, carefully safeguarded the whole party.

Our first group was advancing slowly. The snow was soft and we sank in up to our knees. Lachenal grew worse: he frequently stopped and moaned about his feet. Rébuffat was a few yards behind me.

I was concerned at the abnormal heat, and feared that bad weather would put an end here and now to the epic of Annapurna. It is said that mountaineers have a sixth sense that warns them of danger—suddenly I became aware of danger through every pore of my body. There was a feeling in the atmosphere that could not be ignored. Yesterday it had snowed heavily, and the heat was now working on these great masses of snow which were on the point of sliding off. Nothing in Europe can give any idea of the force of these avalanches. They roll down over a distance of miles and are preceded by a blast that destroys everything in its path.

The glare was so terrific that without glasses it would have been impossible to keep one's eyes open. By good luck we were fairly well spaced out, so that the risk was diminished. The Sherpas no longer remembered the different pitches and oftentimes, with great difficulty, I had to take the lead and be let down on the end of the rope to find the right way. I had no crampons and I could not grasp an axe. We lost height far too slowly for my liking, and it worried me to see my Sherpas going so slowly and carefully and at the same time so insecurely. In actual fact they went very well, but I was so impatient I could no longer judge their performance fairly.

Lachenal was a long way behind us and every time I turned around he was sitting down in the track. He, too, was affected by snow-blindness, though not so badly as Terray and Rébuffat, and he found difficulty in seeing his way. Rébuffat went ahead by guess-work, with agony in his face, but he kept on. We crossed the couloir without incident, and I congratulated myself that we had passed the danger zone.

The sun was at its height, the weather brilliant and the colors magnificent. Never had the mountains appeared to me so majestic as in this moment of extreme danger.

All at once a crack appeared in the snow under the feet of the Sherpas, and grew longer and wider. A mad idea flashed into my head—to climb up the slope at speed and reach solid ground. Then I was lifted up by a superhuman force, and, as the Sherpas disappeared before my eyes, I went head over heels. I could not see what was happening. My head hit the ice. In spite of my efforts I could no longer breathe, and a violent blow on my left thigh caused me acute pain. I turned round and round like a puppet. In a flash I saw the blinding light of the sun through the snow which was pouring past my eyes. The rope joining me to Sarki and Aila curled round my neck—the Sherpas shooting down the slope beneath would shortly strangle me, and the pain was unbearable. Again and again I crashed into solid ice as I went hurtling from one serac to another, and the snow crushed me down. The rope tightened around my neck and brought me to a stop. Before I had recovered my wits I began to pass water, violently and uncontrollably.

I opened my eyes to find myself hanging head downwards with the rope around my neck and my left leg, in a sort of hatchway of blue ice. I put out my elbows towards the walls in an attempt to stop the unbearable pendulum motion which sent me from one side to the other, and I caught a glimpse of the last slopes of the couloir beneath me. My breathing steadied, and I blessed the rope which had stood the strain of the shock.

I simply *had* to try to get myself out. My feet and hands were numb, but I was able to make use of some little nicks in the wall. There was room for at least the edges of my boots. By frenzied jerky movements I succeeded in freeing my left leg from the rope, and then managed to right myself and to climb up a yard or two. After every move I stopped, convinced that I had come to the end of my physical strength, and that in a second I should have to let go.

One more desperate effort, and I gained a few inches. I pulled on the rope and felt something give at the other end—no doubt the bodies of the Sherpas. I called, but hardly a whisper issued from my lips. There was a death-like silence. Where was Rébuffat?

Conscious of a shadow, as from a passing cloud, I looked up instinctively, and low and behold! Two scared black faces were framed against the circle of blue sky. Aila and Sarki! They were safe and sound, and at once set to work to rescue me. I was incapable of giving them the slightest advice. Aila disappeared, leaving Sarki alone at the edge of the hole; they began to pull on the rope, slowly, so as not to hurt me, and I was hauled up with a power and steadiness that gave me fresh courage. At last I was out. I collapsed on the snow.

The rope had caught over a ridge of ice and we had been suspended on either side. By good luck the weight of the two Sherpas and my own had balanced. If we had not been checked like this we should have hurtled down for another 1500 feet. There was chaos all around us. Where was Rébuffat? I was mortally anxious, for he was unroped. Looking up I caught sight of him less than a hundred yards away:

"Anything broken?" he called out to me.

I was greatly relieved, but I had no strength to reply. Lying flat, and semi-conscious, I gazed at the wreckage about me with unseeing eyes. We had been carried down for about 500 feet. It was not a healthy place to linger in—suppose another avalanche should fall! I instructed the Sherpas:

"Now—Doctor Sahib. Quick, very quick!"

By gestures, I tried to make them understand that they must hold me very firm. In doing this I found that my left arm was practically useless. I could not move it at all, the elbow had seized up—was it broken? We should see later. Now, we must push on to Oudot.

Rébuffat started down to join us, moving slowly; he had to place his feet by feel alone. Seeing him walk like this made my heart ache; he too had fallen and he must have hit something with his jaw, for blood was oozing from the corners of his mouth. Like me, he had lost his glasses and we were forced to shut our eyes. Aila had an old spare pair which did very well for me, and without a second's hesitation Sarki gave his own to Rébuffat.

We had to get down at once. The Sherpas helping me up, I advanced as best I could, reeling about in the most alarming fashion, but they realized now that they must hold me from behind. I skirted round the avalanche to our old track which started again a little further on.

We now came to the first wall. How on earth should we get down? Again, I asked the Sherpas to hold me firmly:

"Hold me well because . . ."

And I showed them my hands.

"Yes, sir," they replied together like good pupils. I came to the piton; the fixed rope attached to it hung down the wall and I had to hold on to it—there was no other way. It was terrible; my wooden feet kept slipping on the ice wall, and I could not grasp the thin line in my hands. Without letting go I endeavored to wind it around my hands, but they were swollen and the skin broke in several places. Great strips of it came away and stuck to the rope and the flesh was laid bare. Yet I had to go on down, I could not give up halfway.

"Aila! *Pay attention! . . . Pay attention!*"

To save my hands I now let the rope slide over my good forearm and lowered myself like this in jerks. On reaching the bottom I fell about three feet and the rope wrenched my forearm and my wrists. The jolt was severe and affected my feet. I heard a queer crack and supposed I must have broken something—no doubt it was the frost-bite that prevented me from feeling any pain.

Rébuffat and the Sherpas came down and we went on but it all seemed to take an unconscionably long time, and the plateau of Camp II seemed a long way off. I was just about at the limit of my strength. Every minute I felt like giving up; and why, anyway, should I go on when for me everything was over? My conscience was quite easy: everyone was safe, and the others would all get down. Far away below I could see the tents. Just one more hour—I gave myself one more hour and then, wherever I was, I would lie down in the snow. I would let myself go, peacefully. I would be through with it all, and could sleep content.

Setting this limit somehow cheered me on. I kept slipping, and on the steep slope the Sherpas could hardly hold me—it was miraculous that they did. The track stopped above a drop—the second and bigger of the walls we had equipped with a fixed rope. I tried to make up my mind, but I could not begin to see how I was going to get down. I pulled off the glove I had on one hand, and the red silk scarf that hid the other, which was covered with blood. This time everything was at stake—and my fingers could just look after themselves. I placed Sarki and Aila on the stance from which I had been accustomed to belay them, and where the two of them would be able to take the strain of my rope by standing firmly braced against each other. I tried to take hold of the fixed rope; both my hands were bleeding, but I had no pity to spare for myself and I took the rope between my thumb and forefinger, and started off. At the first move I was faced at once with a painful decision: if I let go, we should all fall to the bottom: if I held on what would remain of my hands? I decided to hold on.

Every inch was a torture I was resolved to ignore. The sight of my hands made me feel sick; the flesh was laid bare and red, and the rope was covered with blood. I tried not to tear the strips right off: other accidents had taught me that one must preserve these bits to hasten the healing process later on. I tried to save my hands by braking with my stomach, my shoulders, and every other possible point of contact. When would this agony come to an end?

I came down to the nose of ice which I myself had cut away with my axe on the ascent. I felt about with my legs—it was all hard. There was no snow beneath. I was not yet down. In panic I called up to the Sherpas:

"Quick . . . Aila . . . Sarki . . . !"

They let my rope out more quickly and the friction on the fixed rope increased.

My hands were in a ghastly state. It felt as though all the flesh was being torn off. At last I was aware of something beneath my feet—the ledge. I had made it! I had to go along it now, always held by the rope; only three yards, but they were the trickiest of all. It was over. I collapsed, up to the waist in snow—no longer conscious of time.

When I half-opened my eyes Rébuffat and the Sherpas were beside me, and I could distinctly see black dots moving about near the tents of

Camp II. Sarki spoke to me, and pointed out two Sherpas coming up to meet us. They were still a long way off, but all the same it cheered me up.

I had to rouse myself; things were getting worse and worse. The frost-bite seemed to be gaining ground—up to my calves and my elbows. Sarki put my glasses on for me again, although the weather had turned gray. He put one glove on as best he could; but my left hand was in such a frightful state that it made him sick to look at it, and he tried to hide it in my red scarf.

The fantastic descent continued and I was sure that every step would be my last. Through the swirling mist I sometimes caught glimpses of the two Sherpas coming up. They had already reached the base of the avalanche cone, and when, from the little platform I had just reached, I saw them stop there, it sapped all my courage.

Snow began to fall, and we now had to make a long traverse over very unsafe ground where it was difficult to guard anyone; then, fifty yards further, we came to the avalanche cone. I recognized Foutharkey and Angawa mounting rapidly towards us. Evidently they expected bad news, and Angawa must have been thinking of his two brothers, Aila and Pansy. The former was with us all right—he could see him in the flesh—but what about Pansy? Even at this distance they started to ask questions, and by the time we reached them they knew everything. I heaved a deep sigh of relief. I felt now as if I had laid down a burden so heavy that I had nearly given way beneath it. Foutharkey was beside me, smiling affectionately. How can anyone call such people "primitive," or say that the rigors of their existence take away all sense of pity? The Sherpas rushed towards me, put down their sacks, uncorked their flasks. Ah, just to drink a few mouthfuls! Nothing more. It had all been such a long time . . .

Foutharkey lowered his eyes to my hands and lifted them again, almost with embarrassment. With infinite sorrow, he whispered: "Poor Bara Sahib—Ah . . ."

These reinforcements gave me a fresh access of courage, and Camp II was near. Foutharkey supported me, and Angawa safeguarded us both. Foutharkey was small and I hung on around his neck and leaned on his shoulders, gripping him close. This contact comforted me and his warmth gave me strength. I staggered down with little jerky steps, leaning more and more on Foutharkey. Would I ever have the strength to make it even with his help? Rousing what seemed my very last ounce of energy, I begged Foutharkey to give me yet more help. He took my glasses off and I could see better then. Just a few more steps—the very last . . .

At Camp II Marcel Ichac had been following our movements for the past two days, noting down the sequence of events minute by minute. Here are some extracts from his log:

Saturday June 3[25] (I)—Camp II:

Oudot and Noyelle left at nine o'clock;[26] at ten-thirty Noyelle arrived back. Something to do with the oxygen? Possibly the mask didn't allow a sufficient flow? Oudot and the three Sherpas are going very slowly up the funnel. Meanwhile I am playing hide and seek with the clouds looking through the telescope of the theodolite, and also watching the parties above the seracs of the Sickle through field glasses. There are four of them; Lionel and Rébuffat, and behind them Couzy and Schatz.

No sign of Maurice. He must be on the final slopes which are less steep, and so invisible from here. The wind is blowing the powder snow violently. But he can't be far from the summit now, perhaps even . . .

Sunday June 4

A dull day. Snow fell during the night—sleet then fine snow with a strong north wind. Annapurna is hidden in the mist. Tired and anxious. What's happening to the others?

By midday eight inches of powder snow. Continual avalanches, visibility zero.

Heard voices about four o'clock and in the mist, which continues for about a hundred yards below the camp, four forms appeared—Oudot and his three Sherpas. Obviously sinking in up to their waists. Nothing to do but to get boiling water ready for them.

They arrived at seven o'clock: that morning Oudot had remained in his tent. Towards one o'clock the bad weather got worse and Adjiba had come to him and said: "It's the monsoon! If we stay here we're done for."

Monday June 5

Will today end better than it has begun? What alarms there have been—for us, anyway! At one time I thought Oudot and myself were the sole survivors of the party of eight who left Le Bourget on March 30!

At six o'clock thought I heard someone calling and went outside: the sun was rising through threatening clouds. Nothing to be seen. Got back into my sleeping bag; immediately heard two distinct shouts and through the field-glasses saw two men on a patch of ice at the height of Camp IV, but well over to the left. They kept on shouting and signalling with their arms. Who could they be? Oudot thought Schatz and Couzy. Their immobility— particularly one of them—was most alarming. Frostbitten feet no doubt. What did they want? Normally it takes six hours to get up so far in fine weather. But in powder snow and with the monsoon striking repeatedly . . . They're still shouting . . . things are getting urgent. Where are the other eight? Higher up near the summit? Their position must be pretty precarious at Camp IV, but what can they be waiting for to descend to Camp III?

8 o'clock: *Oudot is preparing a rescue party. He has no ice-pitons, etc. . . . . Noyelle is going down to Camp I with Adjiba to bring up reinforcements (equipment and Dawatondu). Up here the Sherpas are uneasy. Three of them belong to the same family: Pansy, Aila and Angawa.*

8.30: *Shouting continues. On the off-chance I'm tracing out the letters "VU" in the snow. A few minutes later a man moves quickly towards the seracs which must shelter Camp IV. He's stopped three hundred yards away from it—on the same level—is making signs and has now gone back again. The others are getting up, apparently without difficulty, and are traversing across to Camp IV. Not two of them but four.*

So there are four, plus the one who went to meet them plus his companion or companions. The position of Camp IV near the funnel of the Sickle is more sheltered, and from there one can get down quickly to Camp III or Camp II. The avalanches have now stopped.

9.30: *Saw Noyelle arrive at Camp I.*

10 o'clock: *At last—three men have appeared in the funnel of the Sickle coming down towards Camp III (one Sahib, two Sherpas?).*

Miraculously the weather is holding, with a west wind. Annapurna is completely clear—if only it lasts!

11 o'clock: Two men, unroped and therefore Sahibs, appear and come quickly down the former party's track. At the pace they're going, they should be here by evening. At last we'll know everything!

11.15: A man has appeared exactly at the spot where we saw one this morning, going towards *Camp V. He has stopped and is evidently looking up. His appearance is comforting in one way, for he is certainly not alone at Camp IV. So that he and his probable companion make two, plus those coming down—three and two—seven in all. It looks, then, as if one party must still be somewhere higher up.*

12.20: I'm watching the group of four crossing a very steep slope above Camp III. Behind them is one man alone, lagging a bit. Now, very high up, another man has just left Camp IV and is quickly descending: perhaps one of those I saw a short time ago? Suddenly a cloud of snow—like a volcano—appears to spurt out beneath the feet of the four near Camp III. They are knocked down and go rolling over and over. Then the avalanche passes on, leaving three figures stretched out on the snow; the lowest, who has been swept down 150 feet,[27] is now climbing up the slope again; now two more—ah, thank goodness!—they have separated and revealed a fourth. So they are all safe.

Our Sherpas have realized what's happened. Angawa and Foutharkey have gone off to meet them with ice-axes and glasses which they have lost. The others are continuing to descend. At three o'clock they meet the two Sherpas at the top of the avalanche cone. At last we shall know everything.

We were now quite near the tents of Camp II and Ichac, Noyelle and Oudot rushed up to meet us. I was in a fever to tell them the good news.

"We're back from Annapurna," I shouted. "We got to the top yesterday, Lachenal and I." Then, after a pause: "My feet and hands are frost-bitten."

They all helped me; Ichac held something out to me, and Noyelle supported me, while Oudot was examining my injuries.

My responsibility was now at an end. We had succeeded, and I knew that the others would all be with us in a few minutes.

We were saved! We had conquered Annapurna, and we had retreated in order. It was now for the others to take the initiative, above all, Dr. Oudot, in whom lay our only hope. I would put myself entirely in their hands; I would trust myself to their devotion. Henceforth only one thing would count—the victory that we had brought back, that would remain forever with us as a miraculous consolation. The others must organize our retreat and bring us back as best they could to the soil of France.

My friends all rallied around—they unwrapped my hands, took off my *cagoule;* and settled me into a tent already prepared to receive us. I found this simplification intensely comforting; I appreciated my new existence which, though it would be short-lived, was for the moment so easy and pleasant. In spite of the threatening weather the others were not long in arriving: Rébuffat was the first—his toes were frost-bitten, which made it difficult for him to walk and he looked ghastly, with a trickle of blood from his lips, and signs of suffering written large on his face. They undressed him and put him in a tent to await treatment.

Lachenal was still a long way off. Blind, exhausted, with his frost-bitten feet, how could he manage to follow such a rough and dangerous track? In fact, he got over the little crevasse by letting himself slide down on his back. Couzy caught up with him on his way down and, although desperately weary himself, gave him invaluable assistance.

Lionel Terray followed closely behind them, held on a rope by Schatz, who was still in fine fettle. The little group drew nearer to the camp. The first man to arrive was Terray, and Marcel Ichac went up towards the great cone to meet him. Terray's appearance was pitiful. He was blind, and clung to Ang-Tharkey as he walked. He had a huge beard and his face was distorted by pain into a dreadful grin. This "strong man," this elemental force of nature who could barely drag himself along, cried out:

"But I'm still all right. If I could see properly, I'd come down by myself."

When he reached camp, Oudot and Noyelle were aghast. Once so strong, he was now helpless and exhausted; his appearance moved them almost to tears.

Immediately after, Schatz and Couzy arrived, and then Lachenal, practically carried by two Sherpas. From a distance it looked as though he was pedaling along in the air, for he threw his legs out in front in a most disordered way. His head lolled backwards and was covered with a bandage. His features were lined with fatigue and spoke of suffering and sacrifice. He could not have gone on for another hour. Like myself, he had set a limit which had helped him to hold on until now. And yet Biscante, at such a moment, still had the spirit to say to Ichac:

"Want to see how a Chamonix guide comes down from the Himalaya?"

Ichac's only reply was to hold out to him a piece of sugar soaked in adrenalin.

It was painful to watch Terray groping for the tent six inches from his nose: he held both hands out in front of him feeling for obstacles. He was helped in, and he lay down; then Lachenal, too, was laid gently on a mattress.

Chapter XVI

The Retreat

EVERYONE WAS NOW OFF THE MOUNTAIN AND ASSEMBLED AT CAMP II. BUT IN what a state! It was Oudot's turn to take the initiative, and he made a rapid tour of inspection. Faced with the appalling sight that we presented, his countenance reflected, now the consternation of the friend, now the surgeon's impersonal severity.

He examined me first. My limbs were numb up to well beyond the ankles and wrists. My hands were in a frightful condition; there was practically no skin left, the little that remained was black, and long strips dangled down. My fingers were both swollen and distorted. My feet were scarcely any better: the entire soles were brown and violet, and completely without feeling. The arm which was hurting me, and which I was afraid might be broken, did not appear to be seriously injured, and my neck was all right.

I was anxious to have Oudot's first impression.

"What do you think of it all?" I asked him, ready to hear the worst.

"It's pretty serious. You'll probably lose part of your feet and hands. At present I can't say more than that."

"Do you think you'll be able to save something?"

"Yes, I'm sure of it. I'll do all I can."

This was not encouraging, and I was convinced that my feet and hands would have to be amputated.

Oudot took my blood pressure and seemed rather concerned. There was no pressure in the right arm, and the needle did not respond at all on my left arm. On my legs the needle oscillated slightly, indicating a restricted flow of blood. After putting a dressing over my eyes to prevent the onset of ophthalmia, he said:

"I'm going to see Lachenal. I'll come back in a moment and give you some injections. I used them during the war and it's the only treatment that's any use with frost-bite. See you presently."

Lachenal's condition was slightly less serious. His hands were not affected, and the black discoloration of his feet did not extend beyond the toes, but the sinister color reappeared on his heels. He would probably lose his toes, but that would probably not prevent him from climbing, and from continuing to practice his profession as a guide.

Rébuffat's condition was much less serious. His feet were pink except for two small gray patches on his toes. Ichac massaged him with *Dolpyc* for two hours and this appeared to relieve him; his eyes were still painful, but that was only a matter of two or three days. Terray was unscathed: like Rébuffat he was suffering from ophthalmia—most painful, but only a temporary affliction. Couzy was very weak, and would have to be considered out of action. That was the balance sheet.

Night fell gradually. Oudot made his preparations, requisitioned Ichac and Schatz as nurses, and Camp II was turned into a hospital. In cold and discomfort, and to the accompaniment of continual avalanches, these men fought late in the night to save their friends. Armed with torches they passed from tent to tent, bending over the wounded and giving them emergency treatment, at this minute camp, perched 20,000 feet up on the flanks of one of the highest mountains in the world.

Oudot made ready to give me arterial injections. The lamp shone feebly and in the semi-darkness Ichac sterilized the syringes as best he could with ether. Before starting operations, Oudot explained:

"I am going to inject novocain into your femoral and brachial arteries."

As I could not see a thing with the bandage over my eyes, he touched with his finger the places where he would insert the needle: both groins and in the bends of my elbow.

"It's going to hurt. Perhaps I shan't get the right place first shot. But in any case you mustn't move, particularly when I have got into the artery."

I was not at all reassured by these preparations; I had always had a horror of injections. But it would have to be done, it was the only thing possible.

"Go ahead," I said to Oudot, "but warn me when you are going to stab."

Anyhow, perhaps it would not hurt all that much in my present condition. I heard the murmur of voices—Oudot asking if something was ready, and Ichac answering:

"Here you are. Got it?"

Oudot ran his fingers over my skin. I felt an acute pain in the groin and my legs began to tremble; I tried to control myself. He had to try again, for the artery rolled away from the needle. Another stab, and my whole body was seized with convulsions; I stiffened when I should have relaxed, and felt all my nerves in revolt.

"Gently!" I could not help myself.

Oudot began again: my blood was extremely thick and clotted in the needle.

"Your blood is black—it's like black pudding," he said in amazement.

"That's got it!" This time he had succeeded in spite of my howls which, I knew very well, made the operation all the more difficult to perform. The needle was now in position:

"Don't move!" Oudot shouted at me. Then to Ichac:

"Hand it over!"

Ichac passed him the syringe; I felt the needle moving in my flesh and the liquid began to flow into the artery. I should never, until then, have believed so much pain to be possible. I tried to brace myself to the utmost to keep myself from trembling: it simply had to be successful! The liquid went on flowing in.

"Can you feel any warmth?" asked Oudot, brusquely, while he was changing the syringe. Again the liquid went in; I gritted my teeth.

"Does it feel warm?"

Oudot was insistent—the point was evidently crucial; yet still I felt nothing. Several times the syringe was emptied, filled up, and emptied again:

"Now, do you feel anything?"

"I seem to feel a little warmth, but it's not very definite."

Was it auto-suggestion? The needle was withdrawn abruptly, and while Ichac sterilized the instruments, I had a few moments' respite.

"It's excruciating, the way it hurts," I said, just as if Oudot needed telling!

"Yes, I know, but we must go on."

The performance was repeated on the other leg. My nerves were all to pieces, and to brace myself like this took all of my strength. In went the needle and I howled and sobbed miserably, but tried in vain to keep still. I could see nothing because of the bandage. If only I could have seen the faces of my friends it might perhaps have helped me. But I was in the dark—a terrible darkness—with nowhere to look for consolation but within myself. It was late and we had all had more than enough. Then for that day it was over and the first-aid party moved on to Lachenal's tent. He perhaps, would have more courage in face of physical pain.

It seemed to me, when I vaguely became aware of the end of the session, that the treatment had gone more quickly for him. Terray slept in Lachenal's tent and Couzy and Ichac slept beside Rébuffat who was delirious and moaned about his feet all night. Oudot came and lay down next to me. If anything were to happen, he would be there.

Next day plans were completed for the evacuation of the entire camp: the three injured men would be taken down on sledges, two would be able to walk, with assistance, and four were all right. There were miles of glacier to cover, rock barriers to get down, interminable moraines and scree slopes to skirt around or to traverse, a river to cross, and a pass of over 13,000 feet to get over—and all this in the monsoon!

It was now June 6 and Ichac was worried, for he remembered the Tilman expedition to Nanda Devi, which was held up for three weeks by rivers swollen by the torrential monsoon rains. Should we have time to reach the Gandaki valley where the easier gradient would put fewer obstacles in our way? In a week's time we must be clear of the mountains. Soon Couzy would be fit again, Terray cured of his ophthalmia and Rébuffat able to walk. But there were two serious casualties who would have to be carried on the porters' backs under the most appalling conditions, as far as the main valley.

"It's unbelievable," remarked Ichac, "it's actually fine today."

The medical supplies urgently demanded by Oudot had arrived from Camp I. He began his rounds with me, and was pleased because the injections had been effective and warmth had returned as far as my insteps. He put fresh dressings on my hands, and though I felt no real pain, there was, nevertheless, some sort of feeling in my fingers. Again I put my question:

"What shall I have left?"

"I can't exactly say. Things have not completely settled down yet and I hope to be able to gain an inch or so. I think you'll be able to use your hands. Of course," and he hesitated for a moment, "you'll lose one or two joints of each finger, but if there's enough of the thumbs left, you'll have a pinch hold, and that's of prime importance."

It was grim news, but still, only yesterday I had feared that the consequences would be far worse. For me this meant goodbye to a great many plans, and it also implied a new kind of life, perhaps even a new conception of existence. But I had neither the strength nor the wish to look into the future.

I appreciated Oudot's courage and was grateful to him for not being afraid to tell me the extent of the amputations which he foresaw would be necessary. He treated me as a man and as a friend, with courage and frankness, which I shall never forget.

The injections, which had already done so much good, had to be repeated. This time the session would be even worse and I was terrified at the prospect. I am ashamed to say that the thought of this treatment daunted me, and yet so many people have had to endure it. This time it was to be an injection, not of novocain but acetylcholine, of which a few ampoules had been brought up from Camp I. Terray joined me in the tent and stood close beside me. He, too, could see nothing under his bandage, and he had to be guided if he wanted to move about at all. I pictured his face and touched his features with my forearms while Ichac and Oudot prepared the needles, ether, and ampoules. I whispered to Lionel what a fearful ordeal I found it and begged him to stay close.

"Oudot will warn me before inserting the needle: I mustn't budge then, and you must hold me as tight as you can in your arms."

I hoped that Terray's presence would help me bear the agony. Oudot began with my legs; like the day before, it was too awful for words. I howled and cried and sobbed in Terray's arms while he held me tight with all his strength. I felt as if my foot was burning—as if it had been suddenly plunged into boiling oil. Professionally Oudot was in the seventh heaven and everybody showed his delight in my suffering, which was proof of the success of the treatment. This gave me new courage and at last, after the fourth syringeful, the necessary 100 cc had been injected.

"Now for the arms," announced Oudot.

This session seemed to go on for ever and I was utterly worn out, but there was distinctly more feeling in my right arm. Oudot stormed away—the needles were either too thick or too small, too thin or too long: never just right, and each time it meant a fresh stab. I began to howl like a dog again.

"Hold me tighter," I gasped between sobs to Terray, who was already holding me as tightly as he could. I tried hard not to tremble, but Oudot was still not satisfied:

"Don't move, *nom d'une pipe!* We'll go on as long as we must. It's *got* to succeed."

"Sorry, I'm doing all I can; I'll stay with it."

I held out my arm for a fresh attempt. When Oudot did find the artery, then it was the needle that got blocked—the too-thick blood clotted inside. From the bend of the elbow Oudot gradually tried higher and higher up towards the shoulder so as not to stab in the same place. Twice he touched a nerve: I did not cry but sobbed spasmodically. What an eternity of suffering! I could do nothing. Oudot stopped for a moment. "We'll manage all right," Ichac assured me.

"Stick with it, Maurice!" Terray whispered. "It'll soon be over; it's dreadful, I know, but I'm here beside you."

Yes, he was there. Without him I could never have borne it all. This man whom we thought hard because he was strong, who made himself out to be a tough peasant, showed a tenderness and affection towards me that I have never seen equaled. I hid my face against him and he put his arms around my neck.

"Come on! Get on with it!"

"Too small and too fine," shouted Oudot.

He began to lose patience. All this fuss with the instruments exasperated me, and I wondered if they would have succeeded the first attempt in a hospital.

After several hours, and goodness knows how many attempts, the injection was successfully made. In spite of frightful pain I remained immobile as the syringe was emptied. Deftly Oudot replaced it with another without removing the needle from the artery. With the second syringeful, I felt the warmth spreading, and Oudot was exultant. But this warmth became unbearable. I howled and clung to Terray in desperation, holding my arm out stiff, without, so I hoped, moving it a fraction of an inch. Then I felt the needle being withdrawn and cotton applied.

"Right arm finished! Now for the left!"

Oudot could not find the artery, and this puzzled him. I told him that when I was young I had seriously damaged this arm, and that explained everything: that was why there had been no blood pressure, and why he could feel no pulse. The position of the artery was not normal, and it was not possible to make an injection in the bend of the elbow; it would have to be done at the shoulder—much more difficult. I thought of what it had been like for the right arm! Suddenly, at the fifth or sixth attempt, Oudot shouted:

"I've got it!"

I kept absolutely still: syringeful after syringeful went in.

"I'll have to do a *stellaire*."

I had no idea what this was and Oudot explained that it meant injecting novocain into the nerve ganglion to dilate the arteries and make them easier to find, and improve the blood supply. A long needle was necessary, to be stuck into the neck in the region of the pleura. I was in despair. It was just too much. For hours and hours I had endured this agony—I should never have the strength for more. But Oudot lost no time, the needle was ready, and he began to explore my neck:

"This is a tricky business: You have to insert the needle in a certain direction, then, when you come up against an obstacle you have to push to the left, and you're bound to be in the right spot."

"Warn me before you stick it in."

In the silence that followed I heard things being moved around.

"I'm going to insert the needle," Oudot announced.

I braced myself immediately, and resolved to keep perfectly still. The needle went in—it must have been a tremendous length; it touched a very sensitive part and the pain made me cry out in Terray's arms. Oudot was now maneuvering to get the needle into the ganglion and I could feel it moving deep down. It was in! First shot! The liquid must have started flowing in, but I could not feel it.

"Will it take long?" I asked faintly.

"It's almost finished," he replied holding his breath. "Only another 20 cc to go in."

I felt the awful needle being pulled out. It was over, and now I could relax. Oudot was very pleased: it had been almost a whole day's work, but he had managed to do everything he wanted. Never had I suffered so much in my life; but if my feet and hands were to be saved it would be because of Oudot and his perseverance. Ichac helped him collect the instruments to take along to Lachenal's tent. For the time being he was satisfied with my general condition, but what effect this generalized frost-bite would have on my body in the next few days remained to be seen. The camp was becoming more and more like a hospital: everybody's thoughts and actions hung on the surgeon's words.

That same day began the incredible work of transporting the injured, which ended only after a long and painful retreat, lasting five weeks, beneath torrential rain and over dangerously steep ground. This retreat, during which all the injured slowly recovered, will for ever remain an achievement of the highest order, and it reflects great honor upon all the members of the Expedition.

The sledge we had at our disposal was an extra-lightweight Dufour *luge* mounted on two skis for runners. Naturally, the Sherpas were not familiar with this contraption, so Oudot and Ichac decided to make the least injured of us, Rébuffat, the victim of the first try-out. Schatz took charge of operations, with four Sherpas whom he placed in V formation around the sledge, and the procession started off about two-thirty. Rébuffat was well wrapped up and firmly tied to the sledge in case it should tip over. As night fell the four Sherpas arrived back at camp, bringing a note from Schatz advising the use of six men for subsequent descents.

Meanwhile Oudot had given all his patients injections and the evening was spent in changing the dressings. Soon after nightfall the weather worsened, and again it snowed heavily. The others were alarmed, and decided to get the rest of the casualties down before it was too late. As luck would have it, next morning when we woke up, it was fine. I was to be taken down first, and before I left Oudot inspected my feet and hands and changed the dressings. He was very satisfied and described my progress as "spectacular"! I was dressed and put in a sleeping-bag and laid on the Dufour sledge, and Ang-Tharkey directed the team of Sherpas. I could see nothing under my bandage, but I felt the air was warm and so knew it must be fine; I hated the thought of being transported without being able to see what was going on. I was very glad to hear that Ichac would accompany me down so that I shouldn't be alone if I needed anything. In my heart I dreaded this descent, particularly the passage over the rock barriers. How would they manage? But the Sherpas were intelligent and never had to be shown anything twice. Afterwards, when we were in camp, Ichac told me how much he had admired them: "It would have been difficult to find a team like this in France," he said; "every one of them did his utmost and every move was perfectly coordinated."

With a few jerks the sledge started off. I was weak and slightly deaf but I recognized Oudot's voice in the climber's familiar "*Bonne descente!*" No doubt he was there behind us, waving a hand. Swaddled in all my clothes I began to sweat; I could feel the sun beating down. Now and then Ichac came close and said something, and it did me good to hear him and know he was there. Suddenly the slope steepened, and in spite of the straps holding me in position, I slipped forward. The Sherpas took up their positions in an inverted V in order to brake the sledge. We had reached the big rock band, and as far as I could remember, the angle here was steep. I guessed that Ichac had driven his axe in to keep me in balance.

I heard a hollow echo—seracs—and the pace had to be forced now for there was danger of their collapsing. We came to the rocks—and how these Sherpas managed, I shall never know. The wall was very steep yet I was carried on the sledge itself; Ichac told me later that if my eyes had not been blindfolded I should never have been able to stand the sight of such acrobatics, and of such impossible positions. I heard sighs of relief—we must have reached the glacier at last. The sledge reverted to a horizontal position, and I was on the snow. A few minutes rest, and on we went at what seemed to me a breakneck pace, and I pictured the Sherpas pulling on the ropes all around me and running in the snow, though no doubt this was only imagination. Then we slowed up—we had reached the moraine of Camp I.

I was left alone for a moment while the Sherpas put up a big valley tent into which they carried me a few minutes later. Ichac settled himself beside me—from now on we always shared the same tent and he watched over me, day and night, like a brother. The descent had taken two hours and twenty minutes, and the Sherpas had been marvelous. What should we have done without them?

Ichac briefly explained what was going on. Being blind was most demoralizing; I felt I was nothing but a chattel to be carted about. I knew my ophthalmia was less serious than that of the others and I kept asking for the bandage to be taken off. But since I was nothing but a chattel I had no right to speak.

Although it had clouded over and had begun to sleet, the Sherpas went up again to Camp II with Schatz and Noyelle to fetch Lachenal. About three o'clock snow started to fall. Time dragged as I lay in my tent alone with my thoughts. The silence was broken only by the persistent sound of ice cracking, which rather alarmed me. Where had they placed the tent? Suppose a crevasse suddenly opened? But I was ashamed of these childish fears—surely a mountaineer of many years' experience should know very well that a crevasse doesn't yawn open like that in a second!

Ichac, the only fit Sahib, supervised the organization of Camp I. Towards the end of the afternoon, at about five o'clock, he saw, to his great surprise, Noyelle and Lachenal's convoy emerge through the mist, covered with snow. This time the Sherpas had taken only an hour-and-three-quarters to come down—they had had a terrific day and were worn out. This resulted in some complaints: there was not enough food and part of their equipment had remained up at Camp III and Camp IV! This last point especially bothered them for on Himalayan expeditions the normal practice is for the Sherpas to keep their personal equipment as a perquisite. They bitterly regretted these clothes, which had to be considered as lost, and Ang-Tharkey even declared his intention of going up to Camp III again.

I summoned Ang-Tharkey and warned him that I expressly forbade anyone to return higher than Camp II to fetch anything whatsoever. But at the same time I told him of my very great satisfaction at the magnificent behavior of the Sherpas under his orders, and assured him that they were not to worry about the clothes, for they would all receive generous compensation. Ang-Tharkey went off to give the others the good news.

There was tremendous activity all over the camp where Lachenal was being made as comfortable as possible. Tents seemed to have sprung up as if by magic, and a regular little village was formed at the foot of the great wall of ice.

The next day, after a fine start, the clouds collected again towards eleven o'clock, and it was not long before snow began to fall. Oudot had not yet come down from Camp II. I could hear the avalanches rumbling down in ever closer succession, making an appalling noise which wore my nerves thin. Ichac tried to joke about it.

"Here we are—that's the three thirty-seven freight train. Now for the four o'clock express!" He succeeded in making me smile.

Through the telescope he saw, towards the end of the morning, the last tents of Camp II being taken down, and in the afternoon our doctor arrived with his Sherpas, laden like donkeys. Before even putting down his sack he asked about the condition of his patients: any developments since yesterday?

There was marked improvement: Rébuffat could now walk and his ophthalmia was nearly cured. As for Lachenal, circulation had been restored to his feet, and warmth had returned, except to his toes, though the black patches on his heels would probably leave scars. Improvement was visible on my limbs, too, and Oudot was well pleased. He spoke with a frankness that touched me far more than he will ever know:

"I think that the fingers of your left hand will have to be amputated, but I hope to be able to save the end joints of your right hand fingers. If all goes well, you'll have passable hands. As for your feet, I'm afraid that all your toes will have to go, but that won't prevent you from walking. Of course to begin with it'll be difficult, but you'll adapt yourself all right, you'll see."

I was aghast at the thought of what would have happened if Oudot had not given me the injections so promptly and efficiently. Perhaps they had not yet produced all their effect. More sessions would be necessary and I wondered whether I should be able to overcome the immense lassitude that came over me after all these painful ordeals. In any case I wanted to take every advantage of the respite, and celebrate our success with due ceremony. For the first time since our victory the whole Expedition was assembled together and the condition of the casualties was now such as to warrant a little festivity. We gathered around the one and only tin of chicken in aspic and we uncorked the one bottle of champagne. There was already a lot of us who wanted a drink of it but I was determined that the Sherpas should, somehow or other, join in the general rejoicing. I invited Ang-Tharkey and we drank with him to our victory. Ichac put our thoughts into words:

"You've taken a lot of punishment but our victory will remain."

In spite of the circumstances, the general atmosphere in the tent was remarkably cheerful. We wrote a telegram to be sent off to Devies by the next mail-runner:

FRENCH HIMALAYAN EXPEDITION 1950 SUCCESSFUL STOP ANNAPURNA CLIMBED JUNE 3 1950

HERZOG.

Directly the festivities were over there were more injections—those in my legs were finished fairly quickly. Then Oudot tackled my arms and I knew by experience that these would be the most painful. For an hour all attempts were unsuccessful: the afternoon wore on and Oudot became exasperated.

"Don't move about like that!" he cried.

"Take no notice of the noise I make . . . do what's necessary."

Terray had come close to me. I was writhing in pain, and he held me tight.

"Stick with it! Don't move, don't move, Maurice."

"It's hopeless!" shouted Oudot. "When I do succeed in finding the artery, the blood clots. We'll never manage it!"

He sounded in despair, but his words belied him; he had not the slightest intention of giving up, and neither had I, in spite of the pain. The rest of them were appalled as they listened to the cries coming from the tent where Oudot was in action. The Sherpas were silent. Were they praying for their Bara Sahib? I sobbed so convulsively that I could not stop, and was shaken by continual spasms.

Then, after a short rest, late in the evening at about ten o'clock the injection was successfully accomplished. Ichac passed the syringes to Oudot in the dark. There was blood all over the tent. Ichac and Oudot went out while Terray soothed me with infinite gentleness. Never had I felt so wretched. I was utterly worn out with suffering and fatigue, incapable of resistance. Terray still held me in his arms. "It'll be all right, you'll see, later on."

"Oh but Lionel, everything's over for me, and I simply can't bear what they're doing to me any longer."

"Life's not over," he insisted, "you'll see France again, and Chamonix."

"Yes, Chamonix perhaps, but I'll never be able to climb again."

It was out at last, I had told him, and I let myself go in despair:

"I'll never be able to climb again—I'll never do the Eiger now, Lionel, and I wanted to so much."

Sobs choked me. My head was against Terray's and I felt his tears, for he was crying, too. He was the only one who could fully understand the tragedy that this represented for me, and I could see that to him, too, it appeared hopeless.

"No, of course, not the Eiger, but I'm sure you'll be able to go back to the mountains . . ." and then, very hesitantly, he added, "Not the same sort of climbs as before, of course."

"It will never be the same again. But, Lionel, even if I can't do the sort of climbs I used to, if I could still do easy things, that would be a great deal. The mountains meant everything to me—I spent the best days of my life among them—I don't want to do spectacular climbs, or famous ones, but I want to be able to enjoy myself in the mountains, even if it's only on the old standard routes."

"You'll go back all right, you'll see," said Lionel. "I feel just the same way."

"But mountains aren't the only thing; there are other things in life as well—what shall I do about all that?"

"You'll manage somehow, Maurice."

There was a silence; then he said, "You ought to lie down now."

He settled me with such affectionate care that he accomplished the impossible and left me comforted and soothed. After a last look to see that I was comfortable, he went slowly out. What a friend I had found in Terray!

Next morning Oudot took off my bandage: it was wonderful to be able to see again. I noted that the weather was fine, and I asked the date: the last few days had been one long night.

"Friday, June 9," Ichac told me.

At the moment Lachenal was being made ready to go down to Base Camp. He would travel in a *cacolet*—an arrangement of canvas and webbing for carrying an injured man, who sits in it on a porter's back. It was an awkward and primitive contraption and I had never liked the look of it. Lachenal, on the contrary, who was accustomed to the thing and had himself carried many casualties down by this method, was perfectly ready to descend this way, though later on he wasn't quite so enthusiastic. Soon he started off with his Sherpas, escorted by Couzy and Noyelle. His legs dangled down most uncomfortably and made him groan. In the afternoon the Sherpas came up again followed by Couzy: the descent had taken two hours, and Rébuffat and Lachenal were none the worse for the journey.

While I rested the others made up their loads. The next day, before going off, Oudot examined me and his favorable impression was confirmed: the injections of acetylcholine, which had been abominably painful, had saved a part at least of my feet and hands. Adjiba, Sarki, Foutharkey and Pandy the Chinee were going to take turns at carrying me in the *cacolet*. The route was well marked, there were no stones and the going was straightforward. But I was crushed up against the porter and horribly jolted at every step. I was afraid of falling and clung desperately to his neck with both arms though I tried to do all in my power not to hinder his movements. Whenever his step faltered I was perfectly aware of it. Several times both Adjiba and Pandy slipped, and instinctively I tried to put my arm out, without realizing that it was useless. I was less anxious in the couloirs than on the steep rock slabs where the porter might fall, and kept on being afraid that my hands or my feet might knock against the rock.

"Sarki! . . . *Pay attention!* . . . *Pay attention!* . . ." Again and again I repeated this cry; which became an entreaty. At the awkward pitches they helped each other: one placed the carrier's feet in position, and another would push from behind to maintain his balance. After many difficulties we got over the rocky section and arrived in view of Base Camp.

It felt as if we had been all day on this journey, but in fact it was only two hours and a half, and there had not been the slightest hitch. It was now the turn of the Base Camp to be the center of activity, which it had not hitherto known. Suddenly Ichac dashed into the tent where I had just been laid down and shouted:

"The coolies! The coolies are here!"

Chapter XVII

In the Woods of Lete

THESE WILD-LOOKING CREATURES, MOST OF WHOM WE RECOGNIZED, ARRIVED IN small groups. By a miracle they had kept the rendezvous we had fixed with them a fortnight before, and Ichac was overjoyed. Soon he got the radio going; it was just about time for the weather report. A bulletin, specially broadcast for us, warned us of the approach of the monsoon proper:

"This is All India Radio, Delhi, calling on 60.48 m.

You will now hear a special weather bulletin for the French Expedition to Nepal:

Monsoon extending over all eastern Himalaya will be reaching your area by June 10.

Barometer pressure at Gorakhpur 980 millibars.

I repeat: you have just heard a special bulletin . . ."

So the storms of the last few days, which had added such hazards to our enterprise, were nothing but forerunners of this enormous disturbance which spreads over Asia at this season every year. The rains, which are torrential over the rest of India, become a solid deluge within a few hours of reaching the mountains. Tomorrow the skies would open and the floods would be upon us; but we heard the news calmly enough now that we were clear of the mountain.

A coolie handed a scrap of paper through the door of the tent: it was a note from Schatz, who had gone on ahead to discover an easier crossing of the Miristi Khola gorges than we had made on the way up, and who now wrote that the volume of water had doubled in a single afternoon. So it became urgent to get away from this valley, which might easily become a vast trap, and though we said nothing we were all thinking of what had happened on Nanda Devi.

As forecast, the weather was bad next morning and rain fell ceaselessly. The Sherpas broke camp with feverish haste. We had given them orders to distribute to the coolies, before leaving, all the food we were unable to take down with us. The porters pounced gleefully on the tins and tubes which Sarki and Ang-Tharkey threw into the air by handfuls. Here was unlooked-for *baksheesh*! Oudot, on the contrary, was beginning to run short of essential medical supplies. Bad luck lent a hand, too, for the needles had been dropped, and the syringes broke as he struggled with my arteries which were practically impossible to find.

The situation was serious; there were only two ampoules of acetylcholine left. Lachenal had had his two injections and my arms and right leg were done, and there we had to stop; but I was unmoved by this news which so distressed the others. I lay there like a dying man, in a state of extreme nervous excitement, knowing that these sessions were a terrible strain on my general condition.

While the last loads were leaving the camp under Ang-Tharkey's supervision, Lachenal started down. After a few yards the coolies abandoned the stretcher and the sledge was tried, but with no success. Oudot sent for the *cacolet*.

"We *must* get away at all costs," he said.

Before fixing him in it he gave Lachenal an injection of morphine. For me they found a wicker basket. The Sherpas hoisted me up and tucked my legs into a sleeping-bag covered by a *pied d'éléphant*. Everything was soaked. From the walls all around us came echoes of rumbling avalanches mingled with the continual noise of falling stones loosened by the rain. The porter's naked feet sank into the soggy ground of the moraine on which they were walking, and we sent boulders flying down as we went. We were like the ragged remnant retreating in a disorderly rout from the scene of some catastrophe.

The column, composed of the two invalids, and of Oudot, Terray, Couzy, Ichac, Sarki and eight coolies, moved with painful slowness. Should we be able to reach the pre-arranged stopping-place before night? Judging by the time we had taken on the way up, it *should* have been possible, even easy, but seeing the porters struggling beneath the weight of their burdens, and constantly sliding on the moraine where every step was a problem, we began to have our doubts. Time was passing but the clouds lifted and the rain stopped for a while. We lacked flashlights and food. Ang-Tharkey, unaware of our difficulties, had not made any provision for the party in the rear, so Sarki was sent on ahead with a message.

We were soon completely lost in a featureless country with neither color nor horizon. The scree of the moraine had given place to enormous boulders surrounded with a prickly vegetation which hindered our movements still further. The porters showed great fortitude, and made no complaint. Night fell and three flashlights discovered among our baggage were brought into action. The sahibs guided the coolies in the mist and the rain which had started up again harder than ever. It was past eight o'clock when the porters and their burdens, exhausted and disheartened, halted after an acrobatic descent of a slippery chimney down which somehow we had managed to come.

Lachenal and myself were placed under shelter; the others judged that we were in no fit state to go any farther that night. Terray decided to stay with us, while Couzy, Ichac and Oudot went off rapidly towards the camp. They had only just left us when they met Sarki and Foutharkey coming up—with nothing but a flask of coffee by way of supplies! They sent Sarki on up to us and took Foutharkey back with them to the tents, which they reached after an hour. They told Schatz and Noyelle that it was not possible to carry the two casualties over such dangerous ground at night, and described our wretched bivouac. Immediately Schatz offered to take us up food and equipment, and Dawatondu went with him. In our shelter the situation wasn't ideal, in spite of Terray's efforts to cheer things up. Lachenal was still under the influence of morphine, but I was furious that we had failed to reach the camp, which I knew to be so near.

When we were no longer expecting anyone, Schatz arrived; water streamed down his face as he raised his startled eyes to mine, and with a little smile announced triumphantly that he had brought up sleeping-bags, warm clothing and food. What more did we need? Soon a primus stove was roaring away. None of us had eaten since the morning and the smell of the open cans of food made Terray's mouth water. Meanwhile Dawatondu had inflated the mattresses and, though the food didn't tempt me, I enjoyed the comfort of a mattress. All night long it rained and I couldn't sleep. Deathly cold, my teeth chattering, I was haunted by anxiety and a shameful fear.

In the morning the weather improved. The formation of the clouds had changed, and they now tended to creep along the walls, and move upwards. When this happens in Chamonix it means fine weather. Getting back into my wicker basket was unpleasant, and Lachenal, too, found little pleasure in returning to his *cacolet*. We were in a hurry to reach the camp and every few minutes I kept asking:

"Are we there?"

I always got the same answer, as though I were a child:

"Five minutes more!"

At last we saw the yellow roofs of the tents at the far end of a small flat space. The sky was clear when we reached the camp where Ichac,

Noyelle and Oudot welcomed us. We were not yet at the end of our troubles: the bridge which Schatz had built would not hold out until the evening; already it was only a foot above the water, and would in any case have to be reinforced before the loads and the casualties could be taken across. None of the coolies would volunteer to carry us over; and even the Sherpas thought it dangerous. Finally Adjiba made up his mind, and the others stood by to help him at the start and at the finish. From my tent I heard Lachenal being taken across, then Adjiba returned, I was hoisted on his back and with a firm step he went towards the bridge. This consisted simply of four or five tree-trunks lashed together with liana and fixed somehow or other to either bank; the river went swirling by beneath, only just clearing the bridge, and spray wet the porters' feet, making them liable to slip. The feeling of helplessness was so awful, I wanted to shut my eyes. But I had to look, and though he carried me with great care I whispered in Adjiba's ear:

"Slowly, Adjiba!"

Would he be able to keep his balance on this rickety, slippery foot-bridge? Oudot, who was watching the operation, tried not to show his anxiety; his expressionless smile was intended to be encouraging. The moment we set foot on the bridge I could feel the precariousness of our situation. Adjiba calculated his moves and put each foot forward gingerly.

"Slowly, Adjiba!"

The water raced by, forming eddies which made me dizzy to look at. The Sherpas on the other side were not far off now. I was afraid that my bearer would quicken his steps as we approached terra-firma. Again I murmured:

"Slowly, Adjiba!"

A few inches more—and then helping hands brought us safely to the bank. I heaved a deep sigh of relief, but at the same time felt a strong desire to cry: the inevitable nervous reaction after an ordeal. Adjiba took me at once into a tent and settled me there while the rest of the party hastily crossed the river, which was rising visibly. The coolies lined up to cross, and two hours later everything had been taken over. The Expedition would not be trapped in the Annapurna massif, though by the following morning the bridge would have gone—swept away by the rushing torrent.

Oudot began to examine us at once, for he feared that the cold and damp of the previous night would have caused a deterioration in our condition. Lachenal's feet were very swollen and the improvement of the last few days was arrested. As for me it was mainly my right hand which had suffered from our unfortunate bivouac. Oudot had assured me that the damage would not go beyond the end joints of my fingers. Now he said that at least two joints would have to go. All these emotions tried me sorely.

We all gathered together in one tent for lunch. Schatz, who the day before had gone off to reconnoiter the Miristi gorges, told us that there was not the slightest chance of our being able to follow these gorges direct to Baglung and the Gandaki valley. This route would have avoided a long detour, but it was quite impracticable: gigantic walls fell sheer to the river's edge over a distance of several miles, so that almost immediately we should have been forced to climb up out of the gorge to the ridges above—in other words to take the same route by which we had come on April 27.

We decided to dispatch Pansy as a special messenger to New Delhi to send off the telegrams we had written a few days ago.

I took little part in the conversation. When my attention was not needed I preferred to doze and not think about the present. My strength was ebbing and I dreaded the next stages of the march. After examining me once again Oudot did not hide the fact that it was difficult, in view of the extensiveness of my injuries, to foretell the course things would take. With half-closed eyes I heard him explaining to Ichac how dry gangrene can turn into gas gangrene which necessitates immediate and extensive amputation. Ichac shuddered when Oudot told him that the toxins spreading from the affected parts to the living tissue become diffused over the whole body and produce general septicemia. Or sometimes it concentrated in one organ, the liver for example, particularly after antibiotic injections such as penicillin.

Meanwhile Terray was very adroitly constructing a chair in the shape of a hook, like those used for carrying in the Alps. He made it out of sticks fastened together with wire—it would enable the legs to be supported at the same level as the rest of the body, thus avoiding the wounded man's principal cause of suffering. The Sherpas copied Terray's model for me. The rain drummed ceaselessly on the tents, almost making us wonder whether the canvas would give way beneath the enormous bullet-like drops.

After a bad night I woke slowly and was told that the weather had improved. If only it would keep fine till evening! Today, they told me, we should have to go up from 12,000 to 15,000 feet over extremely steep slopes without any hope of a bivouac site before the pass of April 27. At all events the chairs were satisfactory. Thanks to Terray's ingenuity both

Lachenal and I were slightly less apprehensive about the next stages of our journey.

The coolies climbed up steadily, although there was no track and sometimes steps had to be cut in the earth, so steep was the slope. Noiselessly as ghosts, they labored heroically through the mist to complete the allotted stage before nightfall. Shadows appeared and disappeared, outlines faded into the mist. This retreat would have seemed like a dream, and the men mere phantoms, had it not been for the jolting of my chair which caused pain in every part of my body. I tried my best to keep drowsy and semi-conscious, and envied Lachenal who managed to go to sleep on the back of his porter.

A little before noon the main contingent had ascended the grassy gullies and reached the C.A.F. shoulder—the point at which Schatz had left a Club Alpin Français pennant on the way up. The coolies wanted to camp here, saying that higher up there would be no better site, but Ichac and Oudot turned deaf ears to this suggestion. They sent the casualties ahead and themselves walked with the Sherpas; the coolies were obliged to follow. The long, long traverse across to the pass of April 27 had begun.

Visibility was down to ten yards, and the porters walked in single file. They kept warm while they were moving with their loads, but as soon as they stopped their teeth began to chatter, for their only clothing was a small blanket. I tried to adjust myself to the swaying rhythm of my bearer, but he continually upset my calculations by hesitating, taking a longer or a shorter step, or, in certain awkward places, striding sideways. I could not stop trying to stretch out my arms in an endeavor to hold back or help on, or with the idea of protecting myself. Far away in the depths of its infernal gorges I heard the roar of the Miristi.

At the end of the afternoon we came upon the site of a shepherds' camp, the only one before the pass, which there was obviously no question of our reaching that evening. Prudence demanded that we should remain where we were for the night, and all that I asked was to be put down in a tent where I could lie still.

Dawn was sullen and we left in pouring rain, with visibility less than twenty yards. We had to continue the flanking movement and cross a whole series of streams which would be no easy matter. It was a sad day for me. I felt quite definitely that my condition was getting worse: I was aware that I had no reserves and I was profoundly disheartened.

For some time Schatz had been trying to encourage me with the assurance that the ridge was no longer very far off. There came a shout of triumph, but although Ichac was only a few yards away I could barely hear him:

"Maurice, you're on the Krishna side now!"

I was not particularly elated, although it was an important moment. As I passed in front of Ichac I saw him shooting with his movie camera. It struck me as a crazy proceeding—surely it wouldn't come out—there was no light, and this, as he had often enough told me himself, was essential for color film.

We began to descend gradually to the pass. At each step the porters let themselves slide down the slope, feet foremost, and the violent jerking caused me unbearable pain. To go on was madness, and, moreover, I just didn't feel capable of standing another couple of hours of this torture. I implored Ichac to stop everyone and go up again to the site which we had passed. Very unwillingly those in front retraced their steps, while the Sherpas pitched the tents on the soaking ground.

We had now come to the last really hard day: we should have to descend for some 6,000 feet to the Chadziou Khola and the shepherds' camping ground. How would all the porters manage, especially those who would have to carry the two casualties across the terribly steep slopes on this part of the route?

Right at the beginning, on leaving the gap marked with a *chorten,* one of the coolies slipped and rolled down for fifty yards or so. We feared he would disappear into the river six thousand feet below but he clung on and brought himself to a stop; for a moment he lay stretched out on the ground. The sack he had been carrying went bowling down the slope as well as a container, which burst open. The sack bounced, described a fine curve and disappeared into space. The man was only dazed; he picked himself up and came back towards us. He was a Tibetan from Tukucha, and one of the few who had consented to wear expedition boots!

I heard a frightful yell. I couldn't see what was happening, but I could guess from the shouts: a huge stone had fallen above Lachenal in the couloir. Terray succeeded in diverting it from its course, but the rock had hit Lachenal's bearer. The man fell without being able to protect himself; his arms were caught in his *cagoule,* and the block hit him on the nose. His face was covered with blood and he had an enormous bruise. It was not exactly an encouraging portent.

Ichac, Rébuffat and Schatz went down the great grass couloir, the haunt of the marmots discovered by Rébuffat on the way up. They stopped at the first trees while the rest of the party came carefully down in their turn. To find out the owner of the sack that had fallen into the Chadziou Khola, they decided to check the loads as they were carried past on the porters' backs.

"I think it was mine," said Schatz, "and for once both my fountain pen and wallet were in it!"

Schatz was staring at a porter—he lifted up a sack that was concealing another and saw the name written plainly for all to see on the main pocket: "M. Schatz."

"There's no doubt," said Ichac, proceeding by elimination, "it must be Gaston's."

Rébuffat wasn't pleased. This retreat had been an ordeal for him too: and his frostbitten feet were still giving him some trouble. I saw him sitting down disconsolately, thinking of what he had lost. Suddenly Ichac had an inspiration.

"Gaston, look what you're sitting on!"

He shot up like a jack-in-the-box and read on the sack: "G. Rébuffat." The lost sack turned out to be the only one which belonged to no one: it contained spare clothes.

We were now in the forest, which was extraordinarily thick and tangled; we felt as if we were walking through submarine scenery in a damp, unhealthy jungle, expecting at any moment to meet hideous monsters. It was here that, on the way up, we had seen those giant rhododendrons of such magnificent shades of red. We entered the "triumphal way," a natural archway of flowers, which we had noticed on the outward journey. The coolies in front had stopped here—and why not? There was a general halt and soon fires were crackling. Oudot was of the opinion that the hardest part of this stage still lay ahead, and he wanted to go on at all costs. He gave me fresh injections of morphine and spartocamphor—these were the more painful because I had grown so thin, and I lost consciousness for a few moments. I felt the eyes of the Sherpas and coolies upon me. What a sight I must have been! There was a new expression in their eyes, which I had not seen before. Was it pity, or grief, or a kindly indifference? Before we left, they arranged on my knees a garland of the most beautiful flowers they could find. This gesture touched me deeply, and from now on during the whole course of our long retreat, whenever it was possible, the Sherpas never once forgot to put flowers beside me.

Now began the descent through the dead trees of the dense jungle. The Sherpas went ahead, and with great sweeps of their *kukris* cut away the branches and bamboos that barred the way. The ground was soaking and everyone kept slipping—there was scarcely a man who did not fall that day. Couzy, Ichac, Oudot, Schatz and Terray went on to reconnoiter the route; Noyelle, according to plan, was always one march ahead, and Rébuffat stayed with Lachenal and myself. The injections Oudot had given me were very effective: I was completely worn out, but I felt less pain, and most of the time I dozed with my eyes half shut. Lachenal followed immediately behind me. The last bit before the river was particularly steep, and I would never have given myself one chance in a thousand of coming through alive. The slope was practically vertical and the minute track crossed it at an angle; the coolies had to cling to the trees growing alongside.

My bearer was in trouble; he could move neither backwards nor forwards. Finally he pressed himself up against the wall and went along sideways step by step. The hook-shaped chair in which I was stowed hung right over the precipice. Now and again the Sherpas dug their ice-axes into the wet ground and clung to them desperately the better to help my bearer. I was painfully aware of the slightest jolt. With bulging eyes I looked under my feet at the swirling Chadziou Khola into which I was in danger of falling at every step. If the porter slipped there would not be a chance— perhaps he would be able to stop himself, but who could stop me? I no longer had the strength to fight my fears, and I knew now what fear really was. Lachenal also was petrified by fright. Fortunately for him, his arms were free and occasionally he was able to help himself. Every step was a reprieve, for it brought us nearer our goal. Before we arrived there was one last ordeal. For about five yards the track, which was already sketchy, disappeared entirely. A little ledge ran across a slab of rock and the feet had to be shuffled along it. My bearer carried on with great courage— my admiration for these men who unhesitatingly tackled such dangerous work was unbounded. He moved along sideways, clinging to the smallest holds, and letting the other porters guide his feet into the next steps.

At long last we reached the Chadziou Khola, swollen by the monsoon rains, which we had nonetheless to ford. Lachenal following me over this dangerous crossing, and for all his fear, seemed completely master of himself, while I was a mere human wreck. Standing shoulder to shoulder and holding each other up, the porters succeeded in bracing themselves against the force of the current. We climbed up a hundred yards through strongly scented jungle and then, in the distance, I saw the Shepherds' Camp.

The porters halted before making this final effort, but after a few minutes I asked my bearer to get to the camp as quickly as he could. At the foot of a cliff it seemed to me that he took the wrong direction—on the way out we had traversed across, but the Sherpas who accompanied us seemed to be quite sure of the route. On we went, and the way ran up such a steep grass slope that we had to adopt the technique we would have used for traversing on ice. The Sherpas persisted and here we were embarked on a regular climb. I called nervously to Ichac to intervene, saying that we were about to have a frightful fall, but the porters were obstinate. We were beneath a sort of cornice overhanging a practically vertical wall and the rock was rotten. Perched up on my bearer and sticking out a yard from the rock, I was able to gaze into the very depths of the gorge below me. The Sherpas were worried and told me that my bearer could not turn around; he must go on. I could not stand any more and called for help—but still, I reflected, my luck had held during many a long day. After a few steps the going became easier and we got back onto grass and picked up the track which we ought to have followed from the beginning, and which Lachenal now took, profiting from our experience. We reached the camp just as the rain stopped.

As I went into my tent I longed for nothing but peace and quiet. I scarcely had the strength to speak, but I murmured to Oudot that the hard part was over now—there was a good path as far as Lete. I remembered a larchwood near the village and beautiful meadows dotted with granite boulders which reminded me of the Chamonix valley. During the long retreat I had thought of this idyllic little wood as a welcoming haven. I hoped we should make a long halt there, and my friends agreed. It was unnecessary for everyone to go up to Tukucha and back again to Lete. We would reorganize the whole Expedition in this wood before beginning the long trek homewards through the valleys of Nepal to the Indian frontier.

"Where's my ice-axe?" I asked Schatz.

I set great store by it; as Lachenal had lost his, it was the only one to have been to the top of Annapurna. No one had seen it since we had left Base Camp. Schatz inspected all the Sherpas' axes, but it was not to be found. I felt this loss deeply. Though in itself it was of no importance, I had intended to present the axe to the French Alpine Club on my return. It turned up two days later.

The next day we had only a short march. As Oudot reckoned that we should reach the woods of Lete before midday, there was no need to hurry, and we might as well enjoy the few rays of sun that had appeared as if by magic. The coolies started off and then we, too, left the Shepherds' Camp.

We arrived together at Choya and we were enthusiastically received. The inhabitants rushed towards us and looked at the casualties with curiosity. Dawatondu's throat must have been dry as he remembered the pleasures of the outward journey, and Ang-Tharkey volubly explained to Ichac and Oudot that this would be an excellent place to pitch camp—there was water, wood, and food.

"*Good place!*" insisted our Sirdar. There was also good *chang* at Choya. But somehow the Sahibs didn't seem to understand. *En route!* Unwillingly the party moved on and soon we came to the banks of the Krishna Gandaki. Its clear, pure waters had become a dirty black flood, foaming and swirling and making an infernal noise. We crossed over by a bridge without any incident, and after a short hour's walk at last reached the resting place of which I had dreamed so long.

We chose a good-sized grassy site, bounded by three enormous granite boulders, and surrounded by the soft green of the larches—a cool and restful place. The wind played among the tall trees, and, closing my eyes, I fancied myself back in Chamonix. The tents were pitched where the Sherpas pleased. The sun was warm, and Oudot decided to make his examinations out of doors. One of my feet had begun to suppurate, and my hands were in an awful state. There was a most unpleasant nauseating smell; all the bandages were soaked with pus. Oudot broke into his last reserves of dressings—he knew that fresh equipment would be coming from Tukucha. For the first time he took his scissors and began "trimming," or cutting away the dead and affected parts. My feet did not hurt too badly, but my hands were so sensitive that the slightest touch made me cry out in pain, and I broke down—I could fight no longer. Oudot decided to stop. He painted the wounds with mercurochrome.

"Stay outside while I do Lachenal," he said.

Lachenal's condition had improved. He had come through the ordeals of the retreat very well indeed, and his morale was high, now that we were down in the valley; his excellent appetite had not deserted him.

In the afternoon Ichac, Oudot and Schatz left for Tukucha, where they were welcomed by Noyelle and G. B. Rana. That evening, in the few tents still standing, they talked at length, but not very cheerfully, for their main topic was Lachenal's and my condition. Oudot was of the opinion that I would undoubtedly have to undergo an operation before we reached the Indian frontier, which would not be until the first fortnight of July.

The next day the dismantling of the camp was completed before a circle of coolies and children who squatted there hour after hour, keeping a lookout for tins or old tubes of milk. Noyelle saw to paying off the porters, and there was a grand distribution of rupees. In the afternoon Oudot finished his preparations and left to return to Lete and his patients.

Twenty-four hours later everything was ready for the others to leave the village which had given us such a kindly welcome and had been our headquarters for nearly two months. The coolies and the inhabitants paid their farewell respects to the Sahibs with a series of shouts. At four o'clock everyone was back at Lete.

The condition of the casualties, of myself in particular, was now distinctly alarming; when Oudot returned the day before he pronounced the situation critical. He had been hard at it since morning, resuming the agonizing injections. I presented an increasingly distressing picture. I had lost over forty pounds and became extremely thin. The fever steadily mounted—that evening my temperature was 105°!

"102°" announced Ichac without batting an eyelid.

I was oblivious of everything now, unconscious most of the time, in a coma.

"Heavy dose of penicillin," ordered Oudot.

Shadows appeared close by out of the mist. They leaned over, then disappeared noiselessly. The silence awed me. I no longer suffered. My friends attended to me in silence. The job was finished, and my conscience was clear. Gathering together the last shreds of energy, in one last long prayer, I implored death to come and deliver me. I had lost the will to live, and I was giving up—the ultimate humiliation for a man, who, up till then, had always taken a pride in himself.

This was no time for questions nor for regrets. I looked death straight in the face, besought it with all my strength. Then abruptly I had a vision of the life of men. Those who are leaving it for ever are never alone. Resting against the mountain, which was watching over me, I discovered horizons I had never seen. There at my feet, on those vast plains, millions of beings were following a destiny they had not chosen.

There is a supernatural power in those close to death. Strange intuitions identify one with the whole world. The mountain spoke with the wind as it whistled over the ridges or ruffled the foliage. All would end well. I should remain there, forever, beneath a few stones and a cross.

They had given me my ice-axe. The breeze was gentle and sweetly scented. My friends departed, knowing that I was now safe. I watched them go their way with slow, sad steps. The procession withdrew along the narrow path. They would regain the plains and the wide horizons. For me, silence.

Chapter XVIII

Through the Paddy Fields

I CRIED OUT AS I FELT A LITTLE STAB OF PAIN: ICHAC HAD JUST GIVEN ME HIS FIRST injection, and was quite agitated. The rain poured down incessantly, giving us a melancholy send-off. Oudot had hesitated about giving the order, but it was now June 19 and high time we were off. Lachenal and I were laid on stretchers made for us by G. B. Rana, but before I sank back again into apathy I gave a last fond glance around the little wood.

The party began to move off, with Rébuffat, who had found a horse, prancing beside us. We forded a stream coming down from Dhaulagiri, the coolies standing shoulder to shoulder to brace themselves against the current. Ichac and Oudot undressed and crossed over with great dignity in their underpants. They had lost weight after all the events of the past weeks and their bodies were slim and youthful-looking.

When we came to Dana we felt that we had really left the mountains behind us. Here were fields of corn, banana trees, and heat, as we made our way down towards the main valleys. Even after all we had been through, we hated to feel that we were now leaving—for good, as well we realized—the scene of our great adventure.

One after the other our coolies left us; in spite of all our offers even Pandy would come no further. The valley climate did not suit him, and great beads of sweat rolled down his body. There was also another reason—he had earned a lot of rupees and reckoned it was enough. He would not have known what to do with more money.

On the afternoon of the 20th, as we were going along an easy path, the sun, which we had not seen lately, came out for a few minutes, and we halted under some huge banyan trees for lunch. It was an ordeal for me: I was revolted at the mere idea of food. Oudot had become my tormentor—he insisted on my taking nourishment, and the others all tried to get me to swallow something. Ichac and Terray tried every means: sometimes they reasoned with me, sometimes they cajoled, until at last they got angry and threatened:

"You won't last more than a few days at this rate."

If only they would realize how cold this argument left me! When they had finished their vain appeals, Oudot turned up; he wasted no time in making a tactful approach, but simply commanded me to swallow what I was given:

"You must finish up those kidneys. I'll be back in a moment to see if you have. Surely you don't want to be forcibly fed."

Sarki cut up the beastly kidneys with his dirty, sticky hands and stuck them on the end of his knife to feed me. For ages I chewed away like a child without being able to swallow. Oudot would be certain to come back! He was my bogyman. There! That's one bit down! I felt that it would choke me and that I would bring it up again immediately. Hell! Still all that to swallow! Oudot came back, looking stern: "You're not trying, Maurice!" Turning towards Sarki, he ordered him to carry on . . . Every meal was like that.

Under the banyan trees the air was cool. Nice plump chickens ran about unsuspectingly. If I could have one of these, now, that would be a change from the tough mutton whose very smell nauseated me. A peasant was ready to sell us one on condition that we caught it ourselves. He had hardly finished speaking when G. B. Rana grabbed his gun and fired. The chicken was cut in half and ended its existence in a casserole. Ang-Tharkey brought it to me in triumph, for it was quite an occasion if the Bara Sahib actually wanted to eat something.

My particular coolies, who came from Dana, were extraordinarily expert; four of them carried me as though I were a feather. Among them there was a one-eyed fellow of about fifty who was full of the kindliest attentions towards me. At every halt he would explain that there was not much further to go, and that they knew the paths. My confidence in their strength and ability gave me courage: if a single coolie had stumbled, either Lachenal or I might have been hurled down hundreds of feet. Sometimes the stretcher would be at an angle and I would have to make desperate efforts with knees and elbows to stop myself sliding. When I could not, I called out and a Sherpa would run up and hold me on. These alarms were nerve-racking and I asked for a Sherpa to remain constantly by my side. Sarki was detailed to do this and he stayed by me the whole time. He gave me fresh water and bananas, helped me to eat, and blew up my mattress at each halt to keep the stones on the path from sticking into me. I had grown so thin that the least irregularity hurt me.

One night we camped near Banduk at the foot of a huge waterfall. The rain teemed down as I lay in my tent, but I scarcely heard the onslaughts of the monsoon as I tried to get to sleep. I was thinking of the nightmare descent, and it seemed to me to be physically impossible to bear such a prolonged agony. Though the smell from my dressings made everyone feel ill, no one uttered a word of complaint; but I often came very near to fainting myself.

Ichac slept by my side, and at last I dropped off too. In the middle of the night I woke with a start. An overpowering force made me sit up and a horrible fear held me in its grip. I had the dreadful feeling that I was about to die, and I was deafened by the sound of bells. Where was I? I cried out loud. The light went on, and to my enormous relief I realized that I was in the tent, and remembered I was part of the Expedition. Ichac was alarmed:

"What on earth's the matter?"

I tried to explain to him that appalling sensation of nothingness.

"Must have been a nightmare," he said. But all the same he left the light on and talked gently until I had quieted down again.

First thing next morning I spoke to Oudot about it. He told me that morphine sometimes produces such reactions, and from then on I resolved never to take morphine again; I would rather bear the worst pain than pay that price for relief.

Near Beni we were told there was an epidemic of cholera, so we had to avoid the village by crossing the Gandaki by a bridge spanning the whole breadth of the swirling, unbridled torrent. But this bridge, which was 200 feet long and suspended 50 feet above the river, gave us some anxiety. It was made of two chains with bent rusty rods supporting some old worm-eaten planks, and its length caused disquieting oscillations which could become alarmingly violent. The *cacolet* would have to be used. Lachenal went first, and after a few yards he began to cry out. Some of the Sherpas helped Adjiba, who was carrying him, by holding back the rods to prevent Lachenal's feet from being hurt. When my turn came I tried to bear it all with as much courage as I could muster, but though the Sherpas held back the rods and Adjiba walked as carefully as he could, the swaying made me feel horribly sick. On the other side I joined Lachenal and the two of us howled in concert before the embarrassed coolies.

G. B. Rana intended to make his horse swim across. Several nylon ropes were tied together and from the opposite bank everyone hauled on the animal. The unhappy beast resisted heroically, for he smelled danger. He was thrown into the river willy-nilly and immediately disappeared beneath the water. From time to time his ears, a leg, or a flank appeared— surely he would be a corpse when he arrived. Not a bit of it! A few yards from the bank a head emerged and gradually the horse scrambled onto terra firma and advanced on us with Olympian calm.

It was late and we pitched camp near the river. But cholera was raging on this side too, and the next morning, after an unforgettable session of hand "trimming," we hastened to leave this unhealthy district.

It was raining every day and when we had to find shelter that evening we cursed and swore. We wanted a house where we could all be together, where we should have more room to sort things out and where, too, we should no longer hear the exasperating noise of rain on the roofs of the tents. When we reached the straggling hamlet of Kusma we were in a quandary, for there was no suitable house and the "authorities" whom we had approached conducted us to the *gompa!* We settled ourselves without ceremony, and soon, from the sacred place which we supposed to be no longer in use, there arose a cacophony of bawdy songs.

Some of the party saw to paying off the coolies who had to go back to Dana, and recruiting others to come on with us to Tansing. Schatz collected the equipment and checked the loads; Couzy, who had been unanimously elected cook, peered into all the open containers. Everything was uncertain; we did not know whether we should have enough coolies to enable us all to leave next day. We were told there were another five marches. Actually it took us over ten days.

Some fifty patients awaited the Doctor Sahib. They had all kinds of diseases, mostly inflammation or unaccountable fevers. It would have taken a long time to see all the patients, and required a lot of medical supplies, not to speak of endless patience on Oudot's part. He drew up a standard questionnaire:

1. How old are you?
2. Do you sleep well at night?
3. Have you a good appetite?
4. Where is the pain?
5. Do you cough?

This questionnaire was given to Noyelle who translated it into English for G.B.'s benefit, with the help of a few words of Hindustani, and G.B. translated it into Gurkhali. The replies had to follow the reverse order, but after all these intermediaries they were often pretty queer. The Sherpas were doubled up with laughter. They could only understand part of the conversation—the last bit that began in Hindustani, went on into Gurkhali and then came back in Hindustani. By this stage it had suffered a farcical change!

Oudot had tremendous prestige. People came long distances to see him, for he had become a sort of god. We admired the touching simplicity of these creatures who put their health and sometimes their lives in the hands of a complete stranger. It was the first time they had been examined by a real doctor. When they were ill they consulted the village witch doctor, or so-called "healer." The great panacea was always the same—an ointment of cow-dung.

The patients were not always very tractable; they were bound by the dictates of their religion, and they didn't like it when Oudot touched them. The hardest job was to examine the women, who were excessively modest and would not allow themselves to be touched on any account, still less undressed. On one occasion Oudot succeeded in getting all the finery off a Nepalese girl. When she was half undressed Sarki, who had been helping, discreetly left the tent. Nothing would then persuade the girl to proceed any further.

Medicine had to be dealt out to all of them. Whenever he could, Oudot gave them something relevant to their ailment; otherwise he distributed inoffensive pills which had mainly a psychological effect. But there was no knowing what they might do with the things. They would unhesitatingly swallow anti-sunburn ointment or the most solid of plasters, and cheerfully swap medicines, given for particular illnesses. But they showed great courage in any surgical treatment.

One day an unfortunate youth came along with a double compound fracture of the wrist. The radius stuck out from a mass of pus, the arm was enormous, and the hand swollen out of all recognition. He was certainly in a bad way. Oudot—always by the same complicated process of interpretation—discovered that the accident had happened a fortnight ago. He told the parents that amputation of the arm was the only way of saving their son. They refused, and made it plain that all they wanted was a dressing. Well, it couldn't be helped. Oudot gave the patient morphia and then tried to get things back in place: he succeeded after a fashion and finally put the arm in plaster.

"What will happen?" I asked Oudot anxiously. There would be no one to change the dressing, and in a few days the wound would begin to suppurate again.

"There's nothing else to be done. He'll probably be dead in a fortnight."

He said this with a fatalistic air which rather frightened me. Yet he was right. It was not possible to reason with these people; here we were still in the dark ages. I thought of all these unfortunate people who were a prey to epidemics against which they had no means of protecting themselves: no doctor, no vaccine. In countries like these death gets its own way easily and the process of selection is intensive. On our long homeward march we often met funeral processions, and it was not cheering for Lachenal and myself to see the biers so like our own litters. The corpses were swathed in strangely-colored winding sheets and were preceded by horns whose notes re-echoed back and forth among the mountains. The families and friends of the deceased followed in silence, showing no undue sorrow. Death was but a period of transition and had no distressing implications. Where they not assured of reincarnation in other and more perfect shapes? The bodies were buried along the banks of the Krishna Gandaki, and the monsoon floods would carry them away down to the sacred Ganges.

Every day Oudot attended to the injured members of the Expedition. He was perpetually running after his medicine chest, which was invariably either right on ahead, and then we had to catch up with it, or else far in the rear, and we had to wait ages. But neither Lachenal nor I was ever in any hurry for the doctor to get to work. Gradually the injection of large quantities of penicillin began to take effect; the fever abated and the fear of generalized septicemia receded. I began to talk and to take an interest in what was going on around me. One day on a green sward at Putliket, Oudot began performing on me as usual.

"But don't make such a noise!" he enjoined me.

"Gently, Oudot, please!"

"I'm being as gentle as I can. Does that hurt?"

I braced myself with all my strength to bear the pain, and clenched my teeth:

"It's all right, I didn't feel a thing."

"Good!" said Oudot, and gave a great snip with his scissors.

"Ouch!"

I felt a shock all over me, and Oudot announced:

"The first amputation! The little finger!"

This gave me rather a twinge. A little finger may not be much use, but all the same I was attached to it! Tears were very near. Oudot picked up the joint between his finger and thumb and showed it to me.

"Perhaps you'd like to have it as a souvenir? It'll keep all right, you know! You don't seem very keen?"

"I certainly don't want it. There's no point in keeping a black and moldy little finger."

Throwing the "souvenir" casually onto the lid of a container, Oudot said:

"Well, you're no sentimentalist."

The line of demarcation between the living tissue and the dead was now clearly visible. Oudot worked with a *rugine*,[28] and every day one or two joints, either on my feet or my hands, were removed. All this was done without anesthetics, in the open, how and when it was possible.

One day Oudot would operate in a native house, another by the side of the road, amidst the unavoidable dust; sometimes along the rice swamps in spite of the damp and the leeches; or again in the middle of a field, in the rain, beneath the uncertain shelter of an umbrella held in the shaking hand of G. B. Rana's orderly. Without respite Oudot cleaned, cut and dressed.

While these sessions went on, and we casualties endured our tribulations in a nauseating stench—blood everywhere, pus dripping from the bandages and hundreds of flies sticking to our wounds—we were often, paradoxically, spectators of comic incidents. Now, after the first rains, came the season for planting the rice. All available labor was busy in the rice-fields, and to find porters became the Expedition's worst headache. The others were very perturbed: we *had* to get out of these parts at all costs. Oudot ordered G. B. Rana to use his authority and employ high-handed tactics to recruit coolies. We reminded him that we were under the protection of the Maharajah who would not tolerate our being held up at the moment of leaving his country. G.B. did all he could, but his efforts had no success.

Gradually our attitude hardened. Although we had offered to supplement the ordinary pay, we soon saw that, unless we paid prohibitive prices, the further we penetrated into the densely cultivated areas, the greater our difficulties would become, until we just should not be able to advance. For all their reluctance to act as slave-drivers, my friends were obliged to employ a system of "voluntary" recruitment. The method was simple: we had to get men where they were to be found, take them by the seat of their pants and place them very gently underneath the loads and the stretchers. The men objected strongly at first, but it all ended in smiles. They would get enough rupees to wipe away all regrets on the one side and all remorse on the other. The Sherpas tumbled to the operation perfectly, and I imagine that we were not the first Himalayan expedition to employ this method. They would stroll innocently about the villages sniffing the air, ready to pounce upon the first native whom they judged capable of carrying a load.

Under the lee of a house right in the center of the little village of Garomboree, I lay exhausted after a session with the surgeon's knife during which I had undergone several amputations. I gazed blankly at the bustling activity of the stony main street. The Sherpas had gone coolie-hunting, and a porter belonging to the *Suba* of Tukucha who, the day before, had given me a superb sword of chased silver, had gone with them. He took our side and held forth louder than anyone. He had a stentorian voice, and the teeth of a savage, which terrified me: I was always afraid he would take a bite out of me. Suddenly Sarki, Ang-Tharkey and Adjiba shot out of a nearby alley pushing before them four bewildered rice-planters. In a twinkling all their tools had been taken away and after some "friendly" propelling, here they were! One after the other the "volunteers" arrived at the scene of action as the enrollment went ahead.

We moved along in single file in the rain. As the day was drawing to a close and a strange and restful quiet reigned in the green countryside, the Sherpas spotted a fisherman, going home with his net well filled, walking slowly along ahead of us. Adjiba nudged Foutharkey and Sarki, picked up a cudgel and stepped forward stealthily. There was a sudden scuffle: away went the captive's net and line and his bags of bits and pieces, and a few moments later he found himself at the right front end of my stretcher, marching in step with his new friends. Poor fisherman! The Sherpas softened their tone, explaining that he would have to go on as far as Tansing, but that he would have a handsome number of rupees by way of compensation. The fisherman cried, and begged, and if he hadn't been prevented, would have knelt down and chanted a dirge. But as there was nothing to be done about it, he finished by smiling.

Every day during our retreat, such scenes were enacted, for every night a number of coolies deserted, preferring to forego the rupees owing to them. The situation became critical. The Expedition was scattered over several villages, and sometimes the front and the rear were separated by two days' march. Some groups were brought to a standstill in lonely places where it was impossible to find even the trace of a coolie.

On June 29, at Darjing, twenty-five coolies were missing at the roll call—and the weather was appalling. A former Gurkha N.C.O., who sported a magnificent cap, had, for several days, been playing a queer and rather sinister role as he prowled round the Expedition without any discernible reason. His conversations with the coolies were always followed by desertions; he harangued them and made trouble. Ichac came to Oudot and myself and said:

"If this Gurkha has such a bad influence on the coolies it may be that he has some authority."

"Yes, but if he uses it in this way, we shall end up like Harrer,"[29] replied Oudot.

"Perhaps we could conciliate him and make good use of his influence," suggested Ichac. "Why not employ him—use him as a recruiting sergeant."

So we engaged him at ten rupees a day. He wasn't exactly a desirable character. If he managed to enlist coolies by bringing pressure to bear on the *Subas* of the neighborhood, he also possessed an immoderate liking for *chang* and for the pretty girls of Nepal. In the evening yelling mobs threw themselves into wild dances which went on until far into the night. The next morning our recruiting sergeant reported for duty, seedy-looking and with tired eyes; but he braced himself and was soon on the quest for "volunteer" porters.

For days on end, through the most fantastic country, we descended the high valleys of Nepal to reach the plains. After following the Krishna Gandaki for a whole week to Kusma, we had to abandon the route we had taken on the journey out: the waters of this great river were now so high that the crossings had become hazardous, if not impossible. So at Kusma we left the Gandaki and crossed a range of fairly high hills to rejoin the Andhi Khola valley which runs parallel to the Gandaki, the banks of which were still negotiable. We rejoined our outward route again at Tansing.

The Expedition had turned into a limp and anemic body straggling without much spirit on a course the reason for which escaped us. We were buoyed up by a single wish: to get to India as quickly as possible. This interminable descent of the valleys of Nepal, in endless rain and in the damp heat of the monsoon, had a bad effect on us physically. The others had lost their energy and they dragged themselves miserably along the little walls of the rice-fields, plodding listlessly on and taking no interest in anything.

Couzy and Terray brought up the rear. When we got near to the frontier Noyelle went on to Gorakhpur, with the object of making arrangements with the Indian railways for our return journey. In the center of our formation were Oudot, Ichac, Lachenal, Rébuffat, Schatz and myself. Every day Lachenal was more restive; he could not endure the least delay and swore at the coolies. During halts, we sometimes found ourselves side by side. He was reading the Expedition's only thriller—by small installments, so as to savor it all the better; it was, I gathered, the story of a headless man—I never got farther than that.

"What a lot of time we're wasting!"

"We'll have to be patient, Biscante; things aren't always easy. Think of the difficulty of recruiting volunteers!"

"What about G.B.! Don't you think he could bestir himself a bit?"

"The heat depresses everyone after all this hard going."

"Oh hell!" burst out Lachenal, his patience exhausted. "I just *can't* stand all these characters around us day in and day out, gesticulating, and bellowing a gibberish that you can't understand a single word of! You make signs to them to come near, and they put down their loads! You make signs you want to drink, so they bring you bananas! Oh, for my house in Chamonix, my wife and the kids!"

"There's not much further to go now. After Tansing it's two days' march to India. It's no longer a question of days but of hours. All I ask for is a good hospital with a modern operating room, masses of medical supplies, dressings which are changed continually . . . and nice thick ones at that!"

The fact was that for some time our cotton had been getting scarce, though Oudot saved all the usable pieces. The alcohol had all gone and the needles had to be disinfected in my eau de Cologne.

"Thank God we've got our doctor," said Lachenal. "I can't think what we'd ever have done without him. For one thing, you wouldn't be here now! But don't you think he could be a bit more gentle? God, how he hurts sometimes! You know, these surgeons, when they're on the job they don't worry about whether people are under an anesthetic or not, they go on just the same—cut, snip, stab. Oh, what miserable wretches we are!"

And what a duet we set up! But how pleasant it was to complain!

Chapter XIX

Gorakhpur

THE PARTY HAD BECOME GRADUALLY ACCUSTOMED TO THE NOMADIC LIFE WHICH we had been leading for the last few weeks. Sometimes we made our way along the slippery little walls running between the rice-fields, but the stretchers were too wide for this and had to be carried right through the fields. This reminded me of those medieval lords whom, as a child, I had pictured trampling down flourishing crops for their pleasure. Sometimes we proceeded in single file along tracks that took us right through the middle of strange corn fields where the gigantic plants towered several feet above our heads.

During the halts the coolies would squat around us, taking turns on a puff at the same cigarette. Their religion forbade them to put their lips to tobacco, source of an impure pleasure; but they got around this difficulty by inserting the tip of the cigarette between thumb and forefinger, curled round to form a little bowl; putting their lips to this, they inhaled without touching the tobacco, and so obtained an innocent delight.

As we approached Tansing the weather improved, and it was the sun now that made us suffer. The flies swarmed over my saturated bandages and there was nothing I could do about it. A Brahman came up and embarked on a long prayer; listlessly I answered "Atcha! Atcha!" As far as I could make out he said he was a sun-worshiper: it wasn't quite the best moment for such a declaration, and I wished him and his sun to the devil!

He gesticulated continuously while he droned on. I got tired of him and my eyes strayed to the freshly rain-washed sky. Suddenly my attention was caught by an object—unless I was mistaken it was an umbrella that the Brahman carried under his arm. Immediately I began to take an intense interest in what he was saying, and after a few moments I got him to understand that his umbrella would be most useful to me, and we continued to converse under its restful shade as he held it over us, trotting along beside the stretcher.

Another two hours and we were at the end of our march. While Sarki fed me with an astonishing number of bananas I heard cries and protests: it was Ang-Tharkey hastening the poor Brahman on his way with a few well-placed kicks. I asked our Sirdar what it was all about and he explained as best he could:

"Bara Sahib, he's a robber, not a porter! He wants to be paid four rupees for the march! And where is his load, I should like to know?"

My Brahman, seeing that I was inquiring about him, came up, jabbering incomprehensibly. Ang-Tharkey went on:

"Bara Sahib, he says he worked as he went along, that it tired him greatly, and that it is only natural he should be compensated for his trouble."

"Give him two rupees."

He was bitterly disappointed.

We were nearing Tansing and there was now no danger of the porters deserting us; they all wished to go to the "big town." They trotted along briskly.

"There's Pansy!"

"Can't be!"

Pansy, who had been gone a long while and about whom we were beginning to feel concerned, came up quite unruffled, with his usual pleasant grin, as though he had only been away a few moments. Everyone rushed to greet this splendid Sherpa who had just completed a nineteen days' march with only one halt, at Delhi, where he had stayed for forty-eight hours.

"Here's the mail!"

"Letters?"

It was almost unbelievable; for the first time we were going to get news from France. The letters were soon distributed and faces disappeared behind reams of notepaper.

"My wife's not very well," Ichac told me, "the last letter was written some time ago. I wonder how she is."

"What do you know! There's going to be another Himalayan Expedition!"

This was surprising news.

"Well they must be feeling tough!"

"How many are going?"

"Where are they going?"

There was a cross-fire of questions and answers. Not everybody received good news; and some of the party looked worried or anxious as they resumed the march.

In the distance a green hill appeared. Sarki pointed with his finger:

"Tansing, Bara Sahib, Tansing!"

Were we nearing the end?

Next day after a heavy shower, though we had to go down a very muddy path full of pot holes, the porters no longer walked, they flew. Tansing was only a few hundred yards away: already we were on the outskirts. Here again were the little shops, the motley and inquisitive populace. We crossed the town and came out at last on a wide level place where we pitched our camp. Terray shifted the loads about eagerly and sang at the top of his voice—a good sign—the one and only song he knew: "*Au son joyeux des balalaikas.*" Everyone had taken fresh heart.

Just for a change Oudot did some operating that afternoon. During this session I lost my second big toe and the thumb of my right hand. It began to rain and I was taken into a tent, where for over an hour I listened in terror to Lachenal's cries as he underwent his first amputation. I was terribly upset by his sufferings, especially when I heard him protesting "No! No!" as though he couldn't resign himself to losing anything so precious.

Next day the "authorities" were received at the camp. The Governor, who impressed me most favorably, seemed very well disposed towards us. Why should he not help us to recruit coolies? He promised to do so at once. It was now the morning of July 4 and in a few hours' time porters would be at our disposal—a great relief. Officially, G.B.'s assignment would come to an end in two days' time, at Butwal, but I wanted him to accompany us as far as Katmandu. There was no doubt he would be very useful to us there. But I was chiefly concerned with giving him a richly deserved reward. G.B. was agreeable to accompanying us and promised to make the necessary application to the Maharajah. A few hours later he burst into the tent, his face wreathed in smiles, and announced that the Maharajah had given permission for him to go to the capital.

Before leaving for Butwal, our last stage, I wanted to spruce myself up a bit. I asked for a barber, for I had a beard like an ancient prophet. G.B.'s orderly undertook to go and fetch one; he returned soon after accompanied by a Gurkha with a hang-dog air and revoltingly dirty. I was apprehensive as he approached, but I hugged the thought of his razor which would skim my cheeks so delicately. Water was brought and my Gurkha began to soap me. He used some primitive stuff which was not soapy, nor did it lather, and he rubbed my face with it vigorously. All ten fingers as well as his palms were energetically employed and the massage became painful.

"*Bechtari! Bechtari!*" I said. "Gently!"

But the man seemed quite determined. Soon the beard was ready. He rummaged in his box and drew out an instrument which I did not at all like the look of. It was a small steel blade, very short, fixed between two bamboo sticks. The whole thing looked most peculiar. The barber seized hold of my face roughly with his smelly hands and began to "shave" me. The blade dragged the hairs and with his fingers he plucked them out one by one most conscientiously. I yelled bloody murder, but he scolded me and took not the slightest notice of my protests.

Oudot poked his head into the tent with an almost triumphant expression.

"I'd rather have an amputation," I shouted, "than the attentions of this savage!"

After an hour my cheeks and chin were more or less presentable. Now for the mustache! I was most particular about its shape. He started and I could feel the blade, which really did cut this time. I pursed up my lip— there was nothing left at all! The session was over. My tormentor had the effrontery to demand an exorbitant fee. Marcel Ichac gave him three rupees in a lordly manner and told Sarki to send him packing.

Lachenal was sent on to Butwal in the first contingent, in charge of Rébuffat. I followed in the second. Everything around us was so green that I did not recognize this as the route by which we had come three months ago. Towards evening we topped a hill. Ichac was beside me:

"Look, Maurice!" he said.

He asked the Sherpas to place my stretcher so that I could look back at the country we were leaving. Everything breathed an indefinable melancholy at this twilight hour. Did this feeling come from the sight of these high valleys, of the vast mountains which we could see on the horizon, or from the memory of our almost incredible struggles up there, or was it because we could feel reality already changing imperceptibly into dream? Ichac and I gazed in silence.

In a few minutes we should be back in contact with the world outside. The wonderful adventure which linked us to these mountains would soon belong to the past. Already the porters were preparing to lift me up: the long procession must resume its way. With my forearms I tried to touch my face which felt all wrinkled—and surely my hair must be quite white. My heart was full, and I looked away; jolting along in silence, we went in search of shelter for the night.

Before getting to Butwal next day we met Noyelle, who had returned from his mission to Gorakhpur:

"Hello, boys!" he called out from a distance, as soon as he saw us, and it was not long before he was with us.

"How are you? Is it hot in India?"

"Terribly—like a Turkish bath."

Noyelle told us the carriages would be at Nautanwa station on July 6—which was the next day. There was no time to be lost. In a heavy storm and a deluge of rain we arrived at our old camp at Butwal, where we found Lachenal. The latter part of the day was given up to more operations, and often I nearly fainted.

All the loads were assembled. But the question was whether the trucks would be there next day to take us to the terminus of the Indian railway where we were due at ten o'clock. I begged G.B. to do what he could. So off he went at once, in the middle of the night, through a stretch of thick and unhealthy jungle, to reach Bethari. On the morning of July 6 the trucks arrived! It was a triumph for G.B. and I congratulated him warmly. We paid off the porters and embarked for Nautanwa. The jungle was full of monkeys, who were not in the least alarmed by our presence. One of the trucks had a blowout, and the one I was in broke down. However, it all turned out all right for out of the two trucks we managed to make one workable one.

At last we came to Nautanwa and settled ourselves into the two palatial railway cars reserved for us. By early afternoon all the loads were aboard and the train moved off towards Gorakhpur. All sorts of plans were brewing. Everyone wanted to get back to France without delay. All the members of the party, who for three months had shown exemplary courage and patience, were now ready to do anything to gain twenty-four hours. But the various individual wishes were hard to reconcile. As far as I was concerned I intended to make every effort possible to keep the promise I had given at the start to visit the Maharajah of Nepal. Oudot would accompany me to Katmandu, and Ichac and Noyelle would come too. The others would go on to Delhi and wait there a few days. Lachenal, to avoid the heat, would go up to a hill station, such as Mussoorie.

While these plans were being debated, Oudot was busy at his job, scissors in hand, trimming feet and hands in spite of the temperature—113° in the shade—and the swarms of mosquitoes. We were nearing Gorakhpur. Now for Lachenal, and let's get on with the operations! In another two hours the Expedition would split up, and for nearly a week Lachenal would be deprived of our doctor's care.

In the railway car we were shaken about like dice in a box, and it was difficult for Oudot to operate: he took advantage of the stops to perform his amputations. Between stations everything was made ready: the dressings had to be unwrapped, things sorted out, chemicals prepared, and the scissors held out for Oudot to start work the second the car stopped.

"Come on, your turn, Biscante!" said Oudot hurriedly. "Sarki. . . ."

He made a vague gesture that meant: "Clean up all the muck around the Bara Sahib."

With foresight Lachenal had removed his dressings himself and presented his first foot to the executioner ready for the sacrifice. At the station before Gorakhpur two toes from his right foot went. The three others would have to be done at Gorakhpur itself.

"Gently, Oudot, please, gently!"

"I swear I'm doing everything I can, Biscante. I can't do more. Come on, quick!"

Lachenal held his foot with both hands. With his eyes starting from his head, he pleaded with Oudot.

"Gorakhpur," said Schatz, "we're there!"

The train slowed up. Couzy, Rébuffat, Schatz and some of the Sherpas got ready to jump on to the baggage car. All the equipment had to be rapidly loaded into other cars which were coupled to the Lucknow train, due to leave in an hour.

Great beads of sweat were pouring off Oudot. He trimmed and trimmed again without paying attention to poor Biscante's cries: there was only half an hour and he still had another toe to cut. Altogether it made a considerable number since he had started. This time the scissors were too big.

"Quick, Ichac, the little scissors."

The train stopped at this moment with considerable jolting.

"Damn!" The scissors had fallen down inside the window-slot! Oudot was at his wit's end.

"While I go on, try to get them."

"It can't be done. You can't take a great door like this off its hinges all in a minute!"

This wasn't at all to Lachenal's liking; but that big toe had to be done.

"But I don't want you to do it! Gently, gently . . ." he said between sobs.

Natives appeared at the doors.

"Get the hell out of here!" roared Oudot.

They didn't understand what he said, but they obeyed, which was the main thing.

"No, Oudot, please!"

This time Oudot was at the end of his patience. He stopped and looked at Lachenal:

"Really, it's a bit too much! You might be a little more obliging!"

This left Lachenal speechless. If it is a matter of being obliging, he said to himself, he can cut off both arms and both legs!

The train was due to leave in a few seconds. Crowds were moving about all the time on the platforms, and getting in our way. The moment the bandages were on, Terray seized Lachenal and carried him off. We just had time to call:

"Goodbye, Biscante! Cheer up! See you in Delhi!"

Things had to be cleaned up now; the nauseating smell drove even the natives away. Sarki and Foutharkey set to work, they opened the door wide and with a sort of old broom made of twigs, they pushed everything onto the floor. In the midst of a whole heap of rubbish rolled an amazing number of toes of all sizes which were then swept onto the platform before the startled eyes of the natives. Whistles blew, the cars jolted, and amid cries and shouts the train started. We drew out alongside a mass of humanity. I just had time to spot Terray, who waved us goodbye with a pair of boots.

Lulled by the rhythmical song of wheels on rails, my thoughts turned to that remote capital whither we were bound, a city indeed of the Thousand and One Nights.

Chapter XX

There Are Other Annapurnas

IN OUR COMPARTMENT OF THE INDIAN O.T.R. COMPANY TRAIN ICHAC, NOYELLE, Oudot and I lay silently on the long seats, refreshed by the cool breeze blown onto us by the fan ventilator. Our thoughts wandered, and gradually darkness fell.

After a twenty-four-hour journey across the plain of the Ganges, in what for us was unheard-of comfort, we arrived at Raxaul, on the frontier between India and Nepal. The transfer of our baggage at the Nepalese station was quickly effected under the supervision of Sarki and Pansy, who were accompanying us to Katmandu. Sarki had not left me for an instant since Annapurna, though it had not been an easy job for him. I often thought of his great thirty-six-hour march to establish the liaison upon which the whole fate of the Expedition depended. Katmandu was for him a dream city of which he scarcely dared to think; he had earned this reward a hundred times over and so indeed had Pansy, a Himalayan veteran whose devotion and quiet good nature made him a most lovable character. Our Sirdar, Ang-Tharkey, had not been able to come with us: huge floods in his home district had made him very anxious, for he had a large family, so he had asked us to let him go direct to Darjeeling. The farewell scene at Gorakhpur had been most touching, when the Sherpas received, in addition to their pay, generous *baksheesh* as well as their personal equipment, a matter of considerable value—even by European standards—as it was the very latest thing. Each in turn had come to salute me, with hands joined together, Indian fashion. Some of them, like Foutharkey, bowed slowly with a gesture of respect, then, touching me with one hand, they placed their foreheads against my clothes. For all their satisfaction at being through with this Expedition which would remain for them, as for us, a great memory, they looked sad.

The Maharajah had detailed an officer to look after our comfort and bring us to Katmandu. But there was bad news: the train would not leave till the next day. We were disappointed, but not surprised: the Nepalese rolling-stock consisted of only three engines! Happily the delay was cut short, thanks to the initiative of our three liaison officers—Noyelle, G.B., and this Nepalese officer. General Bijaya, Minister of Foreign Affairs, son of the Maharajah, had telegraphed instructions for a special deluxe car to be put at our disposal, and this would be coupled to the freight train which was due to leave at three o'clock the next morning.

In the middle of the night and to the accompaniment of the piercing noise of crickets, insects and other creatures, we settled ourselves as well as we could in the luxurious compartments. The others were already sound asleep when the train started up; there was such a jolting that I was afraid of being shot out of my bed. The track had a narrow gauge of only two feet! The tiny coach, balanced precariously, pitched and rolled enough to make one sick, and I could not sleep.

We crossed a particular dense and unhealthy jungle, and in the morning reached the terminus where the Maharajah's officer ordered a hearty and delicious breakfast for us. Outside, a Chevrolet truck was waiting for our luggage, and an American station wagon for ourselves. I was put in the front of the car and I sat up for the first time in a month, but I was so thin that I was unable to appreciate this luxury. The nineteen miles to Bhimphedi should only have taken a few minutes to travel but actually it took over two hours. The road was narrow, but good; we crossed numbers of rivers by prefabricated bridges. This is the only road in Nepal and the inhabitants are extremely proud of it; it is, in fact, an important arterial route and the only means of reaching Katmandu.

We climbed up gradually, followed by the truck with the delighted Sherpas perched on top. Here and there the road ascended in zigzags and we noticed that many of the houses had corrugated iron roofs—the ugliest boon that Western industrialism has conferred on these remote people. At eleven o'clock we reached Bhimphedi where horses and "dandies"—a kind of sedan chair—were awaiting us. The road went no further. To get to Katmandu, where we were due to arrive in the evening, we had to follow a mountain path unfit for cars. Oudot was tired out and suffering from very painful boils, so he chose a "dandy" rather than a horse, and so did I.

The path zigzagged up a steep slope, but the coolies were wonderfully skillful in adjusting their steps so that we felt not the slightest jolt; the bearers changed over without slowing down the pace. All day long we continued. The "dandy" was too small for me and I was obliged to curl myself up while trying to protect my bandages. I could not remain seated for long, and Oudot gave me injections of *solucamphor* to help me bear up. Rest houses, at the disposal of the guests of the Maharajah, were spaced out along the route. At one o'clock we came to a fort manned by Gurkhas, a Vauban style building of which the Nepalese were very proud.

After a quick lunch in the rest house, situated in the top of the fort, we set out again; we still had a long way to go, and two passes to cross to reach Katmandu.

My position became unbearable; the only thing I could do was what I had already tried during the dark days at Lete—to sink into a kind of stupor and attempt to forget my present suffering. There was a pass at about 6,500 feet which would take us over the hills that blocked our view. Looking up I saw huge cables going right across the valley; I wondered if it could be a cable railway. So indeed it was—the longest in the world, measuring nearly nineteen miles. It provisioned Katmandu and the surrounding neighborhood, a population of some hundred and fifty thousand people.

The others of the party, who had good mounts, had ridden on ahead. They would wait for us at the beginning of a carriage road. A carriage road? I showed surprise when I was told that a car would take us to Katmandu. How had a car got there? It certainly could not have come along the rough track which we ourselves had had such difficulty in following. I asked about this.

"Cars are brought by coolies."

Turning towards Oudot, I said:

"Then they must be pushed along these paths. It's not possible, just look at the angle!"

In some places two persons could not have walked abreast. And the metal bridge we had just crossed was barely five feet wide.

"They're not *pushed,* they're *carried.*"

It was incredible. There were trucks, too, it seemed. But what about those two passes over 6,000 feet high? Then it was explained to me. The cars, without their wheels, are lashed onto huge platforms carried by from fifty to seventy coolies. They avoid the greater part of our route by following the river beds where the, coolies walk bare-foot. They cross the two passes in the same manner at certain points where the track was wider and the zigzags less sharp. Marching in step, bent under their yoke, the coolies sing rhythmical chants to help them along. It has thus been possible to construct a network of roads for about twelve miles around Katmandu, where there are about a hundred cars in circulation.

It grew dark; the coolies labored as we neared the pass, for they had had a hard day. From this point, I was told, there is a splendid view of the Himalaya. Below, at the opening of this celebrated valley of Nepal, lies the plain where Katmandu, historic bulwark of the country, displays its hundreds of temples, shrines and palaces. It was dark when we arrived at the pass, and I did not know how the porters could see their way. There was no question of making a halt, even though I was so desperately tired that I was ready to give up the ghost. My situation reminded me forcibly of the cages in which Louis XI kept his prisoners.

But there, in the distance, were electric lights! (Next day I learned there was a power station on the banks of the Bragmati.) The hours went by; the lights were desperately slow in drawing nearer. As we passed through the sleeping villages, I had not even strength enough to groan.

About midnight a small village loomed up, shadows flitted about, and I felt that this was the end, and so indeed it was. A little further on an old American car stood waiting. The coolies had to be paid, and the baggage loaded onto a truck, while I took my place beside Oudot in the car. At this precise moment a flat tire was discovered and it took another quarter of an hour to change it. A frightful storm caught us en route and torrential rain drummed on the top of the car. We went up a drive, passed a Gurkha presenting arms, and at one o'clock in the morning came to the Maharajah's rest house. There were shouts of welcome from the others who were waiting for us; Ichac, Noyelle and G.B. came out to meet us, and I was delighted to see our Minister to India, Christian Belle. He was in charge of Nepalese affairs, and in spite of the absence in France of Ambassador Daniel Lévi, had immediately decided to come, to present the members of the Expedition personally to the Maharajah. This very good friend of ours, who already knew all about our adventures, was shocked by my condition.

Here, at last, the first time in months, I should be able to enjoy a few days' rest. There was furniture—a table—a refrigerator! There was even a bathroom. But all this counted for nothing beside what awaited us on the table: a bottle of Alsatian wine! I felt quite giddy and was all set for an orgy—but the dignified turbaned butler dispensed the precious liquid with so much ceremony that I remembered my manners. We were to remain here until July 11, which meant three days of rest and good food for me— for the others, three days of visiting the fascinating capital. All the life of Nepal centers on Katmandu.

My companions got ready to see the sights of the town, but before setting off, Oudot trimmed my four wounds and told me to keep the bandages off my feet and hands for most of the day. This was rather a problem for I must not touch anything. I must keep my four limbs in the air, and be on the look-out for flies and mosquitoes. Time, I feared, would drag while I lay like this, and I had a horror of all these insects that carry every disease—especially the flies—which are much larger than the European kind and have red bellies—they stick like leeches. My fears were only too well justified, when later, at Delhi, Oudot took off my dressings and found that my foot was harboring a batch of wriggling maggots. At the approach of the surgeon's tweezers they withdrew into their holes. By the time we reached Paris the maggots had grown huge, fatter than a pencil, and there was at least half a pound of them. At first I was horrified—I was being spared absolutely nothing! I never got over my horror, in spite of Oudot's paternal explanations that maggots would clean wounds more effectively than any modern chemicals. They were even, he said, deliberately introduced into certain wounds.

My friends came back delighted with their sightseeing. They had visited a number of shrines decorated with designs of carved wood and some extremely original statuettes as Nepal had once known a period of great artistic flowering.

Next day preparations were made for the *durbar*—the audience with the Maharajah. Noyelle told us that the ceremony would be held in the late afternoon and would be divided into two distinct parts: the first would be the official ceremony, the second a reception of a far more personal character. We were all most excited at the thought of the *durbar*—we had heard so much about it. Punctuality was called for: we must be not a minute early, nor a minute late; the protocol was very strict. Apart from Monsieur Christian Belle, who would be in the uniform of a Minister Plenipotentiary, we should all be wearing the precious white dinner jackets we had lugged all the way from Paris.

At the appointed hour, our two large cars entered the palace grounds. At the gates Gurkha sentries presented arms. There was a magnificent approach through a formal French garden, laid out with a lake, around which we drove slowly. Soldiers of a complete mounted unit rode towards us, dressed in red, with long drooping mustaches and carrying tall spears. We came out onto a concrete square in front of the Maharajah's palace, and the others quickly got out and ordered me to be carried in on a chair. Soldiers ran up and helped me to take my seat. Mounting the steps of the palace, we were received by His Highness, Mohun Shumsher Jung Bahadur Rana, Maharajah of Nepal. He came forward to meet us dressed in a white uniform glittering with amazing decorations and jewels of untold value. His headgear alone was made up of outsize precious stones; there was one diamond in the center about four inches across. A mustache in the style of the Emperor Franz-Josef added greatly to his dignity.

He came towards me with a kind and fatherly look, and I greeted him respectfully, Indian fashion, holding my bandaged hands together. He said he was happy to welcome me to his palace and to congratulate me and my friends. We went up the rest of the steps together and entered the great hall ablaze with light where the nobles of the kingdom were assembled in hundreds. Their ranks fell back to make way for us. We went right across the hall to the far end, where seats had been arranged for us near the throne. The Maharajah himself arranged the carrying-chair so that I could follow the ceremony properly. I looked around me in amazement; everyone wore the same uniform as the Maharajah, though of course theirs were not so splendid; the diamonds, emeralds and rubies glittered and sparkled. It is astonishing that there still exist such fabulous treasures and courts so out of keeping with our times.

As we were, after all, a few minutes in advance of the officially appointed time, I had leisure to gaze on the princes of the line placed in order of succession: Baber, Kaiser . . . these names were always completed by Shumsher Jung Bahadur Rana. About fifteen of them were sitting silent and immobile. The Maharajah's official function is that of Prime Minister, a hereditary post that descends, according to well defined rules and regulations, to his brothers or his sons. The King of Nepal, Tribhuvana Shumsher Jung Bahadur Rana, who is practically never seen, even by his subjects, represents the spiritual power. On the right were additional rows of princes, dressed in the same glittering uniforms, and sitting in an exactly defined order of precedence. Then came the ministers, the chiefs of the army, and all the high dignitaries and notables of Nepal.

"How's it going?" whispered Ichac, who was sitting next to me.

"Pretty awful. I don't think I can hold out much longer."

In fact, while I kept this upright position my wounds began to suppurate through the bandages. Ichac, too, was embarrassed: the etiquette here was extremely strict—as strict as anywhere in the world. It was not proper for a guest to take photographs. But photography was highly appreciated in this country, and the assembly shut its eyes to slight lapses of etiquette. From time to time there was a flash as Ichac rose discreetly to take a picture. Then he resumed his role of guest. The official court photographers had enormous cameras on tripods which they adjusted with meticulous care, as if they were afraid of losing their heads should the pictures turn out unsuccessfully. They watched Ichac condescendingly, no doubt writing him off as an amateur—photographs could not be taken casually like that!

Monsieur Christian Belle arose and addressed a speech in English to the Maharajah. He thanked him in the name of France for the special permission granted to us to penetrate into the interior of the kingdom; Nepal now could claim the highest mountain that man had climbed. As a mark of gratitude he presented the Maharajah, on behalf of the President of the French Republic, with a modern Aubusson tapestry. The art is unknown in Nepal, and there was general astonishment when we explained that it was not a carpet to be laid on the floor, but a sort of embroidery meant to be hung on the walls like a picture. The silence, which up till then had been absolute, was broken by murmurs of admiration.

Order was restored when the Maharajah rose in his turn and replied to our Minister. He said he was happy to have given us permission, and it could not have been used to better advantage. This permission, which indeed was something quite exceptional, showed how favorably disposed he was to further the good relations between France and Nepal, which had once bound together his father and Silvain Lévi, the great French scholar and expert on Sanskrit.

While he was speaking the hereditary princes looked furtively at each other and consulted their watches. Only a few seconds to go according to schedule: was etiquette going to be transgressed? No! The Maharajah wound up, and after a few courteous words the ceremony came to an end and the dignitaries disappeared as if by magic.

In a few minutes the unofficial ceremony would begin. Already a number of people had appeared in undress uniform; black suits, hats of trimmed fur, and a single badge—the Gurkhas'—consisting of two gold *kukris* intertwined. The Maharajah reappeared in the hall wearing a single decoration—the Grand Cross of the Legion of Honor. The general tone had changed: the rest of our party were talking with groups of ministers and hereditary princes who were admiring the tapestry on a large table. The Maharajah came towards me and for a few minutes we chatted together with great cordiality. I expressed my great liking for his country, so little known to the rest of the world, and told him what an excellent impression G. B. Rana had made upon me. Immediately he was promoted lieutenant and his pay doubled! G.B. was greatly moved; diffidently, and from a respectful distance, he made profuse signs of gratitude, and, bending double, saluted the Maharajah in the curious fashion with which we were now familiar.

Behind the stiff exterior of these warriors, who, as their history shows, are assuredly not always very gentle, I was surprised to find such gentleness, such kindness. Suddenly, everyone stopped talking, and people came in respectfully bearing some little caskets. What was happening now? The Maharajah arose; I was carried to the center of the great hall and the Court stood around us. The British Ambassador and the Indian Ambassador and his attachés, who had just arrived, were also present. Ceremoniously, and with great dignity, the Maharajah opened the caskets and explained to me that he had been instructed by the King, who was ill, to confer upon me the highest Gurkha order in the country, given only to troops in time of war—the Gurkha Right Hand, for valor.

With deep emotion he spoke these simple words:

"You are a brave man, and we welcome you here as a brave man."

No other decoration could have touched me more deeply than that of these valorous Gurkha warriors. Although I was near to fainting in my chair I endeavored to say a few words. I expressed my thanks for this unexpected distinction, and said that I was but the intermediary and that it was the entire Expedition which had thus been honored. Immediately the Maharajah congratulated me upon the decoration which I had been awarded. Then the princes of the line, the ministers and the diplomats filed past me with their congratulations. The party broke up into small groups. From time to time the Maharajah and his son, General Bijaya, came up to me to inquire if I was all right or to ask questions about the regions of eternal snow. This Annapurna venture had fascinated and disquieted them. We hoped that if national misfortunes followed, they would not attribute them to us for having infringed the divine law.

It was time to leave, I could not bear any more; my duties were over. We said our farewells to our host and His Highness and his son, followed by the other personages, accompanied us with pomp to the great staircase. I was in a fever to lie down, but just as we were descending the steps I heard some brief orders being given, and the cars which were driving slowly up came to a halt. A tune rang out, a kind of waltz which had a familiar sound to French ears. Everyone stood at attention. When the tune came to an end I turned, rather astonished, towards the Minister for Foreign Affairs. I was about to remark, "Nice of you to play us a French tune!" Lucky for me that I said nothing: the Minister leaned towards me and asked in a low voice:

"What do you think of our national anthem?"

"Oh . . . Magnificent, and very moving for us Frenchmen . . ."

At that moment the Marseillaise rang out. We were all surprised and deeply touched to hear it in a country so remote from our own. The performance must have involved laborious practice.

We all fell silent, and the Maharajah bade us a last farewell. We saluted him respectfully and entered our cars. The dignitaries were ranged on the steps on each side of the great staircase. Orders were given; the car moved slowly off, while for a second time the Marseillaise was played.

That evening my companions dined at the British Embassy and sent off a friendly message to Tilman, who was then in the Annapurna region. Next day after a well-earned rest we all visited one of the ancient capitals, Bhadgaon, where we found some Hindu temples whose splendor never ceased to astonish us. In the center of Katmandu, in the square beside the temple, we admired a statue of Kali the Goddess. The others went to see the renowned Buddhist *stupa*[30] at Swayambhonath, crowned with a tower of concentric circles of metal.

The next day, July 12, we left Katmandu, and according to custom, on leaving the rest house, our shoulders were draped with a magnificent garland of sweetly scented flowers. The Maharajah, who was full of thoughtful attentions, had insured that my return should be effected as comfortably as possible, and I was borne on a very luxurious kind of litter carried by eight men. The all too familiar jerky movement, however, began again as we wound up towards the pass.

G.B. accompanied me as far as the first turn. He had served us most loyally and as an expression of my personal appreciation I made him a present of my revolver which, during all the war years, had never left my side. It is an unknown weapon in these parts and he was deeply touched by this memento which, for the rest of his life, would remind him of our joint adventure.

G.B. could not bring himself to leave me. He saluted me with great emotion, walked beside me for a time, and then gradually dropped behind. The path wound up towards the hill and was soon lost in the jungle. The garland of flowers spread its scent around me. G.B. wore an expression of infinite sadness and the tears ran down his brown face. I looked at the mountains in the blue distance. The great giants of the earth were there assembled in all their dazzling beauty, reaching up to heaven in supplication.

The others were far ahead. The jolting began again, bearing me away from what would soon be nothing but memories. In the gentle languor into which I let myself sink, I tried to envisage my first contact with the civilized world in the homeward-bound airplane, and the terrible shock of landing at Orly and meeting family and friends.

But I could never have imagined the violent emotional shock that I should in fact experience when it came to the point, nor the sudden nervous depression which would then take hold of me. Those surgical operations in the field, the sickening butchery that shook even the toughest of the natives, had gradually deadened our sensibilities; we were no longer able to judge the horror of it all. A toe snapping off and thrown away, useless, blood flowing and spurting, the unbearable smell from suppurating wounds—all this left us unmoved.

In the airplane before landing, Lachenal and I would be putting on fresh bandages for our arrival. But the minute we started down that iron ladder, all those friendly eyes looking at us with such pity, would at once tear aside the masks behind which we had sheltered. We were not to be pitied—and yet, the tears in those eyes and the expressions of distress, would suddenly bring me face to face with reality. A strange consolation for my sufferings to have brought me!

Rocked in my stretcher, I meditated on our adventure now drawing to a close, and on our unexpected victory. One always talks of the ideal as a goal towards which one strives but which one never reaches. For every one of us, Annapurna was an ideal that had been realized. In our youth we had not been misled by fantasies, nor by the bloody battles of modern warfare which feed the imagination of the young. For us the mountains had been a natural field of activity where, playing on the frontiers of life and death, we had found the freedom for which we were blindly groping and which was as necessary to us as bread. The mountains had bestowed on us their beauties, and we adored them with a child's simplicity and revered them with a monk's veneration of the divine.

Annapurna, to which we had gone emptyhanded, was a treasure on which we should live the rest of our days. With this realization we turn the page: a new life begins.

There are other Annapurnas in the lives of men.

NOTES

1. Sherpas are Buddhists from a high valley in the east of Nepal. They are mountaineers and are semi-professionals on Himalayan expeditions. They are engaged by contract.
2. Every source of income, without exception, will go to form a fund for subsequent expeditions.
3. The chain of the Himalaya extends for about 1,800 miles. It includes something like 200 summits of over 7,000 meters (23,000 feet), and 14 over 8,000 meters (26,000 feet).
4. The geological investigations of the Expedition have been communicated to the Academy of Sciences (meeting of April 23, 1951). With the aid of the information collected the general lines of structure of the Central Himalaya have been traced.
5. A large river, a tributary of the Ganges, which we were to follow up to Tukucha (map page 10).
6. See maps, pages 22 and 23.
7. This impassable chain (not to be confused with the Nigini Hills of South India) forms an immense screen between Tukucha and Annapurna. To reach Annapurna one would have to skirt the Nilgiris to the south along the Miristi Khola, or to the north.
8. The East glacier lies between the north and south-east ridges. At first sight it appeared to give access to both ridges.
9. See map, page 22.
10. The north buttress of the Pointe Walker on the Grandes Jorasses is perhaps the most difficult climb in the Alps.
11. This unpleasant test left us disagreeable memories; it consisted in blowing into a tube and maintaining in it a pressure of four centimeters of mercury. The session comprised about twenty different tests.
12. Another eight-thousander, 26,640 feet, to the east of Annapurna.
13. "Hail, the jewel in the lotus flower."
14. The way round by Muktinath would save a day's march.
15. Rocks are graded according to their difficulty from grade 1, the easiest, to grade 6, the hardest, reaching the limits of the possible. Only very few climbers get to grade 6. Most of the classic expeditions in the Alps are grade 4. In the Himalaya where the altitude makes every movement more of an effort, parties do their best to avoid all climbing difficulties. Where these are met, they do not generally exceed grade 4.
16. Expedition slang: tins containing main meals.
17. See sketch page 92.

18. At the time I was thinking of the following points:
    I—that adaptability, and speed of adaptability vary with the individual;
    II—that adaptability is determined to a large extent by previous appropriate training;
    III—that above a certain critical height, peculiar to each individual and capable of being progressively raised, people deteriorate—below it they recuperate;
    IV—that for the majority of the party this critical height—owing to the policy followed since the beginning of the expedition—should be at present between 16,000 and 20,000 feet.
    With reference to this subject see the reports by Dr. Oudot in the *Presse Médicale:*
      a) Observations physiologiques et cliniques en haute montagne. (59me année, n°. 15, 7 mars 1951, p. 297 à 300.)
      b) Action des inhalations d'oxygène en haute montagne. (59me année, n°. 17, 17 mars 1951, p. 326 à 327.)

19. A carrying frame made of canvas and straps worn like a rucksack in which an injured climber can sit.
20. We're going now.
21. At this time we still thought that we had been up to 21,700 feet, the height registered by our altimeters.
22. On the way up, between Tukucha and the Base Camp this particular Sherpa had consumed an excessive amount of *chang* and methylated spirits.
23. Astringent anti-sunburn lotion.
24. In May 1952 Lambert, with the Sherpa Ang-Tsering, reached 28,215 feet on Mount Everest, possibly the highest point yet attained. (Translators' note.)
25. The day Lachenal and I left Camp V and were going up towards the summit.
26. Oudot and Noyelle were intending to go up to Camp III to pitch tents to replace those taken on by Gaston and Lionel to Camp IV. For Oudot this ascent was to be a vitally important experiment in the use of oxygen.
27. In fact it was 500 feet.
28. A surgical instrument used for scraping bones and separating living and dead tissue.
29. Harrer was a member of a German expedition who, during an extraordinary trip, crossed the Himalaya, followed the course of the Brahmaputra and finished by settling in Lhasa where it is said he was chief engineer and then commander-in-chief of the Tibetan army.
30. Monument to the dead, enclosing the ashes or relics of the Buddha, or else simply a memorial.

GLOSSARY

Anorak: wind-proof jacket with hood attached.

Arête: ridge, generally one of the main ridges of a mountain.

Belay: to secure the climber to a projection with the rope; the projection itself.

Bergschrund: a large crevasse separating the upper slopes of a glacier from the steeper ice or rock above.

Cagoule: long anorak descending below the knees.

Chimney: a narrow vertical gully in rock or ice.

Chorten: a Buddhist religious monument.

Col: pass.

Cornice: overhanging mass of snow or ice along a ridge, shaped like the curling crest of a wave and generally formed by the prevailing wind.

Couloir: gully or furrow in a mountainside; may be of rock, ice or snow.

Crampons: metal frames with spikes, fitting the soles of the boots, for use on hard snow or ice.

Crevasse: a fissure in a glacier, often of great depth.

Gendarme: rock tower or tooth on a ridge.

Glissade: to slide down a snow slope, either sitting or standing, using the ice-axe to control speed and direction.

Ice-fall: a much torn and crevassed portion of a glacier caused by a change of angle or direction in the slope.

Line: a thin rope used for rappel or roping down.

Massif: group of mountains.

Moraine: accumulation of stones and debris brought down by a glacier forming ridges.

Névé: patches of snow, usually above the permanent snow line.

Pitch: section of difficult ice or rock, anything from 10 to 120 feet in height.

Piton: metal spike with a ring in the head, which can be driven into rock or ice.

Rappel or roping down: system of descending steep pitches by means of a rope doubled around a projection. Usually the thin rope known as line is used.

Rope: attaches members of a party together; a party may be referred to as "a rope."

Scree: slope of small loose stones.

Serac: tower or pinnacle of ice, found mainly in ice-falls.

Slalom: zigzag descent on skis.

Snap-link: large metal spring-loaded clip, which can be fixed to the rope or piton.

Snow-bridge: a layer of snow bridging a crevasse.

Spur: a rib of rock: sometimes use for an arête.

Traverse: to cross a mountain slope horizontally.

Tsampa: roasted and ground barley or other grain.

Verglas: thin coating of ice on rock.

ABOUT THE AUTHOR

Maurice Herzog (1919–) is a legendary French mountaineer and sports administrator. In 1950 he became the first person to conquer an 8,000-meter peak, Annapurna. His accomplishment was surpassed only when Sir Edmund Hillary and Tenzing Norgay reached the summit of Everest in 1953. He lives in Lyon, France.